SIX O'CLOCK SOLUTIONS

The Vancouver Sun

Copyright © 1995 The Vancouver Sun

Inside illustrations copyright © Michael Knox

Published by
Pacific Press Books
2250 Granville Street
Vancouver, B.C.
V6H 3G2

President and publisher: Donald Babick

Canadian Cataloguing in Publication Data
Johnson, Eve
     Six O'Clock Solutions
Includes Index.
ISBN 0-9697356-1-8
     1. Quick and easy cookery.   I. Vancouver Sun (Firm).
     II Title.
TX833.5.J65 1995   641.5'55   C95-910756-8

Design:	Blair Pocock, Fleming Graphics
Cover:	Dan Murray
Inside illustrations:	Michael Knox
Back cover photo:	Peter Battistoni
Home economists:	Brenda Thompson
	Ruth Phelan
Nutritional consultant:	Jean Fremont (RDN),
	delta nutrition systems
Index:	Annette Lorek
Copy editing:	Murray McMillan
Editor:	Daphne Gray-Grant

Printed and bound in Canada by Mitchell Press

First edition

SIX O'CLOCK

SIX O'CLOCK SOLUTIONS
ACKNOWLEDGEMENTS

If you ever want to feel a deep sense of personal indebtedness, may I suggest that you write a cookbook? By the time you've sent your efforts off to the printer, you will know, beyond any doubt, that we're all dependent on each other for what we can accomplish.

The first people I'd like to thank are the readers who nudged me into this project by asking when we were going to publish a Six O'Clock Solutions cookbook. The 900 people who entered our Six O'Clock Solutions recipe contest let us know we'd hit a subject of deep interest. Special thanks go to the readers whose names and recipes are printed in these pages, and to those who shared their quick cooking tips: Carol Billings, Sharon Wyse Boileau, Bernice Booth, Betty Cameron, Edward Galloway, Heather Martin, Jenni Mitchell, Jane Murphy, Sonya Oblak, Janice Ross, Moira Taylor and Michelle Woolf.

We've profited from the generosity of chefs and caterers who continue to reach our readers through The Vancouver Sun's *food pages. Stephen Wong and Anne Milne contributed recipes that add a lustre to our weekly efforts and to this book.*

Food editor Murray McMillan saved me from embarrassing misspellings, reined in my colloquialisms and invented some of the snappiest recipe titles in this book.

Home economist and food stylist Brenda Thompson developed the lion's share of our weekly Six O'Clock Solutions recipes. Brenda's concern for accuracy and consistency borders on the fanatical. We wouldn't be nearly as reliable without her.

Home economist Ruth Phelan joined the food pages two years ago. Many of the salmon recipes in this book are her creations; she also took on weeks of extra testing to fill in the inevitable gaps.

Peter Battistoni, whose extraordinary photographs make us look good in the weekly pages, shot the back cover photograph.

Ian Haysom, then editor-in-chief of The Vancouver Sun, *lent his enthusiastic support to this cookbook, as did deputy managing editor Shelley Fralic. Life editor Valerie Casselton put up with a cookbook-writing leave of absence that needed several extensions.*

Steve Proulx, Debbie Millward and the Press Library staff brought recipes back from electronic storage and taught me how to navigate Infomart.

Craig Ferry and Wayne Smith of editorial systems helped us weave our way through the electronic wilderness. Tom Hemmy and his staff came to our aid in the color lab.

Six O'Clock Solutions 1

Lynne Munro and Jeff Lucas in our promotions department lent their support. Promotional assistance with our contest came from Cecil Kimsing at SilverWing Holidays and Chris Gould on behalf of Braun. Jenafor Shaffer cheerfully took on book-related chores. Carole Bridge and Gordon Hood keep our sales figures straight. Marilyn Chepil handles cookbook sales at the promotions desk. Vanessa Pinniger volunteered to help in the tedious work of proofreading.

Jean Fremont, RDN, of delta nutrition systems, was our nutritional consultant. Annette Lorek compiled the comprehensive index.

Once again, the design team at Fleming Graphics came through with a handsome book. Blair Pocock, Catherine Winckler, Joanne Hogan, Karen Madsen and Doug Fleming share the credit. Dan Murray gave us another fabulous cover and Michael Knox drew the charming illustrations inside.

David McPhail and the crew at Mitchell Press guided this book through printing and provided a binding that lies flat when you use it.

Ron Nadain and the folks at Creative Promotions helped ensure that readers received their copies of our last book promptly and in good order. We're counting on them to do it all over again.

Ann Vallee has taken on the task of publicizing the book with a thoughtfulness and enthusiasm that's already impressive.

With a project like this, it helps to have someone at the top who believes in you. Pacific Press publisher Don Babick gave this cookbook his support from the beginning.

Daphne Gray-Grant's energy and ideas permeate this book. If this were a film, her titles would include producer, executive producer and editor. Daphne's genius for organization kept me on track; her unfailing patience and good humor made the book a pleasure to work on.

From January through May, Kris Neely was my own personal six o'clock solution. Every Wednesday evening she brought her good nature, good taste and hard work to my kitchen; together we developed recipes for the seafood and vegetarian chapters and tasted our way through bruschettas, raitas, salad dressings and desserts.

The dinners that followed were sampled and commented on by a hardy crew of tasters, all of whom gamely insisted that it was fun to eat a meal consisting of an appetizer and three different main course pastas. Sincere thanks to all of you.

And especially and always, thanks to Alan.

Eve Johnson
Vancouver, B.C.
July 1995

TABLE OF CONTENTS

MAKING PEACE WITH DINNERTIME.........4

MEAT 12

CHICKEN, TURKEY, DUCK 50

SEAFOOD 92

VEGETARIAN 134

APPENDICES 176

INDEX...181

MAKING PEACE WITH DINNERTIME

I know two otherwise ethical people who play what one of them calls "an elaborate game of chicken" to see who can get home from work last. Why? Because the first one in is supposed to start dinner.

You won't find it in your heart to blame them if, like me, you have stood, hand on the cupboard door, staring at pasta packages, praying for inspiration. Those of us who have seen the six o'clock problem at its worst know what happens next. When, at last, an idea breaks through, it inevitably calls for a large amount of an ingredient you ran out of yesterday.

In the past when this happened to me, I felt not only frustrated, hungry and tired, but also ashamed. I'm a food writer. Wasn't I supposed to have this problem licked? In time I saw the obvious: you can't chop vegetables while you're working on a computer. I have as much time to cook dinner as anyone else who works for a living, which is to say, not enough. So in January, when I started writing this cookbook, I privately wondered if any true six o'clock solution

existed. To begin with, pulling together more than 150 quick, delicious, reliable recipes is no easy task.

When we started running a weekly quick-cooking column called Six O'Clock Solutions in *The Vancouver Sun*'s food pages, we set some stringent rules for the test kitchen. A Six O'Clock Solution has to be ready in roughly half an hour from the moment preparations start — or, as is the case with three recipes in this book, must justify an extra 15 minutes on the grounds of superb taste.

A Six O'Clock Solution can't call for roasted red peppers or cooked chicken breasts. It also can't marinate overnight in the fridge. Marinating food and cooking with leftovers are great quick-cooking strategies, but we wanted recipes for days when all systems have failed. We wanted dinners you could turn to and make in half an hour, on evenings when you didn't have the faintest glimmer of an idea of what you'd like to eat. Four years later, we remain committed to finding and developing new quick recipes. All of them are tested in the newspaper's kitchen and placed in front of a panel of tasters who judge them either "good" or "excellent." (When a recipe is judged as only "fair" we rework it and retest it, or abandon it.) They may not all appeal to you. Still, follow the directions, and they'll work.

Now the recipes have been gathered together, and I'm confident that they span a wide enough range of tastes and occasions to keep a household fed. But what if the six o'clock problem is something more complicated than access to recipes?

A cookbook is a tool. It won't make dinner any more than a lawnmower will keep the grass cut. The question is not, can you find a good cookbook, but can you manage to use it? Can you eat well? Can you sit down most nights, happy and relaxed, to a meal that nourishes you, body and spirit? In short: can you make peace with dinnertime?

It's April now, and the book is written. I walked up my street today in a sun-shower of cherry blossoms that drifted across the pavement and collected in the gutters like snow might, if snow here were ever that dry. My private doubts have mostly evaporated. Ask me, and I'll say yes, you can make peace with dinnertime. You can do it without spending more than half an hour in the kitchen, and you can do it without feeling guilt over what you feed yourself and your

family. The secret is to take a long look at how you think about time.

MARKING TIME

I would bet that somewhere in the back of your mind is a being we might, borrowing from inner-child theorists, call the inner Benjamin Franklin. Even if you've never met him, you've heard his voice, the one that whispers about the Devil finding work for idle hands to do, or, on Friday morning, demands to know exactly what you did with the week, and why it wasn't more.

Settle into a quiet spot and wait. Sooner or later, he will step out of the shadows and, by way of greeting, ask: "Keeping busy?" To the inner Ben Franklin, activity is unquestionably good.

"Wasting time must be the greatest prodigality, since lost time is never found again," he says, putting an arm around your shoulder as you walk. "Remember, time is money. And God helps those who help themselves."

Franklin was a printer, scientist and diplomat. He proved that lightning is electrical energy and helped draft the American Declaration of Independence. He also published 25 years of *Poor*

Richard's Almanacks, collections of homespun wisdom largely borrowed from previous authors, then rewritten in ways that have lodged themselves in the collective mind.

"Time is money," after all, might as well be printed on our T-shirts, so general is our agreement on that truth. Much more rarely do we turn the equation around, and notice that money is also time. Look deeply enough, and you may find that underneath the laudable ideal of using time well lurks the nasty little thought that time not spent in making money is time wasted.

Try to root that weed out of your mind and the inner Ben Franklin will lean forward to say: "He that can earn 10 shillings a day by his labor, and goes abroad, or sits idle one half of that day, though he spends but a sixpence during his diversion or idleness, ought not to reckon that the only expense; he has really spent, or rather thrown away, five shillings."

Nonsense, of course, but potent nonsense. In truth, the world is a good place to be abroad in, especially since we only pass here once. The best ideas, we learn from those who have them, favor idle hours when work has been set aside. If what you're doing is harmful, doing nothing would be an improvement. And happiness beats money as a proof of time well used.

Still, for most of us, each day arrives with a new demand.

Still, for most of us, each day arrives with a new demand. American anthropologist Edward Hall argues that if you drew the average North American's buried concept of time, it would look like a line of empty containers. In his 1983 study of time and culture, *The Dance of Life: The Other Dimension of Time*, he says we picture each day as one in a series of empty containers, like a boxcar on an infinitely long train.

We have to make every moment count, because each boxcar is divided into hours, minutes and even into seconds. "If time is wasted," Hall writes, "the container slips by only partially filled and the fact that it is not full is noted. We are evaluated by how those containers look. To have done little or nothing means no containers are filled.

"Sitting around passing the time of day with others, incidentally, is in the 'nothing' category."

Hall doesn't say so, but in the eyes of our culture, making dinner is pretty much in the nothing category, too. The reasons are simple. Cooking is both repetitive and

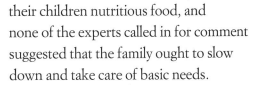

ephemeral. Dinnertime comes up once a day, and the most thoughtfully prepared meal, once it's eaten, is as gone as fast-food hamburger. Over time, wholesome, peaceful dinners may add up to well-being; day by day the one sure result of cooking and eating is dirty dishes.

Talk about dinner, in fact, and the inner Ben Franklin loses interest, goes fuzzy around the edges and starts to fade. Listen as he slips back below the level of consciousness, and you may catch a last piece of advice: "Eat to live," he whispers, "not live to eat," and then he's gone.

What happened to dinner?

No wonder we think of dinner as the last hurdle at the end of the day, a necessary chore. Or, as a woman in a recent newspaper story on how time-poverty affects children's diets put it: "Dinner is something you have to do, but it gets in the way."

The first time I read the story, my eyes slipped over those words. There were more startling things to read. Here, for example, were parents too busy to feed their children nutritious food, and none of the experts called in for comment suggested that the family ought to slow down and take care of basic needs.

Because the story interested me I clipped it and read it again. This time, reading that dinner "gets

What we'd really like at six o'clock is someone else to cook dinner for us.

in the way" was like stepping on a rake. I saw what the words really mean: "Nourishing myself and people I love is a chore that keeps me from doing more important things."

Check reports from nutrition researchers and you'll find them unanimous on one score: fresh, whole foods, the kind you can't get from packages or fast-food outlets, promote good health and offer protection against disease. What is it, you might wonder, that's more important than good health?

Graze through food magazines and you could easily assume that ours is a society of hedonists. Bookstores burst with luscious cookbooks. Kitchenware stores do a booming business. For anyone with money to spend on eating out, it's a mark of sophistication to know how to eat in Thai restaurants, sushi bars and wonton houses. Television networks run Saturday afternoon cooking shows back to back, testimony to the power and importance of food in our lives.

Yet our own day-to-day meals are chores, bothersome duties that get in the way of hockey practice, night school classes and surfing the Internet. We set goals for ourselves, and scramble after them. Sometimes the goal is an expansive one, sometimes it's economic survival. In either case, you aren't likely to write "make dinner" in the spot your daytimer reserves for high priority items.

What we'd really like at six o'clock is someone else to cook dinner for us, a desire that often comes with a little stab of guilt. But take a backward look and you'll see that this is not a whiny new demand that shows we aren't quite the calibre of people our parents were.

The full-time wife is departing with the speed of the live-in cook.

Until the beginning of the First World War, many families employed a cook, whose full-time job was shopping and cooking. Then cooks disappeared, along with gardeners, housekeepers and laundry maids. The authors of *The Joy of Cooking* wrote their encyclopedic book, they tell us, to teach wives newly without kitchen help how to fend for themselves. They begin their introduction, written in 1931, by quoting Saki: "The cook was a good cook, as cooks go, and as cooks go, she went."

Now the full-time wife Irma and Marion Rombauer hoped to tutor is departing with the speed of the live-in cook. Planning, shopping and cooking dinner are still essential tasks. This time around, there's no one left to take on the job.

And who would want to, given how we think about time? Making family dinners doesn't fill boxcars. Viewed from the perspective of the working world, feeding a family is strictly maintenance. When we measure gross national product, we don't count the labor of making dinner, or any other household labor. It's not, in our understanding, real work. Eating dinner adds nothing to your list of accomplishments either, unless it's a business dinner that results in a deal. Children don't make business deals at dinner, so for them, eating dinner is time away from music lessons, sports, homework and television.

So we rush to get things done, blind to the knowledge that time is finite, but work isn't. Fevered by hurry sickness, we've forgotten that food is a source of pleasure, that cooking and eating can bring us back to our senses. The truth is, the more we slow down to notice the sheen of a red pepper, the scent of cumin roasting or the flavor of a raspberry, the more alive we become.

At the speed of life

Chop an onion or taste a soup with full attention, and sooner or later you will stumble on a fundamental truth: eating food means eating life. Meat, fish, grains and vegetables all pass the life they contain on to us; apples in your fruit bowl are breathing as you read this. Food is a continuous chain that passes life from the living soil to the plants that grow in it, to the animals that eat the plants, and then back to the soil, dust into dust.

How you frame this understanding doesn't much matter. You can see food on your plate as life forms sustaining your life, or say, with poet William Carlos Williams, "There is nothing to eat, seek it where you will, but the body of the Lord." All that matters is that you recognize that dinner connects you to life. When you do, you will find your hand resting on a gateway to peace.

You may still have only half an hour to cook, and that half hour may still come at the end of a busy day. But once you know the worth of that half hour, and the time at the table that follows, you can make a commitment to put pleasure back into dinner.

Does that seem impossible to do in the time you have? Stare through the lens of disappearing time and that's how it looks, a landscape of desperation and guilt. You'll never have the time your mother had to cook.

Switch lenses and focus on how food and cooking have changed, and you'll see that your mother could never cook like you. With the ingredients and techniques we have at our disposal, we no longer need more than half an hour to cook a satisfying meal.

If you could open the door on a supermarket of the early 1960s you would search in vain for the foods most useful to anyone who wants to eat well in a limited amount of time. Ripe red peppers, papayas, mangoes, parmesan cheese (ungrated, in blocks), sun-dried tomatoes, fresh basil, balsamic vinegar, extra virgin olive oil, ginger, low-fat yogurt, ready-to-heat tortillas, fresh salsa, canned black beans: all of them entered our kitchens in the last 30 years. You may not be able to make a baked dessert every night like your mother did. If you have a ripe mango, or a pear and a good piece of cheese, do you care?

We have a whole new vocabulary of strong, basic tastes that don't need to be fussed with. When you add chopped sun-dried tomato to a pasta sauce, you've taken a shortcut to flavor, but it's a different kind of shortcut than the one cooks used to take with a can of cream-of-mushroom soup. Can-of-soup cuisine tried to duplicate intricate sauces and ended up tasting predominantly of salt. High-intensity cooking, if we can call it that, lets good, honest flavors speak simply.

As I worked on this cookbook, I gradually came to understand that this is the way I cook by choice. Pasta is ready in less time than it takes to peel, cook and mash potatoes, but the main reason I eat it so often is that I like it. Steamed sea bass with black bean sauce takes only minutes to prepare; you couldn't improve on it if you labored all day. My mother spent entire afternoons rolling flank steak around a bread dressing and baking it (a dish that for reasons I've never understood she always called duck). A beef stir-fry using flank steak goes together in 15 minutes. Put them side by side, and I suspect most of us would rather eat the stir-fry.

ABOUT THIS BOOK

It turns out that the real challenge isn't cooking dinner in the time we have, it's conquering the mental exhaustion that makes cooking anything at all look far too complicated.

When the six o'clock problem strikes, a sort of amnesia sets in. Not until you've already phoned for pizza or taken yourself off to a restaurant do you remember that neither eating out nor ordering in pay off in time saved or in satisfaction.

You can make a great pizza from scratch in 35 minutes, less time than it takes to have a mediocre one delivered. Unless you can afford to eat frequently in very good restaurants, you will wait for your food in an atmosphere less pleasant than your home.

What you need first is a storehouse of delicious, quick, reliable meals. Then turn your attention to grocery shopping. Make it a habit to keep the pantry well stocked. Whenever you're low on an ingredient, make a note on your central grocery list.

I can rarely predict what I'd like to eat for dinner tomorrow, much less a week in advance, so I've never been able to shop for a week's worth of menus at one time. Instead, I've learned to buy food I know I like, and to let appetite guide me when dinnertime arrives. The cook who keeps a stock of spices, chutneys, pastas, canned tomatoes, canned or frozen beans, frozen hamburger and chicken breasts, cheese, ready-made tortillas, salsa and relatively sturdy vegetables (such as broccoli, cauliflower, bell peppers, onions and garlic) on hand need never make more than a quick stop at the market on the way home.

(A herb garden is a kind of living pantry: nothing enlivens quick meals more than fresh herbs. In the summer, I keep herbs in pots near the kitchen door, all of them easy to care for and infinitely rewarding. The world has yet to see the person who can't grow mint, or the garden that won't sustain it.)

The recipes in this book range over several levels of difficulty. To find the simplest, look for the Extra Fast logo, or check the chart on page 176 (where you'll also find a guide to recipes that are Kids' Faves, Low Fat and Great for Entertaining).

For your most hurried evenings, learn a dinner or two that you can make in 15 minutes with one hand tied behind your back. It's best if it needs only ingredients you can keep in the pantry. My own 15-minute meal is Black Bean Burritos, which is as easy and delicious as a recipe can be. You'll be amazed how it

becomes second nature after you've made it once or twice.

When six o'clock comes around, flip through this cookbook, check the pantry, make a decision — and rejoice. The hard part is over.

Then take a deep breath and remember why it's worth slowing down. Congratulate yourself for having your values in order, and notice that you're at home, in your own kitchen, with plenty to eat. If you aren't going to take pleasure in cooking and eating today, when will you?

Six o'clock will keep on arriving as long as people tell time. "Time goes, you say? Ah no!/ Alas, Time stays, we go," wrote English poet and man of letters Austin Dobson, who left this time-bound world in 1921.

He's right, you know. Our lives drift by like cherry blossoms. We have no time to waste being unhappy with dinner. ⏱

CHAPTER ONE

MEAT

Back when my Mom made dinner, home cooks had three things to bring together on one plate: meat, potatoes and a vegetable.

If you want to cook well in a limited time, it makes sense to merge at least two of those elements whenever you can. Meat and vegetables in a stir-fry need only rice to round out a meal. Pasta dishes put the meat together with today's equivalent of the potato, and some of them manage to include the vegetables, too. The Black Bean and Sausage Soup that begins this chapter makes a meal with nothing more to add than a salad and a loaf of bread.

When you make meat the centrepiece, it's surprising how often the result turns out to be a guest-worthy dinner. The effect is heightened if you choose pork tenderloin or lamb chops — cuts that lend themselves to fast and elegant presentations.

Looking for a homier surprise? Then try Upside-Down Pizza at the end of the chapter: easy enough for kids to make, goofy enough for them to love.

Black Bean Soup with Hot Italian Sausage and Spinach

Makes 4 servings

Why is it that when Europeans first started cooking South American beans in the 16th century, they enthusiastically adopted the lima bean and the kidney bean but left the better tasting, better looking, black bean alone? It's a culinary mystery, and one that only grows deeper when you make a dish like this spicy, robust bean-and-sausage soup.

Because the greens show up in your bowl, this is a true one-dish meal, demanding nothing more than a loaf of bread on the side. If you'd like more, set out carrot sticks and olives to whet appetites before dinner.

1	tablespoon (15 mL) olive oil
¾	pound (350 g) hot Italian sausages, cut into ½-inch (1 cm) pieces
1	small onion, chopped
2	garlic cloves, chopped fine
1	(540-mL) can tomatoes (undrained), chopped coarse
1½	cups (375 mL) chicken stock
1	(398-mL) can black beans, drained and rinsed
2	tablespoons (30 mL) chopped, drained sun-dried tomatoes (packed in oil)
1	tablespoon (15 mL) chopped fresh oregano
1	teaspoon (5 mL) chopped fresh thyme
1	bunch spinach, chopped coarse
	Salt and pepper

In large heavy saucepan, heat oil over medium-high heat. Add sausages and saute for 5 minutes or until cooked. Remove sausages and set aside.

Add onion and garlic to saucepan; saute about 3 minutes or until tender. Stir in tomatoes, stock, beans, sun-dried tomatoes, oregano, thyme and sausages; bring to a boil. Add spinach and cook for about 1 minute or until wilted. Add salt and pepper to taste. ⟳

SCISSOR HAPPY

When a recipe calls for a can of tomatoes, chopped, the smartest thing to do is buy them chopped in the can. If all you have is whole canned tomatoes, pull out the kitchen shears. Remove the lid, but don't empty the can. Instead, use the scissors to chop them in the can. You'll save a little chopping time and a lot of cleanup.

Speedy Chili with Sun-Dried Tomatoes

Makes 4 servings

Whether this bright and sunny dish of squash, green bell pepper, tomatoes, white kidney beans and sun-dried tomatoes should really be called a chili is open to question. What's beyond doubt is that it performs the loaves-and-fishes miracle of stretching half a pound of ground beef to feed four — and brings you closer to the eat-more-vegetables spirit of Canada's new food guide, to boot.

1	tablespoon (15 mL) olive oil
½	pound (250 g) lean ground beef
1	cup (250 mL) diced peeled butternut or other winter squash
1	onion, chopped
1	green bell pepper, chopped
1	garlic clove, chopped fine
1	(796-mL) can tomatoes
1	(213-mL) can tomato sauce
¼	cup (50 mL) chopped sun-dried tomatoes (not packed in oil)
1	tablespoon (15 mL) chili powder
1	teaspoon (5 mL) salt
½	teaspoon (2 mL) dried oregano
½	teaspoon (2 mL) dried basil
1	(540-mL) can white kidney beans, drained and rinsed
½	teaspoon (2 mL) Tabasco sauce or to taste
	Grated parmesan cheese

In large heavy saucepan, heat oil over medium-high heat. Add beef, breaking up with back of spoon. Add squash, onion, green pepper and garlic; saute for 5 minutes or until beef is no longer pink and vegetables are tender.

Add tomatoes, tomato sauce, sun-dried tomatoes, chili powder, salt, oregano and basil. Cook over medium heat for 10 minutes.

Add beans and cook for 5 minutes. Stir in Tabasco sauce.

Serve with parmesan cheese. ○

WHAT ARE WHITE KIDNEY BEANS?

Dark red kidney beans are robust and meaty. White kidney beans not only look different, they taste different: milder, with a subtle nut-like flavor. You'll sometimes find small white kidney beans packaged as cannellini beans; they're the traditional choice for minestrone and bean salads.

Flank Steak with Chipotle Marinade

Makes 4 servings

Perhaps it's the salt in the corn chips. Perhaps it's the perverse cooling effect of hot chili peppers. Whatever the reason, when the heat goes up, Mexican flavors are irresistible. If you're ready to press on past the familiar territory of cumin and cilantro, try this flank steak, flavored with smoky chipotle peppers, for a quick summer meal. But don't get over-confident: chipotles are hot chilies. Use just one, at least the first time.

With rice, corn on the cob and a green salad, dinner's made. To keep people amused while the cooking is under way, set out corn chips, guacamole and fresh tomato salsa.

¼	**cup (50 mL) loosely packed fresh oregano leaves**
1	**canned chipotle pepper in adobo sauce, chopped coarse**
1	**shallot, cut into small pieces**
1	**garlic clove, chopped coarse**
½	**teaspoon (2 mL) salt**
¼	**teaspoon (1 mL) pepper**
¼	**teaspoon (1 mL) brown sugar**
¼	**cup (50 mL) olive oil**
2	**tablespoons (30 mL) red wine vinegar**
1	**pound (500 g) flank steak**

In blender or small food processor, combine oregano, chipotle pepper, shallot, garlic, salt, pepper, sugar, oil and vinegar; process until oregano is finely chopped. Put in shallow glass baking dish large enough to hold steak in single layer. Add steak, turning to coat well. Let marinate for 5 minutes.

Remove steak from marinade and place on greased broiler pan; reserve marinade. Broil for about 10 minutes or until cooked, turning once and brushing with marinade. To serve, cut across the grain into thin slices. ☾

WHAT ARE CHIPOTLE PEPPERS?

Chipotles are jalapeno peppers, dried, smoked and, more often than not, packed in a can with adobo sauce — a mixture of onions, tomatoes, vinegar and spices.

Chipotles have a characteristic smoky taste that one chili expert describes as "imposing." Translation: a little goes a long way. Transfer leftover chipotles from the can to a freezer container and freeze them for future use.

WHAT IS EXTRA-THICK YOGURT?

Anyone who makes yogurt at home knows that you get thicker results if you add skim milk powder. Although the full process is a bit more complicated, that's essentially what Astro Dairy Products, maker of extra-thick yogurt, has done to come up with a nutritionally superior sour cream substitute.

A cup of extra-thick yogurt contains 8.2 grams of fat, compared to 36 grams in the same amount of regular sour cream, and 13.8 grams in the same amount of light sour cream.

Because of the skim milk powder, extra-thick yogurt is also higher in protein, calcium and carbohydrates than either light or regular sour cream, and lower in calories and cholesterol.

You can substitute extra-thick yogurt for sour cream, measure for measure, in most cooking.

Cheeky Stroganoff with Ground Beef

Makes 4 servings

True, it takes a certain amount of brass to call a ground-beef-and-mushroom dish a stroganoff, especially when extra-thick yogurt takes the place of sour cream. But ground beef is inexpensive and quick-cooking — two virtues that count for a lot. And extra-thick yogurt gives the sauce the same thick, creamy texture as sour cream, with a fraction of the fat. Broad noodles are the traditional choice to serve beneath the sauce, but almost any pasta you have on hand will do. Add sliced carrots, steamed or boiled and tossed with a little butter and dill, for a welcome splash of color on the plate.

6	cups (1.5 L) broad noodles
2	tablespoons (30 mL) vegetable oil
¾	pound (350 g) lean ground beef
1	medium onion, chopped
2	cups (500 mL) sliced mushrooms
1	garlic clove, chopped fine
1	tablespoon (15 mL) flour
½	teaspoon (2 mL) salt
½	teaspoon (2 mL) paprika
¼	teaspoon (1 mL) pepper
¼	teaspoon (1 mL) dried thyme
¼	teaspoon (1 mL) dried marjoram
1	cup (250 mL) beef stock
1	cup (250 mL) extra-thick plain yogurt

Cook noodles in large amount of boiling salted water until tender; drain.

Meanwhile, heat oil in large heavy frypan over medium-high heat. Add beef and saute for 3 to 5 minutes or until no longer pink. With slotted spoon, remove meat and set aside.

Reduce heat to medium and add onion, mushrooms and garlic to frypan; saute about 4 minutes or until vegetables are tender. Return beef and sprinkle with flour, salt, paprika, pepper, thyme and marjoram; stir to mix. Stir in stock and cook for 1 minute. Stir in yogurt (do not let boil). Serve over noodles. ⟳

Far East Burgers

Makes 4 servings

The danger in letting hamburgers become one of your quick dinner habits is that you can quickly find yourself saddled with a bad case of same-old-thing syndrome. If you'd still like a burger, but boredom is creeping in, try this Pacific Rim variation. Pop the patties in buns and add the standard lettuce and tomato trimmings, or, if the smell of ginger leads you off in another direction, serve them with a heap of stir-fried vegetables and some steamed rice.

1	pound (500 g) lean ground beef
2	teaspoons (10 mL) grated fresh ginger
2	teaspoons (10 mL) hoisin sauce
2	teaspoons (10 mL) soy sauce
2	teaspoons (10 mL) dry sherry
1	green onion, chopped fine
⅛	teaspoon (0.5 mL) pepper
1	tablespoon (15 mL) vegetable oil

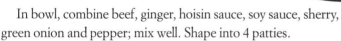

In bowl, combine beef, ginger, hoisin sauce, soy sauce, sherry, green onion and pepper; mix well. Shape into 4 patties.

In heavy frypan, heat oil over medium heat. Add patties and cook for about 12 minutes or until no longer pink inside, turning once. ○

Satay Beef and Bok Choy Stir-Fry

Makes 4 servings

Chinese satay is a paste made from shrimp, chili, soy sauce, spices and sometimes peanuts. Indonesian saté is a way of grilling meat, which, once grilled, is often served with peanut sauce. For this recipe, you want a Chinese satay paste (we used Chiu Chow brand; look for a gold label with a panda logo). Stephen Wong, who writes about the Pacific Rim for our food pages, brought this handsome stir-fry into the test kitchen: a bed of green and white bok choy topped with spicy strips of beef. All you need to add is rice.

1	pound (500 g) flank steak, cut into thin slices about 2 inches (5 cm) long
2	tablespoons (30 mL) vegetable oil

HAMBURGER SAFETY

Protect family and friends from E. coli, *the culprit in hamburger disease, by cooking hamburgers thoroughly.*

When you split the burgers apart, the juices should run clear and any tinge of pink on the inside should disappear after two or three seconds.

Don't try to cook an inch-thick burger on the grill. The outside will burn before the inside cooks. Instead, serve two thinner patties.

Don't let raw meat or its juices come into contact with food that will be eaten raw. Once you've put the burgers on the grill, take the plate that held the raw meat back into the kitchen. Put the cooked meat on a clean plate.

Don't forget the barbecue tongs or spatula that lifted the raw meat on to the grill. Rest the business end of the tool over the grill so the heat can kill any bacteria.

5 slices (¼-inch or 5-mm thick) peeled fresh ginger
1 large shallot, sliced thin
Salt

Marinade
1 tablespoon (15 mL) cornstarch
1 teaspoon (5 mL) sugar
2 tablespoons (30 mL) water
1 tablespoon (15 mL) soy sauce
1 tablespoon (15 mL) vegetable oil
2 tablespoons (30 mL) oyster sauce

Vegetables
1 tablespoon (15 mL) vegetable oil
1 pound (500 g) bok choy, trimmed and cut into 3-inch (7 cm) long pieces
1 large garlic clove, chopped fine
½ teaspoon (2 mL) salt
½ teaspoon (2 mL) sugar
1 tablespoon (15 mL) water
1½ teaspoons (7 mL) sesame oil

Sauce
2 teaspoons (10 mL) satay sauce
¼ cup (50 mL) water
1 teaspoon (5 mL) cornstarch

Marinade: In medium bowl, combine cornstarch, sugar, water, soy sauce, oil and oyster sauce. Add beef and stir to coat; let marinate for about 10 minutes.

Vegetables: Heat wok over medium-high heat; add vegetable oil. Add bok choy, garlic, salt and sugar; stir-fry for 1 minute. Add water and stir briefly; cover and cook for 2 minutes or until bok choy is just tender. Add sesame oil and toss to mix; transfer to serving platter and keep warm.

Sauce: In small bowl, combine satay sauce, water and cornstarch; set aside.

Heat 2 tablespoons (30 mL) vegetable oil in wok over high heat. Add ginger and shallot; stir-fry for 15 seconds. Add beef and stir-fry for 2 minutes. Stir sauce mixture; add to wok and cook, stirring constantly, for about 1 minute or until sauce has thickened. Add salt to taste. Pour evenly over vegetables and serve immediately. ⟳

WHAT IS BOK CHOY?

Bok choy is a Chinese cabbage with thick white stalks ending in glossy, dark green leaves. Baby bok choy is more tender and delicate in flavor; but even the mature plant has a sweet, mild taste.

Bok choy is so good stir-fried that most people need no further inducement to eat it. But those seeking peak nutrition should know that bok choy is a good source of iron and potassium, and an excellent source of C and A vitamins. A cup of cooked bok choy provides 160 mg of calcium, one-fifth of an adult's daily requirement.

Beef Stir-Fry with Chinese Broccoli

Makes 4 servings

Black bean sauce goes with beef and stir-fried greens like mint sauce goes with lamb. But do you make your own black bean sauce, or do you buy it already prepared? Kay Leong, who heads South China Seas Trading Co. on Granville Island, brought this recipe into the test kitchen to show that making your own is almost as easy as spooning sauce out of a jar.

½	teaspoon (2 mL) sugar
1	tablespoon (15 mL) mirin (Japanese rice wine)
1½	teaspoons (7 mL) dark soy sauce
2	teaspoons (10 mL) sesame oil, divided
¾	pound (350 g) boneless top sirloin steak, cut into ¼-inch (5 mm) strips
2	tablespoons (30 mL) salted Chinese black beans, rinsed and lightly mashed
1	tablespoon (15 mL) finely chopped garlic
2	tablespoons (30 mL) peanut oil, divided
¼	teaspoon (1 mL) salt, divided
1	(1-inch or 2.5-cm) piece young ginger, julienned
½	to 1 teaspoon (2 to 5 mL) hot chili paste
1	pound (500 g) Chinese broccoli, trimmed and cut diagonally into 2-inch (5 cm) pieces
⅓	cup (75 mL) chicken stock
2	teaspoons (10 mL) cornstarch
1	green onion, sliced diagonally (for garnish)
	Julienned ginger for garnish

In bowl, combine sugar, mirin, soy sauce and 1 teaspoon (5 mL) sesame oil. Add beef and stir to coat; let marinate for about 15 minutes.

Mash black beans, garlic and remaining 1 teaspoon (5 mL) sesame oil lightly together; set aside.

Heat wok or large heavy frypan over high heat. Swirl in 1½ tablespoons (22 mL) peanut oil and ⅛ teaspoon (0.5 mL) salt. When oil starts to smoke, add beef and stir-fry for 40 seconds or until almost cooked. Remove beef and keep warm.

Heat remaining ½ tablespoon (8 mL) peanut oil and ⅛ teaspoon (0.5 mL) salt in wok. Add black bean mixture and saute for 5 seconds. Add ginger and chili paste; saute for 5 seconds.

WHAT IS CHINESE BROCCOLI?

A close cousin to the broccoli we most often buy, Chinese broccoli has slim, dark green stalks, tender leaves and small, four-petalled yellow flowers.

Chinese cooks call it gai lan *and prize its flavor. Anyone looking for nourishment will also appreciate its iron, calcium and vitamins A and C.*

Before cooking Chinese broccoli, trim a half inch from the top and bottom, and remove any yellow or blemished leaves. Look for it at public markets and some Asian groceries. If you can't find it, either regular broccoli or bok choy can stand in.

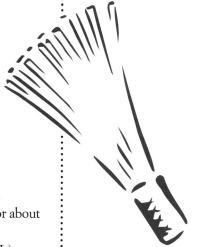

Add Chinese broccoli and stir-fry for 1 minute to coat with black bean mixture. Add accumulated juices from beef; reduce heat to medium, cover and cook for 1 to 2 minutes. Combine stock and cornstarch; set aside.

Increase heat and return beef to wok. Stir cornstarch mixture; add to wok, stirring constantly for 30 seconds or until sauce thickens. Garnish with green onion and ginger. ○

Beef, Bell Pepper and Snow Pea Stir-Fry

Makes 4 servings

A good stir-fry recipe is a diving board, not a straitjacket. So if the price of yellow peppers has gone stratospheric, buy red ones. If the green beans look fresher than the snow peas, make the switch. All you really need to add is rice.

½   cup (125 mL) beef stock
1   tablespoon (15 mL) soy sauce
1   teaspoon (5 mL) cornstarch
3   tablespoons (45 mL) vegetable oil, divided
¾   pound (350 g) flank steak, cut into thin strips
1   jalapeno pepper, seeded and chopped fine
1   garlic clove, chopped fine
1   tablespoon (15 mL) finely chopped fresh ginger
½   pound (250 g) snow peas, trimmed
1   small yellow bell pepper, sliced thin
     Salt and pepper
     Roasted sesame seeds

In small bowl, combine stock, soy sauce and cornstarch; set aside.

In wok or large heavy frypan, heat 1 tablespoon (15 mL) oil over medium-high heat. Add beef and stir-fry for about 2 minutes or until cooked. Remove beef and set aside.

Heat remaining 2 tablespoons (30 mL) oil in wok over medium heat. Add jalapeno pepper, garlic and ginger; stir-fry 1 minute. Add peas and yellow pepper; stir-fry for 2 minutes or until vegetables are tender-crisp. Stir cornstarch mixture; add to wok, stirring constantly. Return beef and simmer for about 1 minute or until sauce thickens, stirring frequently. Add salt and pepper to taste. Place on platter and sprinkle lightly with sesame seeds. ○

HOT AND COLD HONEYDEW MELON

While your family or guests are waiting for the stir-fry, divert their attention with this spicy, no-fat appetizer.

½   honeydew melon, cut into cubes
     Juice of 1 lime
1   to 1½ teaspoons (5 to 7 mL) chili powder

Put melon in bowl and sprinkle with lime juice and chili powder; stir. Serve on cocktail picks.

Barbecued Orange Beef

Makes 4 servings

When it's time to throw a steak on the barbecue, this is the recipe to choose. It not only looks good — cooked, sliced and laid out on a platter with orange slices and cilantro sprigs — it's so full of orange-and-spice flavor no one will notice the modest quarter-pound per person serving.

Don't be put off by the long list of ingredients. Pacific Rim columnist Stephen Wong, who brought this recipe into the kitchen, notes that all but three of them go into the marinade; once it's mixed you can leave it alone to do its work. Rice and a stir-fried green vegetable are all you need to complete the meal.

1	pound (500 g) top sirloin steak
6	orange slices
3	cilantro sprigs

Marinade

4	pieces dried orange peel
2	tablespoons (30 mL) boiling water
3	large garlic cloves, chopped fine
2	green onions, cut into 2-inch (5 cm) pieces and smashed
1	(1-inch or 2.5-cm) piece peeled fresh ginger, smashed
1	tablespoon (15 mL) oyster sauce
2	tablespoons (30 mL) soy sauce
2	tablespoons (30 mL) dry sherry
2	tablespoons (30 mL) frozen orange juice concentrate
2	teaspoons (10 mL) garlic chili paste or to taste
1	teaspoon (5 mL) Worcestershire sauce
1	teaspoon (5 mL) sugar
1	tablespoon (15 mL) cornstarch

Marinade: In small bowl, soak orange peel in the boiling water for about 10 minutes. Squeeze peel over bowl; discard peel and set juice aside.

In shallow dish, combine garlic, green onions, ginger, oyster sauce, soy sauce, sherry, orange juice concentrate, chili paste, Worcestershire sauce, sugar, cornstarch and orange peel juice. Add steak, turning to coat well. Let marinate for about 10 minutes.

Remove steak from marinade. Pour marinade through fine

How to Dry Orange Peel

You can buy dried orange peel in Asian groceries, but, depending on where you live, it may be easier to make your own.

Choose a tangerine or mandarin orange with a fragrant skin. Peel it, then scrape off as much white pith as possible. Dry the peel on a wire cookie rack for three days, or until it's dry and curled, but still slightly pliable. Store at room temperature in a jar with an air-tight lid. It will keep indefinitely.

mesh strainer, pressing with back of spoon to extract juices; set aside for basting.

Cook steak on greased barbecue grill for about 4 minutes per side or until desired degree of doneness, basting once or twice on each side.

Cut steak into ¼-inch (5 mm) thick slices and arrange on serving platter. Garnish with orange slices and cilantro. ◐

Lone Star Tamale Pie
Makes 4 to 6 servings

Some meals have a natural affinity for summer cottages and ski cabins: they're quick, inexpensive and filling; they cook in a frypan; and the ingredients sit easily in any well-stocked pantry. Piling virtue on virtue, Lone Star Tamale Pie is also good looking in a down-home way and offers the Tex-Mex flavors we've all grown so fond of. In case you were wondering, the corn meal expands as it cooks; to serve this "pie" you cut it in wedges.

1	**tablespoon (15 mL) vegetable oil**
¾	**pound (350 g) lean ground beef**
1	**medium onion, chopped**
1	**(398-mL) can whole kernel corn (undrained)**
1	**(398-mL) can stewed tomatoes, drained and chopped**
1	**cup (250 mL) sour cream**
1	**cup (250 mL) yellow cornmeal**
1	**(125-mL) can sliced ripe olives, drained**
1	**tablespoon (15 mL) chili powder**
1	**teaspoon (5 mL) salt**
½	**teaspoon (2 mL) ground cumin**
1	**cup (250 mL) grated monterey jack cheese**
	Salsa

In heavy, 10-inch (25 cm) ovenproof frypan, heat oil over medium-high heat. Add beef and onion; saute for 3 to 5 minutes or until meat is no longer pink. Drain off fat.

Stir in corn, tomatoes, sour cream, cornmeal, olives, chili powder, salt and cumin; mix well. Cover, reduce heat to low and simmer for 20 minutes.

Uncover and sprinkle cheese over top. Broil for 2 to 3 minutes or until golden. Serve with salsa. ◐

SLICE ADVICE

Slice onions the easy way: cut the onion in half lengthwise, then trim the top and peel away the skin, leaving the root intact. Put the cut side down on the chopping block and slice crosswise, starting at the top. The root will hold the onion together as you slice.

Almost Beef Picadillo Enchiladas

Makes 6 servings

Ever since prepared tortillas started showing up in supermarkets, new doorways have opened for time-pressed cooks. Wrap a tortilla around just about anything and you can make an inexpensive, satisfying, almost-Mexican meal in half an hour. If these were authentic enchiladas, the tortilla would be corn. Instead, this recipe wraps a flour tortilla around a close-to-traditional picadillo sauce enlivened with almonds, raisins and red bell pepper.

Add a green salad and dinner's complete. If the Grade 9 boys' basketball team is coming for dinner, add rice on the side and set out a large quantity of nachos while the enchiladas bake.

1	tablespoon (15 mL) vegetable oil
1½	pounds (750 g) lean ground beef
1	(398-mL) can stewed tomatoes
1½	cups (375 mL) medium salsa, divided
1	red bell pepper, chopped
¼	cup (50 mL) coarsely chopped slivered almonds
¼	cup (50 mL) raisins
	Pinch ground cinnamon
1	garlic clove, crushed
10	(8-inch or 20-cm) flour tortillas
1½	cups (375 mL) grated monterey jack cheese
	Salsa, optional

In large heavy frypan, heat oil over medium-high heat. Add beef and saute for 3 to 5 minutes or until no longer pink. Add tomatoes, ¾ cup (175 mL) salsa, red pepper, almonds, raisins, cinnamon and garlic; bring to a boil. Reduce heat and simmer for 10 minutes or until most of the liquid has evaporated.

Spoon ½ cup (125 mL) beef mixture down centre of each tortilla; roll up and place seam side down in greased 13x9-inch (33x23 cm) baking pan. Spoon remaining ¾ cup (175 mL) salsa evenly over enchiladas. Cover pan with foil.

Bake at 350 F (180 C) for 20 minutes or until heated through. Sprinkle with cheese and place under broiler until cheese is melted. Serve with salsa. ☽

WRAP IT!

Enchiladas: *corn tortillas, rolled around a meat or cheese filling, often baked, always served with chili sauce.*

Burritos: *flour tortillas that completely enclose a meat, bean, cheese or sour cream filling. Sometimes fried, often baked.*

Tostadas: *crisp-fried tortillas, corn or wheat flour, topped with beans, chicken or beef and any combination of: lettuce, tomatoes, cheese, sour cream, olives and guacamole. Can be served as a side salad or a whole meal.*

Tacos: *folded corn tortillas, usually crisp-fried, filled with anything that would go on top of a tostada. Think of it as a Mexican sandwich.*

Beef Fajitas

Makes 4 servings

An authentic fajita involves a skirt steak marinated at least 24 hours in a mixture of oil, lime juice, chili and garlic before being grilled, sliced and wrapped in a warm tortilla with onions and bell pepper. We won't be doing that here. Start with a more tender cut of beef and you don't need a long marinating time; stir-fry the beef and it will cook faster than it would on a grill. Then wrap it in a warm tortilla, add sauteed onions and bell pepper, and top with salsa, guacamole, cheddar cheese or a dab of sour cream. Add a salad for a light meal. If you'd like a more substantial dinner, serve the fajitas with steamed rice.

8	(8-inch or 20-cm) flour tortillas
1	tablespoon (15 mL) vegetable oil
¾	pound (350 g) top sirloin steak, cut into thin strips
1	medium onion, sliced thin
½	cup (125 mL) julienned red bell pepper
½	cup (125 mL) julienned green bell pepper
¾	cup (175 mL) mild or medium salsa
½	teaspoon (2 mL) ground cumin
	Toppings: grated cheddar cheese, guacamole, salsa and sour cream

Stack tortillas and wrap in foil. Bake at 350 F (180 C) for 5 minutes or until heated through.

In large heavy frypan, heat oil over medium-high heat. Add beef and saute for 1 minute. Add onion and red and green peppers; saute for 3 minutes or until peppers are tender-crisp and beef is cooked. Reduce heat to medium and stir in salsa and cumin; heat through.

Place an equal portion of beef mixture in centre of each tortilla. Fold bottom of each tortilla (side closest to you) up over the filling; then fold the sides in, overlapping. Serve with desired toppings. ○

GUACAMOLE

2	medium-size ripe avocados, mashed
2	tablespoons (30 mL) finely chopped onion (optional)
4	teaspoons (20 mL) lemon juice
½	teaspoon (2 mL) ground roasted cumin seeds
	Salt to taste
	Few drops Tabasco sauce or to taste

Combine all ingredients in bowl. Garnish with a black olive and a sprinkling of roasted cumin seeds.

Pork Stir-Fry with Broccoli and Lemon

Makes 4 servings

Slice boneless pork into thin strips and you can cook it quickly, a fact not lost upon the early Chinese who invented stir-frying to conserve fuel and came up with one of the great fast cooking techniques of all time.

Flavor the pork with lemon and rosemary and serve it with pasta, and only a purist will notice that there's something about dinner that isn't quite Italian. To fill out the corners of this one-dish meal, pick up spicy olives to eat before dinner, fresh focaccia bread and dark greens for a salad to eat after the pork and broccoli.

¾	**pound (350 g) fettuccine**
¾	**pound (350 g) lean boneless pork, cut into thin strips**
	Grated zest of 1 medium lemon
½	**teaspoon (2 mL) salt**
½	**teaspoon (2 mL) pepper**
1	**teaspoon (5 mL) chopped fresh rosemary**
2	**tablespoons (30 mL) butter, divided**
2	**tablespoons (30 mL) vegetable oil, divided**
4	**cups (1 L) broccoli flowerets**
¾	**cup (175 mL) chicken stock**
	Juice from ½ medium lemon
3	**garlic cloves, chopped fine**

Cook fettuccine in large amount of boiling salted water until tender; drain.

Meanwhile, toss pork with lemon zest, salt, pepper and rosemary. In wok or large heavy frypan, heat 1 tablespoon (15 mL) butter and 1 tablespoon (15 mL) oil over medium-high heat. Add pork mixture and stir-fry for about 3 minutes or until lightly browned. With slotted spoon, remove pork and set aside.

Add remaining 1 tablespoon (15 mL) butter and 1 tablespoon (15 mL) oil to wok. Add broccoli and stir-fry for 2 minutes or until tender-crisp. Remove and set aside.

Add stock, lemon juice and garlic to wok. Bring to a boil, stirring and scraping browned bits from bottom of wok. Boil for 3 to 4 minutes or until slightly thickened. Return pork and broccoli to wok; simmer over low heat for 1 minute. Serve over pasta. ◷

GOING AGAINST THE GRAIN

To get the most tender meat for your stir-fries, cut it into thin strips across the grain, not with it.

Muscles are made up of long thin muscle fibres, held together by sheets of connective tissue. When you cut across the longitudinal structure of the muscle, you cut through the connective tissue and make the meat easier to chew.

Slicing meat for stir-fries is easiest when the meat is slightly frozen. Half an hour in the freezer is enough time to make it firmer; if you're defrosting meat to use for supper, do the slicing before it's fully thawed.

Pork Chops Sicilian Style
Makes 4 servings

PUMPING UP
SPINACH SALAD

*If you're bored with simple
spinach salads, try adding oyster
mushrooms, sauteed in olive oil
with garlic and a little rosemary,
and topped with a lot of basil
sprinkled on at the end. Or add
any combination of the following:*
- *fresh dill*
- *chopped fennel*
- *specialty olives*
- *red onion rings*
- *navel orange chunks*
- *red peppers, roasted or raw*
- *sun-dried tomatoes, chopped*

*Just because they're called fast-fry pork chops doesn't mean that's the
only way to cook them. The proof is this recipe, inspired by reader Kelly
Saunders's entry in our Six O'Clock Solutions contest. Saunders quickly
browns her chops, then bakes them under a topping of bread crumbs,
raisins, pine nuts, capers and parmesan cheese.*

*Add baby carrots, steamed and tossed in butter and parsley, and
either rice or pasta to make a warming meal. Several small bowls of
olives with a range of flavors — herbed, hot and spicy, sun-dried —
and a loaf of Italian bread would be a good way to start dinner; a salad
of spinach or arugula (a peppery green) would end it nicely.*

2	tablespoons (30 mL) olive oil, divided
1	small onion, chopped
1	garlic clove, crushed
¾	cup (175 mL) fresh bread crumbs
¼	cup (50 mL) raisins
¼	cup (50 mL) pine nuts, lightly toasted (see note)
1	tablespoon (15 mL) drained capers
¼	cup (50 mL) grated parmesan cheese
2	tablespoons (30 mL) chopped fresh parsley
¼	teaspoon (1 mL) salt
¼	teaspoon (1 mL) pepper
4	bone-in, fast-fry pork chops (about 1 pound or 500 g total)

In 12-inch (30 cm) frypan, heat 1 tablespoon (15 mL) oil over
medium heat. Add onion and garlic; saute for 5 minutes or until
tender. Transfer to bowl and stir in bread crumbs, raisins, pine
nuts, capers, cheese, parsley, salt and pepper.

In same frypan, heat remaining 1 tablespoon (15 mL) oil over
medium-high heat. Add pork chops and saute about 2 minutes or
until golden, turning once.

Arrange chops in 9-inch (23 cm) square baking dish. Spread
crumb mixture over chops. Bake at 375 F (190 C) for about
8 minutes or until chops are cooked.

Note: Spread pine nuts on baking sheet and bake at 375 F
(190 C) for 3 to 4 minutes or until golden. ○

SIX CLOCK

Pork Chops with Maple Syrup and Balsamic Vinegar

Makes 4 servings

A fast-fry pork chop is a handy thing to have in a kitchen because you can cook it in jig time — less than two minutes a side. The drawback? On its own, a thin little chop is far from an inspiring main course. So let maple syrup and balsamic vinegar come to the rescue. Add them to shallots and chicken stock, cooked in the pan you used for the chops, to make a sweet and darkly mysterious sauce that tastes like you've been cooking for hours.

Boiled nugget potatoes and steamed acorn squash, dusted with cinnamon, round out the dinner plate. Add a green salad and a good loaf of bread and you're golden.

1	**pound (500 g) boneless fast-fry pork chops**
	Salt and pepper
1	**tablespoon (15 mL) butter**
1	**tablespoon (15 mL) vegetable oil**
2	**tablespoons (30 mL) finely chopped shallots**
¾	**cup (175 mL) canned chicken broth (undiluted)**
1	**tablespoon (15 mL) maple syrup**
1	**tablespoon (15 mL) balsamic vinegar**

Lightly sprinkle both sides of pork chops with salt and pepper.

In large heavy frypan, heat butter and oil over medium-high heat. Add chops and saute for about 3½ minutes or until cooked, turning once. Remove chops and set aside.

Add shallot to frypan and saute for about 30 seconds. Stir in stock and boil for 3 to 5 minutes or until reduced to about ½ cup (125 mL). Stir in maple syrup and vinegar; simmer until slightly thickened, about 2 minutes. Return chops with accumulated juice to frypan and heat through, about 1 minute. ○

ABOUT MAPLE SYRUP

Even if you keep an inexpensive pancake syrup on hand for Saturday morning pancake breakfasts with the kids, you need a jar of the real thing — the boiled down sap of a sugar maple — for fine cooking and special occasions.

Pure maple syrup is usually offered in light, medium and dark grades. Amber, full-flavored medium is the right choice most of the time. Light syrup is paler and milder tasting. Dark can taste too much like molasses.

Store pure maple syrup in the fridge once it's been opened.

Pork Chops with Sweet-and-Sour Cabbage

Makes 4 servings

Cabbage is an old-time vegetable with newly discovered virtues: as a member of the cruciferous family, it contains health-promoting anti-oxidants. But if you've ever had a cabbage threaten to take up permanent residence in the vegetable crisper, you'll know there's sometimes a gap between what you ought to eat, and what you want to eat.

One answer: braise the cabbage in chicken stock; season it with cider vinegar, honey and thyme; then serve it with quick-cooking pork chops. Add egg noodles, a green salad and a loaf of good bread, and you have a hearty, sustaining dinner so good you'll find yourself buying cabbage more often.

3	tablespoons (45 mL) cider vinegar
3	tablespoons (45 mL) apple juice
2	teaspoons (10 mL) liquid honey
1	tablespoon (15 mL) butter
1	tablespoon (15 mL) vegetable oil
1	pound (500 g) boneless fast-fry pork chops
1	small onion, chopped
4	cups (1 L) shredded green cabbage
½	cup (125 mL) chicken stock
2	teaspoons (10 mL) chopped fresh thyme
	Salt and pepper

In small bowl, combine vinegar, apple juice and honey; set aside.

In large heavy frypan, heat butter and oil over medium-high heat. Add pork chops and saute for about 3½ minutes or until cooked, turning once. Remove chops and keep warm.

Drain off all but 1 tablespoon (15 mL) fat from frypan. Add onion and saute for 3 minutes or until just tender. Add cabbage and stock; reduce heat to medium and cook, covered, for 5 minutes. Remove cabbage and set aside.

Add vinegar mixture and thyme to frypan; bring to a boil, stirring and scraping browned bits from bottom of pan. Return cabbage to frypan and heat through, stirring frequently. Add salt and pepper to taste. Serve with pork chops. ⟳

*T*AKING STOCK

Most of the recipes in this book are based on reconstituted canned chicken or beef broth, because that's what the quick cook is more likely to have on hand — but, if you can manage it, fresh stock is far better. Not only is it usually lower in sodium (you control the amount of salt you add), it also tastes better. If you don't make your own, look for a specialty shop where you can buy it in plastic bags or tubs. If all else fails, look for a low-sodium canned variety.

Flash-in-the-Pan Pork Schnitzel

Makes 4 servings

It's been years since German food cut a swath through glossy food magazines. So it may not have occurred to you that a schnitzel, defined as any thin slice of meat that's been dipped in egg, breaded and fried, is as quick to cook as a boneless chicken breast. To make a sustaining winter supper, serve these cutlets, spiked with cayenne pepper, with mashed potatoes and braised cabbage, and add a bowl of applesauce on the side.

And yes, you can make mashed potatoes in under half an hour. The secret is to cut the peeled potatoes into chunks small enough that they'll cook in 20 minutes.

¼	cup (50 mL) flour
1	teaspoon (5 mL) dried thyme
1	teaspoon (5 mL) dried sage
½	teaspoon (2 mL) garlic powder
½	teaspoon (2 mL) cayenne pepper
1	egg
2	tablespoons (30 mL) water
¾	cup (175 mL) dry bread crumbs
1	pound (500 g) pork leg cutlets
1	tablespoon (15 mL) butter
1	tablespoon (15 mL) vegetable oil

Combine flour, thyme, sage, garlic powder and cayenne pepper. In shallow dish, beat egg with water. Put bread crumbs on a plate.

Dredge pork cutlets in seasoned flour; shake off excess. Dip in egg mixture, then coat with bread crumbs.

In heavy frypan, heat butter and oil over medium-high heat. Add cutlets and saute about 3 minutes or until cooked, turning once. ☾

GARLIC POWDER AND WHY YOU MOSTLY SHOULDN'T USE IT

Garlic powder is made from dehydrated garlic flakes, ground to a powder. It turns rancid quickly in the jar and even when fresh, its harsh, one-note taste has none of the charms of fresh garlic.

Garlic powder's one advantage: it can be incorporated evenly into a dry mixture, such as the coating for speedy schnitzels. Store it in the fridge, and smell it before you use it.

Pork Chops with Papaya Salsa

Makes 4 servings

Nine times out of 10, we use the word salsa to mean a mixture of tomatoes, onions, chilies and cilantro. This is the tenth time. Here, salsa is a colorful, slightly sweet, slightly hot relish, with all of its flavors bouncing off the lush flesh of a ripe papaya. Pair it with pork chops marinated in cumin, lime juice and cayenne whenever you need to give an everyday pork dinner a culinary boost. (If you don't have a papaya, but there are two perfect peaches or nectarines on your kitchen counter, go ahead: the magic will still work.) Add rice and steamed broccoli or asparagus to round out the meal.

4	boneless pork loin chops (about 14 ounces or 400 g total)
⅓	cup (75 mL) lime juice, divided
1	tablespoon (15 mL) vegetable oil
2½	teaspoons (12 mL) ground cumin, divided
	Pinch cayenne pepper
	Pinch black pepper
1	ripe papaya, peeled, seeded and diced
¼	cup (50 mL) chopped red onion
1	tablespoon (15 mL) finely chopped jalapeno pepper
1	tablespoon (15 mL) chopped fresh cilantro
1	teaspoon (5 mL) liquid honey
	Salt and pepper

Place pork chops in shallow glass baking dish just large enough to hold them in a single layer. Stir together half the lime juice, oil, 2 teaspoons (10 mL) cumin, cayenne pepper and pinch black pepper; pour over chops. Cover and marinate for about 20 minutes.

Remove chops from marinade and place on broiler pan; reserve marinade. Broil for 12 to 16 minutes or until cooked, brushing frequently with marinade and turning once.

Meanwhile, prepare salsa. Stir together papaya, onion, jalapeno pepper, cilantro, honey, remaining lime juice and ½ teaspoon (2 mL) cumin. Add salt and pepper to taste. Serve with pork chops. ⏱

Finding A Good Papaya

Look for fruit that's turned golden yellow and grown tender enough to yield to a gentle touch. Shun fruit that shows bruises, soft spots or mould.

A papaya that's still hard and more green than gold will ripen at room temperature. You can speed the process by putting the papaya in a loosely closed paper bag.

Barbecued Pork Tenderloin with Plum Sauce and Rosemary

Makes 4 servings

Some people are never happier than when they're standing a tradition on its head. If that's you, try this twist on the time-honored pairing of pork and fruit: make the fruit an Asian plum sauce and temper it with the lemon-pine astringency of rosemary. Who knows? With this kind of kitchen-level fusion, in a generation or two there could be people who think rosemary and plum sauce together taste like home.

Because it's boneless, a pound of pork tenderloin comfortably feeds four. That makes it relatively economical for an informal company dinner. Add rice or buttered noodles and a plate of snow peas, steamed, then flashed quickly in a frypan with oil, salt and julienne strips of ginger.

1	**pound (500 g) pork tenderloin**
	Salt and pepper
½	**cup (125 mL) plum sauce**
1	**small shallot, chopped fine**
1	**garlic clove, chopped fine**
1	**tablespoon (15 mL) seasoned rice vinegar**
1	**teaspoon (5 mL) soy sauce**
1	**teaspoon (5 mL) chopped fresh rosemary**
	Rosemary sprigs

Lightly sprinkle pork tenderloin with salt and pepper. In small bowl, combine plum sauce, shallot, garlic, vinegar, soy sauce and rosemary.

Brush plum sauce mixture over tenderloin. Place on greased barbecue grill over medium-high heat. Close lid and cook for 15 to 20 minutes or until cooked, turning and basting with plum sauce mixture every 5 minutes.

Remove tenderloin from grill and cut crosswise into ½-inch (1 cm) thick slices. Garnish with rosemary sprigs. ⟁

WHAT IS PLUM SAUCE?

A thick, sweet-and-sour preserve made from plums, apricots, sugar and seasonings, plum sauce gets its second name — duck sauce — from its standard role in Cantonese restaurants: the faithful companion to barbecued duck.

Its play of sweet and tart tastes makes plum sauce a good accompaniment for pork and spareribs, too. Most supermarkets sell plum sauce in the Asian section; store the opened jar in the fridge.

Barbecued Pork Tenderloin with Ginger and Soy Sauce

Makes 4 servings

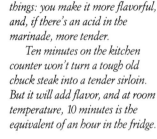

HIGH-SPEED MARINATING

Marinate meat overnight in the fridge and you accomplish two things: you make it more flavorful, and, if there's an acid in the marinade, more tender.

Ten minutes on the kitchen counter won't turn a tough old chuck steak into a tender sirloin. But it will add flavor, and at room temperature, 10 minutes is the equivalent of an hour in the fridge.

Who wants to spend a warm summer evening in the kitchen? If dinner's on your shoulders and the meal can't be a simple salad, try this strategy: grill red peppers, mushrooms and zucchini along with marinated pork tenderloin. Add a bowl of nugget potatoes, which will cook by themselves while you play with the barbecue, and you'll barely have to come inside at all.

Be sure to buy long, slender strips of pork tenderloin instead of short, fat ones. They'll cook more quickly, and you can use the minutes of cooking time you save to let the pork soak in a ginger, sherry, soy and honey marinade.

¼	cup (50 mL) soy sauce
2	tablespoons (30 mL) dry sherry
2	tablespoons (30 mL) vegetable oil
1	tablespoon (15 mL) brown sugar
1	tablespoon (15 mL) grated fresh ginger
1	teaspoon (5 mL) liquid honey
1	garlic clove, crushed
1	pound (500 g) pork tenderloin

In small bowl, combine soy sauce, sherry, oil, sugar, ginger, honey and garlic; stir to mix well. Pour marinade into large plastic bag and add pork tenderloin; seal bag. Let marinate for 10 minutes.

Remove tenderloin from bag; reserve marinade. Place on greased barbecue grill over medium-high heat. Close lid and cook for 15 to 20 minutes or until cooked, turning once and basting frequently with marinade.

Remove tenderloin from grill and cut crosswise into ½-inch (1 cm) thick slices. ○

Pork Tenderloin with Dried Cranberries and Blueberries

Makes 4 servings

I'd bet serious money that few children ever stumble intuitively on to the kinship between grapes and raisins, and even fewer grasp the unity of plums and prunes. Why should they, when dried and fresh fruit are so vastly different? That difference explains part of the excitement of finding dried blueberries and cranberries on grocery shelves: it's like discovering two entirely new foods.

Plumped up in chicken stock and brandy, tempered with shallots and thyme, dried berries make a complex, startlingly quick sauce for pork tenderloin. Add rice and squares of acorn squash, steamed or cooked in the microwave and tossed with butter, and bring out a salad of mixed dark greens after the main course.

1	cup (250 mL) chicken stock
⅓	cup (75 mL) brandy
¼	cup (50 mL) dried cranberries
¼	cup (50 mL) dried blueberries
1	pound (500 g) pork tenderloin, cut into 1-inch (2.5 cm) thick slices
	Salt and pepper
1	tablespoon (15 mL) butter
1	tablespoon (15 mL) vegetable oil
1	large shallot, chopped
1	teaspoon (5 mL) chopped fresh thyme

In heavy saucepan, combine stock, brandy, cranberries and blueberries. Cover and simmer for 5 minutes or until berries are plumped; set aside.

Pound pork slices until ½-inch (1 cm) thick. Lightly sprinkle with salt and pepper.

In large heavy frypan, heat butter and oil over medium-high heat. Add pork and saute for about 3 minutes or until cooked, turning once. Remove pork and set aside.

Add shallot to frypan and saute for 30 seconds. Stir in berry mixture and bring to a boil. Reduce heat and simmer for 3 minutes or until slightly thickened. Stir thyme into sauce. Add salt and pepper to taste. Return pork and heat through. ○

GREAT FOR ENTERTAINING

HOW NEW ARE DRIED CRANBERRIES?

During the Second World War, food processors began drying cranberries as food for the troops. "Crannies" were packed in brick form and had to be rehydrated before use.

But dried cranberries have a history that reaches back much further than 50 years. They were mixed with dried meat and fat, then shaped into cakes, to make pemmican, the survival rations native North Americans carried on hunting trips.

Lamb Burgers

Makes 4 servings

The great appeal of burgers is that they're meant to be picked up and eaten with no knife and fork intervening between you and your food. Ground beef and hamburger buns are incidental: the same atavistic pleasures can easily be had with other patties and other breads. Try, for example, lamb patties, flavored with fresh rosemary, served burger-style in pita breads with tomato, cucumber, lettuce and a dollop of yogurt. Add a salad to make dinner complete — Skinny Orange Vinaigrette is a good partner for spinach.

1	pound (500 g) ground lamb
2	tablespoons (30 mL) fine dry bread crumbs
1	tablespoon (15 mL) water
2	small shallots, chopped fine
1	garlic clove, chopped fine
1	teaspoon (5 mL) finely chopped fresh rosemary
¾	teaspoon (4 mL) salt
¼	teaspoon (1 mL) pepper
4	hamburger-style pita breads, top third cut off
	Sliced tomato
	Sliced cucumber
	Lettuce
	Plain low-fat yogurt

In medium bowl, combine lamb, bread crumbs, water, shallots, garlic, rosemary, salt and pepper. Shape into 4 patties.

Place patties on lightly greased broiler pan and broil for 10 minutes or until cooked, turning once.

Place each patty in a pita bread with tomato, cucumber and lettuce. Top with a dollop of yogurt. ⏱

SKINNY ORANGE VINAIGRETTE

¼	cup (50 mL) orange juice
2	tablespoons (30 mL) olive oil
2	tablespoons (30 mL) white wine vinegar
2	tablespoons (30 mL) coarsely chopped fresh parsley
1	garlic clove
	Salt and pepper to taste

Combine all ingredients in a blender or mini food processor and blend until garlic is chopped fine. Makes about ½ cup (125 mL).

Lamb and Eggplant Meal-in-a-Pocket

Makes 4 servings

Eggplant is not normally a quick-cooking vegetable. That's because the big, round, dark purple eggplants we know best are bitter inside and need to be sliced, salted and left to drain for half an hour before they're fit to cook. So how can you make a Greek-inspired lamb and eggplant saute in 20 minutes? Use long, skinny Japanese eggplants instead. You get much of the same texture and taste with none of the time-consuming preparation.

This meal-in-a-pita contains tomatoes, cucumber, feta and olives along with the lamb and eggplant — enough to tide you through a movie or a night-school class. If the evening's going to be more leisurely, set out a bowl of hummus with pita bread and olives. Add a salad of dark greens, such as spinach, arugula or mizuna, to eat with the pita.

1   tablespoon (15 mL) vegetable oil
1   shallot, chopped
1   garlic clove, chopped fine
½   pound (250 g) ground lamb
2   cups (500 mL) diced Japanese eggplant
     (about 2 eggplants)
1   large tomato, seeded and chopped
⅓   cup (75 mL) chopped English cucumber
½   cup (125 mL) crumbled feta cheese
¼   cup (50 mL) sliced ripe olives
2   tablespoons (30 mL) chopped fresh oregano
     Salt and pepper
4   hamburger-style pita breads, cut in half
     Plain low-fat yogurt

In large heavy frypan, heat oil over medium heat. Add shallot and garlic; saute for 30 seconds. Add lamb and eggplant; saute for 5 to 7 minutes or until lamb is cooked and eggplant is tender.

Drain excess fat from frypan and return to heat. Add tomato, cucumber, feta cheese, olives, oregano and salt and pepper to taste; cook for 1 minute or until heated through.

Spoon an equal portion of lamb mixture into each pita half and top with a dollop of yogurt. ↺

HUMMUS

1   (398-mL) can chickpeas, drained and rinsed
5   garlic cloves
¼   cup (50 mL) water
½   cup (125 mL) tahini (sesame seed paste)
     Juice of 2 lemons
2   tablespoons (30 mL) olive oil
     Salt and pepper

In food processor, pulse chickpeas and garlic. Add water and pulse. Add tahini and lemon juice; puree until smooth. Mix in olive oil and salt and pepper to taste. Makes 2 cups (500 mL).

Anglo-Indian Curried Lamb

Makes 4 servings

When microwave ovens first appeared, they were supposed to revolutionize home cooking. Twenty years later, most of us use the zapper to reheat leftovers and rejuvenate the occasional cup of cold tea. This Anglo-Indian curry, sweetened with raisins and apples, and spiced with a powerful dose of prepared curry powder, might just change your habits. Serve the lamb with rice, mango chutney and a cooling East Indian dish, known as a raita. Heat whole-wheat chapatis (Indian flatbreads you'll find in supermarkets beside the tortillas, which they much resemble) in a frypan, or if you have a gas stove, over a direct flame. Add a salad to satisfy cravings for something green. The spicy Indian crackers called pappadams, puffed in a quarter to a half inch of hot oil, would make a good pre-dinner snack.

1	pound (500 g) ground lamb
½	cup (125 mL) sliced celery
¼	cup (50 mL) chopped onion
1	garlic clove, crushed
¼	cup (50 mL) flour
3	to 4 teaspoons (15 to 20 mL) curry powder
2	teaspoons (10 mL) instant chicken bouillon
¼	teaspoon (1 mL) pepper
2	tablespoons (30 mL) chopped mango chutney
1	cup (250 mL) coarsely chopped apple
1	cup (250 mL) water
1	cup (250 mL) milk
⅓	cup (75 mL) raisins
	Salt

Crumble lamb in 2-quart (2 L) microwaveable casserole. Add celery, onion and garlic. Cover and microwave at high for 5 to 7 minutes or until lamb is no longer pink and vegetables are tender, stirring once. Drain off fat.

Add flour, curry powder, bouillon and pepper; stir to mix well. Stir in chutney, apple, water, milk and raisins. Microwave, uncovered, at high for 10 minutes or until thickened and bubbly, stirring every 2 minutes. Microwave at high for an additional 1 minute. Add salt to taste.

BANANA-MINT RAITA

1	cup (250 mL) plain low-fat yogurt
1	medium banana, cut into small pieces
1	tablespoon (15 mL) unsweetened medium coconut
1	tablespoon (15 mL) finely chopped jalapeno pepper
1	tablespoon (15 mL) lime juice
1	tablespoon (15 mL) finely chopped fresh mint
	Salt to taste

In small bowl, combine all ingredients. Cover and refrigerate until serving time. Makes 1¾ cups (425 mL).

Lamb Kebabs with Raspberry Sauce

Makes 4 to 5 servings

Ellen Mackay of Duncan stumbled on this prize-winning recipe when she looked in the fridge one day and saw lamb, fresh raspberries and some of the "tons of mint" she grows in her garden. She marinated the lamb, barbecued it and made a sauce from the raspberries — an idea so good it won the meat category in our Six O'Clock Solutions contest. For an easy company dinner, all you need to add is rice and either green beans or asparagus.

2　pounds (1 kg) boneless leg of lamb, trimmed

Marinade

2　tablespoons (30 mL) extra virgin olive oil
1　tablespoon (15 mL) ketjap manis or soy sauce
1　tablespoon (15 mL) crushed garlic
½　teaspoon (2 mL) freshly ground coarse pepper

Raspberry sauce

2　cups (500 mL) fresh raspberries or 300-g package frozen raspberries, thawed or partially thawed (see note)
3　tablespoons (45 mL) mint jelly
2　tablespoons (30 mL) balsamic vinegar

Cut lamb into 1-inch (2.5 cm) cubes.

Marinade: In large bowl, combine oil, ketjap manis, garlic and pepper. Add lamb cubes and stir to coat well. Let marinate for 10 minutes.

Meanwhile, prepare sauce: In medium saucepan, combine raspberries, mint jelly and vinegar. Place over medium-low heat for about 15 minutes or until sauce is hot, stirring occasionally. Put sauce in blender or food processor and puree. Strain sauce and return to saucepan; keep warm.

Put lamb cubes on 4 or 5 skewers and cook on greased barbecue grill or under broiler for 8 to 10 minutes or until cooked, turning once.

Spoon a small amount of sauce on to each serving plate and place 1 skewer on top. Pass remaining sauce separately.

Note: To partially thaw raspberries, place in large bowl and microwave at high for 2 minutes. ○

WHAT IS KETJAP MANIS?

Ketjap manis is an Indonesian soy sauce sweetened with molasses or brown sugar. It's darker and much less salty than regular soy sauce. You can find ketjap manis in supermarket specialty foods sections and in Asian groceries.

And yes, ketjap (also spelled kecap) is the source of our word ketchup, which hung on, even when the sauce it described turned into a tomato preserve.

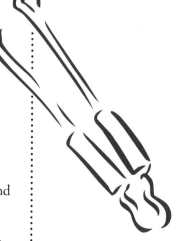

Lamb Chops with Honey Rosemary Glaze

Makes 4 servings

It's tempting to put lamb into one of two categories: British, with mint, and Greek, with rosemary. These lamb chops may sound Greek on the surface, but the honey and rosemary play against the ginger and soy sauce to produce a sweet-tart bite that would have astonished Zorba. Trot them out whenever you need an elegant dinner in a hurry. Serve with orzo (a rice-shaped pasta) or small white potatoes, sprinkled with parsley in either case. Round out the meal with steamed asparagus, a crusty loaf of Italian bread and fresh fruit for dessert. If it's June, very little beats strawberries with balsamic vinegar and pepper.

8	loin lamb chops, about 1-inch (2.5 cm) thick
1	tablespoon (15 mL) vegetable oil
1	tablespoon (15 mL) liquid honey
2	teaspoons (10 mL) soy sauce
1	garlic clove, chopped fine
1	teaspoon (5 mL) finely chopped fresh ginger
1	teaspoon (5 mL) finely chopped fresh rosemary
⅛	teaspoon (0.5 mL) salt

Trim excess fat from lamb chops.

In small bowl, whisk together oil, honey, soy sauce, garlic, ginger, rosemary and salt.

Place chops on lightly greased broiler pan; brush lightly with honey mixture. Broil chops for 8 minutes or until cooked, turning once and brushing with honey mixture. ⏱

BALSAMIC VINEGAR WITH STRAWBERRIES

Vinegar and pepper on strawberries? Yes, if it's fragrant, slightly sweet balsamic vinegar, and freshly ground black pepper.

Allow a cup (250 mL) of strawberries per serving. Portion the berries into bowls and sprinkle each serving with a teaspoon (5 mL) balsamic vinegar, then grind on a moderate amount of pepper.

GREAT FOR ENTERTAINING

Lamb Chops with Fresh Mint and Jalapeno Pepper

Makes 4 servings

Roast leg of lamb with mint sauce used to be one of the emblems of the British Empire. Tastes change: modern cooks are far more likely to broil lamb chops than roast a leg of lamb. And even when they want to find mint and lamb on the same fork, they're likely to slip in some cumin, garlic and jalapeno pepper to jazz it up. Queen Victoria would not be amused.

Lamb chops are expensive enough to reserve for special occasions. Serve them with nugget potatoes if they're in season, rice when you can't get nuggets, and either steamed green beans or snow peas.

8	loin lamb chops, about 1-inch (2.5 cm) thick
3	tablespoons (45 mL) olive oil
2	tablespoons (30 mL) chopped fresh mint
2	large garlic cloves, chopped fine
1	small jalapeno pepper, seeded and chopped fine
1	teaspoon (5 mL) salt
½	teaspoon (2 mL) ground cumin
¼	teaspoon (1 mL) pepper

Trim excess fat from lamb chops.

In small bowl, combine oil, mint, garlic, jalapeno pepper, salt, cumin and pepper.

Spread mint mixture over both sides of chops. Place on lightly greased broiler pan and let stand for 5 minutes.

Broil chops for about 8 minutes or until cooked, turning once. ⟳

JALAPENO PEPPERS: HOT AND NOT

Jalapenos, named after the Jalapa region in the Mexican state of Veracruz, are short, stubby chili peppers with thick walls. They're a quick way to add color, crunch and a zap of chili heat to a huge range of foods.

The tricky part of using them is figuring out in advance how hot the pepper will be.

This isn't just a question of normal variations in chili heat, caused by soil and weather. Since the mid-1980s, pepper breeders in Texas have refined and put on the market a new, mild jalapeno. It looks identical to a hot pepper but has very little of a traditional jalapeno's bite.

For that reason, be sure to taste your jalapenos before you add them to other ingredients. If you've found mild ones, you may want to increase the quantity, or, if they're beyond rescue, add a dash of Tabasco to the dish.

Spaghetti with Beef and Mushrooms

Makes 4 servings

SPAGHETTI SPOON

If there were a Mies van der Rohe "less-is-more" award for kitchen gadgets, I'd nominate the spaghetti-testing wooden spoon. So simple you could mistake it for a decoration, the notch cut half an inch from the end of the handle is the best tool ever devised for pulling a strand of spaghetti out of the pot.

Spaghetti takes 10 to 14 minutes to cook. If you forgot to set your timer, pull a strand from the water, cut it in half and look for a solid white dot at the centre. The minute the dot disappears, the spaghetti's cooked.

Supermarket shelves are lined with prepared spaghetti sauces for a good reason: they're the easiest route to a pantry meal. But on days when you need a simple pasta, don't you also need to eat something fresher and livelier than shelf-stable food? So doctor the sauce: add a modest amount of ground beef, an onion, a cup of mushrooms and plenty of fresh basil. And throw in a secret ingredient: a chopped fresh tomato to add taste and texture to the sauce. Serve a salad on the side, or steam spears of broccoli and squeeze a lemon over them just before they go to the table. Either one will do, as long as you also have a satisfying loaf of bread.

¾	**pound (350 g) spaghetti**
1	**tablespoon (15 mL) olive oil**
1	**onion, chopped**
3	**garlic cloves, chopped fine**
1	**cup (250 mL) sliced mushrooms**
½	**pound (250 g) lean ground beef**
3	**cups (750 mL) spaghetti sauce**
1	**medium tomato, chopped**
¼	**cup (50 mL) chopped fresh basil**
¼	**teaspoon (1 mL) dried crushed hot red pepper**
	Pinch ground cinnamon
	Salt and pepper
	Grated parmesan cheese

Cook spaghetti in large amount of boiling salted water until tender; drain.

Meanwhile, heat oil in large heavy frypan over medium heat. Add onion and garlic; saute for 3 minutes. Add mushrooms; saute for 3 minutes. Remove vegetables and set aside.

Add beef to frypan and saute for 3 to 5 minutes or until no longer pink. Stir in spaghetti sauce, tomato, basil, dried red pepper, cinnamon and mushroom mixture. Cook for 3 minutes or until heated through. Add salt and pepper to taste.

Serve beef sauce over spaghetti. Sprinkle with parmesan cheese. ○

Penne with Hot Sausage, Red Pepper and Broccoli

Makes 4 servings

Outside the kitchen, once you've reduced something, there's less of it. But if you reduce chicken stock (by boiling away some of the liquid), you'll get more flavor and a more substantial consistency — a paradox that lies at the heart of some of the world's great sauces. In this case, helped along by a modest amount of light cream and the magic powers of reduction, chicken stock binds broccoli, Italian sausage, red peppers and the tube-shaped pasta called penne into a robust and satisfying one-dish meal. All you really need to add to dinner is a loaf of bread. If you'd like to sit around the table longer, offer antipasto on crackers before dinner and a butter lettuce salad with a lemon-and-basil vinaigrette after the pasta's been served.

¾	pound (350 g) hot Italian sausages, casings removed
4	cups (1 L) penne
1	tablespoon (15 mL) olive oil
1	medium onion, chopped fine
2	garlic cloves, chopped fine
4	cups (1 L) broccoli flowerets
2	red bell peppers, chopped
1¼	cups (300 mL) chicken stock
½	cup (125 mL) light cream
⅓	cup (75 mL) finely chopped fresh parsley
	Salt and pepper
	Grated parmesan cheese

In large heavy frypan, cook sausage over medium heat for 5 minutes or until cooked, stirring and breaking up any lumps. With slotted spoon, remove sausage and set aside.

Cook penne in large amount of boiling salted water until tender; drain and return to pot.

Meanwhile, add oil to frypan and heat over medium-high heat. Add onion and garlic; saute for 3 minutes or until tender. Add broccoli and red peppers; saute for about 3 minutes or until broccoli is tender-crisp, stirring frequently. Remove vegetables and set aside.

Add stock to frypan and bring to a boil; boil 1 minute, stirring and

LEMON AND BASIL VINAIGRETTE

1	tablespoon (15 mL) lemon juice
3	tablespoons (45 mL) extra virgin olive oil
1	tablespoon (15 mL) finely chopped fresh basil
	Salt and pepper to taste

In a small bowl, whisk together ingredients.

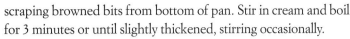
scraping browned bits from bottom of pan. Stir in cream and boil for 3 minutes or until slightly thickened, stirring occasionally.

Return sausage and vegetables to frypan. Add parsley and salt and pepper to taste.

Add sausage mixture to pasta and toss. Serve with parmesan cheese. ○

Red, White and Green Rotini with Bacon
Makes 4 servings

Never underestimate the power of color on appetite. Put a dish as pretty as this one on the table, its white pasta spirals studded with asparagus and strips of red pepper, and you'll start to understand some of the subtle power of the Italian flag, and why it seems to hang unofficially in so many kitchens. An unexpected bonus: despite the bacon, this is a low-fat recipe, coming in at well under 15 grams of fat per serving. Add a loaf of bread and dinner's done.

3	cups (750 mL) rotini
2	tablespoons (30 mL) vegetable oil
1	shallot, chopped fine
1	large garlic clove, chopped fine
1	pound (500 g) asparagus, trimmed and cut diagonally into 2-inch (5 cm) pieces
1	(175-g) package sliced back bacon, cut into ¼-inch (5 mm) strips
½	cup (125 mL) chicken stock
1	small red bell pepper, julienned
	Salt and pepper

Cook rotini in large amount of boiling salted water until tender; drain and return to pot.

Meanwhile, heat oil in large heavy frypan over medium-high heat. Add shallot and garlic; saute for 30 seconds. Add asparagus and bacon; saute for 3 minutes or until asparagus is almost tender.

Add stock and red pepper; cover and cook for 2 minutes. Uncover and cook for 1 minute or until vegetables are tender-crisp.

Add asparagus mixture to pasta and toss. Add salt and pepper to taste. ○

STALKING ASPARAGUS

To trim asparagus, break off the woody end of the stalk. How far up the stalk is it woody? Never try to guess, and don't bother cutting it with a knife. Instead, let the asparagus give you the answer. Grasp the stem end in one hand, the tip in the other, and bend gently. The stalk will break at the point where the asparagus is tender enough for the table.

Spaghettini with Pork, Shiitake Mushrooms and Sage

Makes 4 servings

The Romans thought of sage as an aid to digestion and ate the fresh leaves, dipped in batter and deep-fried, before dinner. North Americans have spent the past 200 years thinking of sage as a dried, somewhat musty herb to eat in turkey stuffing and sausages. But fresh sage is on the comeback trail, and a foray into this recipe will show you why. Paired with pork tenderloin and shiitake mushrooms, fresh sage cuts through the richness of the dish with a sharp, resinous, minty taste.

You could make this a one-dish meal with a plate of raw vegetables to blunt pre-dinner appetites. In that case, all you need to add is a loaf of bread. If it's a more leisurely dinner, serve a salad of mixed greens after the pasta, with a simple oil-and-vinegar dressing.

¾	**pound (350 g) spaghettini, broken in half**
1	**tablespoon (15 mL) olive oil**
1	**large onion, chopped coarse**
3	**garlic cloves, chopped fine**
¾	**pound (350 g) pork tenderloin, sliced thin**
½	**pound (250 g) fresh shiitake mushrooms, stemmed and sliced thin**
1	**small red bell pepper, julienned**
2	**tablespoons (30 mL) finely chopped fresh sage**
½	**teaspoon (2 mL) salt**
¼	**teaspoon (1 mL) pepper**
¼	**teaspoon (1 mL) dried crushed hot red pepper or to taste**
½	**cup (125 mL) chicken stock**
	Chopped fresh parsley
	Grated parmesan cheese

Cook spaghettini in large amount of boiling salted water until tender; drain and return to pot.

Meanwhile, heat oil in large heavy frypan over medium-high heat. Add onion and garlic; saute 3 minutes. Add pork, mushrooms, bell pepper, sage, salt, pepper and dried red pepper; stir-fry for 3 minutes.

Add stock, stirring and scraping browned bits from bottom of

WHAT ARE SHIITAKE MUSHROOMS?

Once you've encountered fresh shiitake mushrooms, with their dense texture, woody odor and rich flavor, you'll know why mushrooms are called the poor man's meat.

Because they're grown commercially, shiitakes are available year round, with peak seasons in the spring and fall. The Japanese have been raising shiitakes for more than 2,000 years by injecting mushroom spores into shii and oak trees — essentially the same process used today. (The name comes from the shii *tree;* take *means mushroom.)*

Look for shiitakes with large tops and small stems. Avoid mushrooms that look shrivelled or have blemishes or slimy spots. Brush shiitakes lightly with a dry pastry brush or paper towel to clean; store them, unwashed, in paper towels in a paper bag in the fridge.

We appreciate shiitakes for their taste. In China and Japan they're also a folk remedy for colds, and researchers believe they strengthen the immune system.

frypan. Reduce heat, cover and simmer for 2 minutes or until pork is cooked.

Add pork mixture to pasta and toss. Sprinkle with parsley. Serve with parmesan cheese. ⏱

Spaghetti with Mushrooms, Pancetta and Sage

Makes 4 servings

WHAT IS PANCETTA?

We call the cut of meat "side bacon," Italians call it pancetta (from pancia, *belly).*

Pancetta (pronounced pan-CHEH-tuh) is cured in salt and spices, but, unlike our bacon, it's not smoked. In cooking, pancetta lends a savory-sweet taste to sauces, pasta dishes and vegetables.

Don't worry about buying more than you need for one recipe: tightly wrapped pancetta can be refrigerated for up to three weeks, or frozen up to six months.

Back in the 1950s, a entire school of cuisine grew up devoted to doctoring canned soup. To my mind, it reached its apogee in consomme with chopped chives and a drop of sherry — still a warming sight on a cold evening. Now that supermarket shelves bloom with hundreds of spaghetti sauces, quick cooks are getting equally adept at making the off-the-shelf pasta sauce taste home-made. This quick sauce, with sage, mushrooms and pancetta, is just one example. Add a green salad and a loaf of bread, and dinner can be on the table in less than half an hour.

¾	**pound (350 g) spaghetti**
1	**tablespoon (15 mL) vegetable oil**
1	**small onion, chopped**
1	**garlic clove, chopped fine**
1	**cup (250 mL) sliced mushrooms**
2	**ounces (60 g) pancetta, chopped**
3	**cups (750 mL) spaghetti sauce**
½	**teaspoon (2 mL) dried sage**
	Grated parmesan cheese

Cook spaghetti in large amount of boiling salted water until tender; drain.

In large heavy frypan, heat oil over medium heat. Add onion, garlic, mushrooms and pancetta; saute for 5 minutes or until vegetables are tender. Stir in spaghetti sauce and sage; heat through. Serve sauce over pasta. Serve with parmesan cheese. ⏱

Fettuccine with Mushrooms, Prosciutto and Basil

Makes 4 servings

Ralph Waldo Emerson was probably not thinking about pasta when he wrote: "Nothing is more simple than greatness; indeed, to be simple is to be great." Still, it's arguable that the best pasta dishes are the simplest.

What makes them memorable is the quality of their basic ingredients. So if you want to taste greatness in this pasta, use fresh basil and buy your parmesan as a chunk of cheese to grate just before you use it. Stay simple for the rest of dinner, too: add a green salad, enlivened with chunks of orange or grapefruit, and a loaf of country-style Italian bread.

¾	pound (350 g) fettuccine
2	tablespoons (30 mL) olive oil
3	cups (750 mL) sliced mushrooms
4	green onions, chopped
¼	pound (125 g) prosciutto, chopped
¾	cup (175 mL) light cream
½	cup (125 mL) grated parmesan cheese
⅓	cup (75 mL) chopped fresh basil
	Salt and pepper
	Grated parmesan cheese

Cook fettuccine in large amount of boiling salted water until tender; drain and return to pot.

Meanwhile, heat oil in large heavy frypan over medium-high heat. Add mushrooms and saute for 4 minutes or until almost tender. Add green onions and saute for 1 minute. Stir in prosciutto. Add cream and simmer for 1 minute or until slightly thickened. Stir in ½ cup (125 mL) parmesan cheese and basil.

Add cream mixture to pasta and toss. Add salt and pepper to taste. Serve with parmesan cheese. ☽

WHAT IS PROSCIUTTO?

Prosciutto (pronounced pro-SHOO-to) is a hog's hind thigh, or ham, salted, then hung to dry in the air while the salt draws off the excess moisture. Prosciutto di Parma, the standard by which all others are judged, hangs for a minimum of 10 months.

Buy prosciutto sliced paper thin and wrap it around slices of melon or pear, or serve it with fresh figs.

Barbecued Pizza with Pesto, Pepper and Prosciutto

Makes 4 to 6 servings

If you've ever looked at the huge array of Italian-style bread shells hanging in supermarkets you already know that this could be a bad time to buy shares in a take-out pizza business. Here's something you may not know: pre-baked shells are sturdy enough to go on the barbecue. That brings grilled pizza — a crisp crust and the taste of food cooked over a flame —within the grasp of anyone who can open a plastic bag. Add a butter lettuce salad with a home-made vinaigrette, and dinner's ready in less time than it takes to order in.

You could, of course, use the same combination of toppings on a shell baked in the oven, and once you've tried it, you may want to repeat this pizza one evening when the barbecue's covered with snow. If you keep prepared pesto in your fridge, you can pick up the rest of the ingredients on a weekly shopping trip and achieve instant pizza potential.

4	cups (1 L) grated provolone cheese
½	cup (125 mL) grated parmesan cheese
1	cup (250 mL) pesto
2	(12-inch or 30-cm) Italian-style bread shells
2	medium tomatoes, sliced thin
1	small yellow bell pepper, cut into thin strips
½	small red onion, sliced thin
½	pound (250 g) thinly sliced prosciutto, slivered

Set one side of the barbecue at high heat.

In small bowl, combine provolone and parmesan cheeses.

For each pizza, spread half the pesto evenly over bread shell, leaving ½-inch (1 cm) border all around. Top with half the tomatoes, yellow pepper, red onion and prosciutto. Sprinkle with half the cheese mixture.

Place 1 pizza on unheated side of barbecue grill and close lid. Cook for 10 to 15 minutes or until cheese has melted and toppings are heated through, rotating pizza frequently to ensure even heating. Repeat with remaining pizza. ○

TOP THAT PIZZA

As time goes by, it becomes increasingly clear: there's no natural limit to the number of possible pizza combinations. Here are a few you might not have considered:

• Grainy mustard, thin slices of cooked potato, strips of roasted red pepper, finely chopped fresh rosemary and cheese (mozzarella, parmesan or a mixture of the two).

• Caramelized onions, gorgonzola and fresh rosemary.

• Pesto, tomatoes and bocconcini, with chopped fresh basil sprinkled on after baking.

• Caramelized onions, diced green peppers, black Italian-style olives and provolone cheese.

• Barbecue sauce, caramelized onions, barbecued chicken and green hot and spicy olives.

• Bacon, spinach and sun-dried tomatoes with or without feta cheese.

Upside-Down Pizza

Makes 4 servings

Neapolitans and anyone with a stuffy attitude toward pizza should stop reading right now. This recipe is for people who get anxiety attacks when they think about making bread dough. It's also for parents who have a tough time persuading their children to eat dinner, as well as for those who'd like to ease their kids into cooking.

Here's the concept: a crust made of ground beef, moistened with tomato juice and eggs, pressed into a pizza pan and baked till it browns. Add tomato, peppers and cheese to the top of the pizza and all you need to make a complete dinner is a green salad and a loaf of bread.

1	(796-mL) can diced tomatoes
1	pound (500 g) lean ground beef
1	cup (250 mL) crushed salted soda crackers
2	large eggs, lightly beaten
¼	teaspoon (1 mL) pepper
1½	teaspoons (7 mL) dried oregano
½	cup (125 mL) diced green bell pepper
1½	cups (375 mL) grated mozzarella cheese
¼	cup (50 mL) grated parmesan cheese

Drain tomatoes; reserving juice. In large bowl, combine beef, cracker crumbs, eggs, pepper and reserved tomato juice; mix well. Spread evenly into 12-inch (30 cm) pizza pan with sides.

Bake at 425 F (220 C) for about 15 minutes or until browned. Drain off fat.

Spoon tomatoes on top of beef crust and sprinkle with oregano, green pepper and cheeses. Return to oven for 5 to 8 minutes or until cheese is melted. Cut into wedges to serve. ○

KIDS' FAVE

FEEDING PICKY EATERS

As a picky eater myself, I have always been grateful to my mother for never forcing me to eat any food I loathed.

When she baked a lemon pie, she put some of the filling aside for me in a custard cup, because I didn't like piecrusts. From time to time, she made raisin faces on my porridge.

Apparently the strategy worked. Here are a few more ideas that may suit your child's age and temperament:

Cut sandwiches into whimsical shapes such as stars or trees.

Make dinner a shish-kebab: put everything on a skewer so your picky eater can have the fun of taking it off again.

Surprise your kids: have breakfast at dinner (pancakes and sausages) or dinner at breakfast (a pizza with lots of vegetables). Throw a tablecloth on the living room floor and have a picnic.

Pepperoni Pizza with Light Cheese

Makes 4 to 6 servings

LOWER-FAT CHEESE

Traditional cheddar cheese usually contains 30 per cent or more milk fat. With today's demand for lower-fat foods you can now buy cheeses ranging from 4 to 18 per cent milk fat.

Keep in mind, that a "light" cheese is not always a low-fat food. The percentage of milk fat on the label refers to fat as a percentage of weight, rather than a percentage of total calories. Calculated that way, the cheddar cheese is actually 75 per cent fat by calories.

Still, common sense should prevail. Keep in mind that the goal of consuming 30 per cent or less of your calories in the form of fat is based on the entire day's food intake. Fruit, vegetables and grains are naturally low in fat; over the course of a day they balance out foods such as nuts, avocados and cheese.

Pepperoni and mushroom pizza with plenty of cheese defines what most kids think a pizza ought to be. But take-out pizza, topped with greasy cheese, can spell high-fat nutritional disaster. Make it at home and you can cut the fat painlessly by using a good, flavorful reduced-fat cheese. (Buy a prepared pizza shell and the kids can make dinner themselves.)

Slice the pepperoni extra thin if you want it to be crisp around the edges. Encourage raw vegetable consumption by putting out a tray of broccoli, cauliflower, carrot sticks and cherry tomatoes.

1½	**cups (375 mL) grated part-skim mozzarella cheese**
1½	**cups (375 mL) grated (light) white cheddar cheese**
1	**cup (250 mL) pizza sauce**
2	**(12-inch or 30-cm) unbaked pizza crusts (Quick Pizza Dough recipe, page 169) or Italian-style bread shells**
1	**cup (250 mL) thinly sliced pepperoni (about 1 inch or 2.5 cm in diameter)**
1½	**cups (375 mL) sliced mushrooms**
¼	**cup (50 mL) grated parmesan cheese**

Combine mozzarella and cheddar cheeses; set aside.

For each pizza, spread half the pizza sauce evenly over unbaked crust or bread shell, leaving ½-inch (1 cm) border all around. Sprinkle with ¾ cup (175 mL) cheese mixture. Top with half the pepperoni and mushrooms, then sprinkle with ¾ cup (175 mL) cheese mixture. Sprinkle with half the parmesan cheese.

If using home-made dough, bake at 500 F (260 C) for 8 minutes, then slide pizzas from pans directly on to oven rack; bake an additional 1 to 2 minutes or until bottoms of crusts are crisp and golden. (On bread shells, bake at 450 F or 230 C for 10 minutes.) ○

CHAPTER TWO

Chicken
Turkey
Duck

Boneless chicken breasts are the faithful friend of time-pressed cooks everywhere.

In the pages that follow, you'll find enough boneless chicken breast recipes to inspire you through weeks of quick meals. The high-flavor cooking principle that's common to almost all of them? If dinner can't wait while flavors mingle and develop, use ingredients that will sing out on the slightest provocation. Spunky foods such as fresh herbs, sun-dried tomatoes, hoisin sauce, balsamic vinegar and fruit chutney make up in flavor what you lack in time.

You can have even more fun if you widen your scope. Try turkey cutlets for quick company dinners, spicy turkey sausage in pasta, duck breast in an elegant salad, or barbecued duck on a pizza.

Chicken Noodle Soup with Snow Peas and Fresh Herbs

Makes 4 servings

Just because you don't have time to nurse a stewing hen through to glory doesn't mean you have to get out the can opener if you crave a bowl of chicken noodle soup. This one-dish meal, with its fragrant base of sauteed leeks, mushrooms, carrots and celery, comes together in half an hour from a standing start. Any cold day is an excuse to make it, but it's almost mandatory when you or someone you care for is getting over the flu. If circumstances call for a truly restorative moment, make a plate of buttered toast for dipping into the soup.

2 tablespoons (30 mL) vegetable oil
2 leeks, sliced thin
1 cup (250 mL) diced celery
1 cup (250 mL) diced carrots
1 cup (250 mL) sliced mushrooms
8 cups (2 L) chicken stock
2 cups (500 mL) broad noodles
½ pound (250 g) boneless chicken thighs, skinned and cut into ½-inch (1 cm) pieces
1 cup (250 mL) snow peas, trimmed and cut diagonally in thirds
1 tablespoon (15 mL) chopped fresh rosemary
2 teaspoons (10 mL) chopped fresh thyme
Salt and pepper

In large heavy saucepan, heat oil over medium-high heat. Add leeks, celery, carrots and mushrooms; saute for 2 minutes. Add stock and bring to a boil. Add noodles and boil for 3 minutes. Add chicken, snow peas, rosemary and thyme; cook for about 3 minutes or until noodles are tender and chicken is cooked. Add salt and pepper to taste.

HOW TO CLEAN LEEKS

Unless you're planning to cook leeks whole, chop them, then wash and drain them. You'll save five minutes of peeling back layers and rinsing out sand.

Grilled Chicken and Red Onion Salad with Feta Cheese

Makes 4 servings

Red onions, cut into slices and grilled, are one of the great joys of barbecue season. Combine them with grilled chicken breasts, feta cheese and greens from the garden, and you have a brilliant summer answer to the quick dinner dilemma. If you're making this salad on a supremely lazy summer day, buy olives, hummus and roasted red peppers at a deli for an instant first course. The only other essential: a loaf of good bread.

½	**cup (125 mL) vegetable oil**
¼	**cup (50 mL) lemon juice**
½	**teaspoon (2 mL) Tabasco sauce**
¼	**teaspoon (1 mL) salt**
¼	**teaspoon (1 mL) pepper**
1	**tablespoon (15 mL) chopped fresh oregano**
2	**whole boneless chicken breasts, skinned and halved**
8	**(½-inch or 1-cm thick) slices red onion**
8	**cups (2 L) mixed torn salad greens**
	Salt and pepper
1	**cup (250 mL) crumbled feta cheese (about 4 ounces or 125 g)**

In small saucepan, whisk together oil, lemon juice, Tabasco sauce, ¼ teaspoon (1 mL) salt, ¼ teaspoon (1 mL) pepper and oregano; set dressing aside.

Place chicken and onions on baking sheet. Drizzle 2 tablespoons (30 mL) dressing over chicken and onions; turn to coat. Let stand for 5 minutes.

Place saucepan with remaining dressing over low heat and keep warm.

Place chicken and onions on greased barbecue grill over medium-high heat; cook for about 8 minutes or until chicken is no longer pink inside, turning once. Cut chicken into thin slices. Separate onion rings.

Place salad greens in large bowl; add chicken and onion. Add warm dressing and toss to coat. Add salt and pepper to taste. Place an equal portion of salad on each of 4 plates. Sprinkle each with ¼ cup (50 mL) feta cheese. ○

BONELESS BARGAIN

If you've ever felt a little stab of guilt when you bought a boneless chicken breast — imagining that if you just had time to bone your own, you could save a bundle — let me put your mind at ease.

With boneless breasts, there's no waste. Factor in the weight of the breastbone and ribs and the cost is about the same.

Chicken with Balsamic Vinegar and Fresh Basil

Makes 4 servings

Gently Italian in tone, this approach to boneless chicken breasts depends for its charm on a balsamic vinegar, shallot and chicken stock sauce. Serve the chicken with fettuccine on the side, tossed with a teaspoon of olive oil and sprinkled with parmesan or chopped parsley, and, when the main course is cleared away, a salad of mixed greens.

2	whole boneless chicken breasts, skinned and halved
2	tablespoons (30 mL) vegetable oil, divided
1	shallot, chopped fine
1	large garlic clove, chopped fine
⅓	cup (75 mL) chicken stock
1	tablespoon (15 mL) balsamic vinegar
	Pinch brown sugar
1	tablespoon (15 mL) chopped fresh basil
	Salt and pepper

Pound chicken breasts until about ½-inch (1 cm) thick.

In large heavy frypan, heat 1 tablespoon (15 mL) oil over medium-high heat.

Add chicken and saute for about 8 minutes or until no longer pink inside, turning once. Remove frypan from heat. Transfer chicken to serving platter and keep warm.

Add remaining 1 tablespoon (15 mL) oil to frypan and place over medium-low heat. Add shallot and garlic; saute for about 1 minute.

Add stock to frypan and bring to a boil, stirring and scraping browned bits from bottom of pan. Boil for 2 minutes or until slightly reduced. Reduce heat and stir in vinegar, brown sugar, basil and salt and pepper to taste; cook for 1 minute. Pour over chicken. ○

WHAT IS BALSAMIC VINEGAR?

Balsamic vinegar is made from the cooked and concentrated juice of white Trebbiano grapes.

The brands you'll find in supermarkets and Italian delis have a small amount of caramelized sugar added, giving the vinegar its characteristically sweet and sharp flavor.

True aceto balsamico tradizionale, *the kind that Lucrezia Borgia is said to have sniffed like smelling salts while giving birth to her first son, is also made from Trebbiano grapes. But this vinegar must be aged in wooden casks a minimum of 10 years. Made in small quantities, it carries such a high price tag that it's more likely to be sipped as a liqueur than sprinkled open-handedly on salad greens.*

SEASONED BREAD CRUMBS

If you don't keep commercial seasoned bread crumbs on hand, here's a quick recipe for making your own.

- ¼ **teaspoon (1 mL) salt**
- ⅛ **teaspoon (0.5 mL) pepper**
- ¼ **teaspoon (1 mL) dried thyme**
- ½ **cup (125 mL) dry bread crumbs**

Mix together and use to coat chicken or fish before frying.

Chicken Breasts with Orange Glaze

Makes 4 servings

When you want to keep things simple, not much beats the direct approach to boneless chicken breasts: dip them in seasoned bread crumbs and fry them. This recipe takes you one rewarding step further. With marmalade and orange liqueur, Dijon mustard and Worcestershire sauce, you make a quick glaze in the same pan that cooked the chicken: citrusy, with a little mustard bite and plenty of bass notes from the Worcestershire sauce.

Steamed rice and brussels sprouts could round out the plate in the fall and winter; go for green beans in the spring and summer. If it's a company dinner, add a spinach, red onion and mushroom salad, sprinkled with toasted pine nuts. For a quick family meal, cut some carrot sticks and trim a bunch of radishes for pre-dinner snacking.

- 2 **whole boneless chicken breasts, skinned and halved**
- 1 **egg, beaten**
- ½ **cup (125 mL) seasoned dry bread crumbs**
- 2 **tablespoons (30 mL) vegetable oil**
- 1 **garlic clove, chopped fine**
- ¼ **cup (50 mL) orange-flavored liqueur**
- 2 **tablespoons (30 mL) orange marmalade**
- 1 **tablespoon (15 mL) water**
- ½ **teaspoon (2 mL) lemon juice**
- ¼ **teaspoon (1 mL) Worcestershire sauce**
- ¼ **teaspoon (1 mL) Dijon mustard**
  Salt and pepper

Pound chicken breasts until about ¼-inch (5 mm) thick.

Dip chicken in egg, then in crumbs to coat well. Shake off excess crumbs.

In large heavy frypan, heat oil over medium-high heat. Add chicken and garlic; saute for about 6 minutes or until no longer pink inside, turning once. Remove from pan and keep warm.

Add liqueur to frypan and bring to a simmer, scraping up browned bits from bottom of pan. Stir in marmalade, water, lemon juice, Worcestershire sauce and mustard. Reduce heat to low. Return chicken to frypan; cover and cook for 2 minutes, turning chicken once. Add salt and pepper to taste. ☺

Chicken with Creamy Lemon Sauce

Makes 4 servings

When you need a dinner that's effortless and still luxurious, think of this gentle lemon and cream sauce for chicken. With orzo (rice-shaped pasta), steamed baby carrots and a wild greens salad, it's a meal you can easily put together for company, even after a day's work.

Don't be scared away by the third of a cup of whipping cream in the sauce. Divided among four people, that's a little more than a tablespoon each, which helps keep this recipe to less than 15 grams of fat per serving. Complete the meal with a salad and set out a plate of fresh lychees or other exotic fruit for dessert.

2	whole boneless chicken breasts, skinned and halved
1	tablespoon (15 mL) butter
1	tablespoon (15 mL) vegetable oil
1	tablespoon (15 mL) water
⅛	teaspoon (0.5 mL) instant chicken bouillon
½	teaspoon (2 mL) grated lemon zest
1	tablespoon (15 mL) lemon juice
⅓	cup (75 mL) whipping cream
	Salt and pepper
2	tablespoons (30 mL) grated parmesan cheese

Pound chicken breasts until about ½-inch (1 cm) thick.

In large heavy frypan, heat butter and oil over medium-high heat. Add chicken and saute for about 8 minutes or until no longer pink inside. Transfer chicken to 8-inch (20 cm) baking pan.

Drain fat from frypan. Add water, bouillon, lemon zest and juice; place over medium heat. Slowly add cream, stirring constantly, until hot (do not let boil). Add salt and pepper to taste.

Pour lemon sauce over chicken and sprinkle with parmesan cheese. Broil until lightly browned. ○

NO-OIL YOGURT SALAD DRESSING

1	tablespoon (15 mL) lemon juice
2	teaspoons (10 mL) sweet grainy mustard
1	garlic clove, chopped fine
	Salt and pepper
¾	cup (175 mL) plain low-fat yogurt
3	tablespoons (45 mL) chopped fresh parsley or mixed herbs

In small bowl, combine lemon juice, mustard, garlic and salt and pepper to taste. Whisk in yogurt and parsley. Makes about 1 cup (250 mL).

Glazed Apricot-Walnut Chicken

Makes 4 servings

One of the general principles of quick cooking is to take shortcuts whenever they offer themselves. In this case, the direct route runs through a jar of apricot jam. Mixed with vinegar and nutmeg to take the edge off the sweetness, and combined with walnuts for a satisfying texture, it's the basis for an almost-instant fruit-and-nut sauce.

To complete the meal, add new potatoes with chopped chives and a side dish of thin slices of young zucchini (buy both green and yellow for a prettier dish), sauteed in olive oil and garlic, with a squeeze of lemon and a generous grinding of black pepper.

1	tablespoon (15 mL) butter
1	tablespoon (15 mL) vegetable oil
2	whole boneless chicken breasts, skinned and halved
1/4	cup (50 mL) coarsely chopped walnuts
	Salt and pepper
1/3	cup (75 mL) apricot jam
1	tablespoon (15 mL) white wine vinegar
1/4	teaspoon (1 mL) ground nutmeg

In large heavy frypan, heat butter and oil over medium-high heat. Add chicken breasts and walnuts; saute for about 10 minutes or until chicken is no longer pink inside, turning occasionally. Transfer chicken to serving platter, reserving juices and nuts in frypan. Lightly sprinkle chicken with salt and pepper; keep warm.

Stir jam, vinegar and nutmeg into juices in frypan. Cook and stir over medium heat for 1 to 2 minutes or until mixture is heated through. Spoon glaze over chicken breasts. ⟳

ABOUT KEEPING WALNUTS

If you think you don't like the taste of walnuts, it may be that you've just never tasted one that wasn't rancid. They spoil easily at room temperature because, like all nuts, they have a high fat content.

If you're buying them in the shell, choose walnuts that feel heavy. Don't buy them if the shell has cracks or holes, or if the nut rattles when you shake it. In a cool, dry place, walnuts in the shell will keep for up to three months.

Buy shelled walnuts in vacuum-packed tins for maximum freshness. After opening, store them tightly covered in the fridge, or in the freezer for up to eight months.

Cinnamon Chicken with Orange Juice, Raisins and Capers

Makes 4 servings

When Keep It Simple, *Marian Burros's quick cookbook, first came out in paperback, I kept a copy in my desk drawer at work. I'd make a shopping list at lunch time, shop on the way home and then refer to my kitchen copy of* Keep it Simple *to cook dinner. Chicken cooked in orange juice, cinnamon and cloves was one of my favorites. This adapted version maintains the mildly Mexican flavor of the original.*

Corn chips and salsa will keep hunger at bay before dinner; serve rice and a spinach salad with the chicken.

2	whole chicken breasts (bone in), halved
1/4	teaspoon (1 mL) ground cinnamon
1/4	teaspoon (1 mL) ground cloves
	Salt and pepper
2	tablespoons (30 mL) vegetable oil
3/4	cup (175 mL) chopped onions
2	garlic cloves, crushed
3/4	cup (175 mL) fresh orange juice
2	tablespoons (30 mL) raisins
1	tablespoon (15 mL) drained capers

Season chicken breasts with cinnamon, cloves, salt and pepper.
In large heavy frypan, heat oil over medium-high heat.
Add chicken, skin side down, and saute for 3 to 4 minutes or until browned. Add onions and garlic. Turn chicken and saute for 3 to 4 minutes or until browned, stirring onions and garlic frequently. Drain fat from frypan.

Add orange juice, raisins and capers to frypan. Reduce heat to low; cover and cook for about 15 minutes or until chicken is no longer pink inside. ○

MEASURING TIME

If you often find yourself stopping to clean your measuring spoons while cooking, buy an extra set or two. You'll achieve substantial time savings at a minimal cost.

Raspberry-Vinegar Chicken
Makes 4 servings

Fruit vinegars had the look of a fad when they first appeared in specialty food stores and magazines several years ago. But they've earned an honest place on our kitchen shelves for one good reason: if you start with a rich, fruity vinegar, you don't have to go far to make a resonant sauce. In this case, a touch of sugar, some onion, the juices left from sauteing the chicken and a minute of boiling in the pan is all it takes.

Serve rice-shaped orzo pasta, scattered with chopped chives, with the chicken. Fresh peas with mint would be wonderful, but only if you have a kitchen helper to shell them. If you don't, look for sugar snap peas that can be cooked and eaten in their pods.

2	**whole boneless chicken breasts, skinned and halved**
	Salt
1	**tablespoon (15 mL) butter**
1	**tablespoon (15 mL) vegetable oil**
¼	**cup (50 mL) finely chopped onion**
1	**tablespoon (15 mL) sugar**
¼	**cup (50 mL) raspberry vinegar**

Lightly sprinkle chicken breasts with salt.

In large heavy frypan, heat butter and oil over medium heat. Add chicken and saute for 5 minutes. Turn chicken and add onion; saute for 5 minutes or until chicken is no longer pink inside. Transfer chicken to serving platter and keep warm.

Stir sugar into raspberry vinegar and add to frypan. Bring to a boil and boil 1 minute or until slightly reduced, stirring and scraping browned bits from bottom of frypan. Pour over chicken. ⏱

MAKING FRUIT VINEGARS

Raspberry isn't the only fruit that makes a great vinegar. Apricots, blackberries, blueberries, cherries, figs, gooseberries, huckleberries, kiwis, mangoes, papayas, plums, strawberries and even watermelons have all been used with success.

The process is easy: put the fruit, lightly mashed or cut up, into a glass jar with a tight lid. Then pour on enough vinegar to completely cover the fruit. You can use almost any wine, sherry, champagne or rice wine vinegar: just be sure it's good enough quality that you like the taste of it even without fruit flavor.

Cover the jar tightly, then store it in a cool, dark place, stirring daily. Check the flavor after a week. If you want it stronger, continue steeping for as long as a month. For more intense flavor, strain the vinegar, add fresh fruit and continue steeping.

When you like the flavor, strain the vinegar into a non-reactive saucepan, add sugar or honey to taste (from none at all to a quarter cup (50 mL) of sugar per cup (250 mL) of vinegar). Bring the mixture to a simmer and cook three minutes. Pour into sterilized bottles through a funnel. Store tightly capped in a cool dark cupboard.

Chicken with Ginger, Mint and Yogurt

Makes 4 servings

While not as well known as writer's block, cook's block is, I suspect, equally widespread. What's most likely to bring it on is the terrifying emptiness of the blank slate: for the writer, the empty page; for the cook, the boneless chicken breast. Yes, the possibilities are endless, but try to pin one down and it flees.

The next time you find yourself hyperventilating in front of the fridge, reach for the yogurt, then add a set of assertive herbs and spices. Rice goes best with this recipe's mildly Asian seasonings; for a vegetable side dish, steam green and yellow beans together and toss them in hot oil and garlic when they're just barely cooked.

1	cup (250 mL) plain low-fat yogurt
½	cup (125 mL) coarsely chopped fresh mint
¼	cup (50 mL) coarsely chopped fresh cilantro
¼	cup (50 mL) chopped green onions
1	tablespoon (15 mL) chopped fresh ginger
3	garlic cloves, crushed
¼	teaspoon (1 mL) ground cumin
1	tablespoon (15 mL) lemon juice
¼	teaspoon (1 mL) hot chili paste
2	whole boneless chicken breasts, skinned and halved

In bowl, combine yogurt, mint, cilantro, green onions, ginger, garlic, cumin, lemon juice and chili paste. Add chicken breasts, turning to coat. Let stand 10 minutes.

Place chicken on greased broiler pan and broil for 6 to 8 minutes per side or until no longer pink inside, basting with yogurt mixture. ○

*R*ICE COOKING TIPS

• *Before cooking, rinse rice in cold water until the water is no longer cloudy.*

• *Once the rice comes to a full, rolling boil, lower the heat to a simmer. The surface of the water should be just gently moving. If your element's lowest heat is too high, use a flame spreader between the saucepan and the element.*

• *Don't peek, or if you must, peek just once to make sure there's enough heat to keep the rice cooking.*

• *Don't stir, ever.*

• *After 20 minutes for white rice, 45 minutes for brown, turn off the heat and let the rice "relax" for five minutes: the grains will get dryer and fluffier.*

YOGURT

Chicken with Mushrooms, Lemon and Fresh Rosemary

Makes 4 servings

POULTRY POUNDING

When a recipe asks for a chicken breast or turkey cutlet pounded to an even thickness, put the poultry between two layers of wax paper or plastic wrap before you start pounding. If you have both on hand, you're better off using the wax paper. It's easier to separate from the poultry.

Once you've reached the desired thickness, using a meat mallet, or failing that, the blunt edge of a cleaver, peel the paper away.

Now that rosemary is readily available most of the year, this gentle chicken dish is an option for any evening when dinner must not only be on the table in record time, but has to live up to a certain civilized standard seldom attained by, say, pizza. Speed comes from pounding the chicken breasts into thin scallops, which cook in about six minutes. Civility accrues when you saute sliced mushrooms in the chicken juices, then, when both chicken and mushrooms have left some of their flavor in the pan, make a sauce with broth, wine, lemon juice and fresh rosemary. The rest of dinner should be equally easy: rice and a vibrant green vegetable. As long as it isn't overcooked, nothing is as eye-poppingly green as broccoli.

2   whole boneless chicken breasts, skinned and halved
     Salt and pepper
2   tablespoons (30 mL) vegetable oil, divided
1   tablespoon (15 mL) butter
1   shallot, chopped
2   large garlic cloves, chopped fine
2   cups (500 mL) sliced mushrooms
¼   cup (50 mL) chicken stock
1   tablespoon (15 mL) dry white wine
2   teaspoons (10 mL) lemon juice
1   teaspoon (5 mL) finely chopped fresh rosemary

Pound chicken breasts until about ¼-inch (5 mm) thick; lightly sprinkle with salt and pepper.

In large heavy frypan, heat 1 tablespoon (15 mL) oil and butter over medium-high heat. Add chicken and saute for about 6 minutes or until no longer pink inside, turning once. Transfer to serving platter and keep warm.

Reduce heat to medium and add remaining 1 tablespoon (15 mL) oil to frypan. Add shallot and garlic; saute for 30 seconds. Add mushrooms and saute for about 5 minutes or until mushrooms start to brown. (If necessary, add extra oil to frypan.) With slotted spoon, remove mushrooms and place on top of chicken.

Add stock, wine, lemon juice and rosemary to frypan; boil until reduced to about 3 tablespoons (45 mL). Drizzle over chicken and mushrooms. ⏱

Chicken Breasts with Mushrooms and Creamy Mustard Sauce

Makes 4 servings

Chicken breasts, cream and button mushrooms are a trio of classic comfort foods: white, calming and devoid of surprises. Brought together with just a bit of Dijon mustard, they offer the culinary equivalent of Mom saying: "There, there, dear, don't you fret." Add either rice or bulgur wheat and steamed green beans, and a warming little dinner can be on the table in less than half an hour.

2	**whole boneless chicken breasts, skinned and halved**
2	**tablespoons (30 mL) flour**
¼	**teaspoon (1 mL) salt**
	Pinch pepper
2	**tablespoons (30 mL) vegetable oil**
1	**tablespoon (15 mL) butter**
1	**small onion, chopped**
1	**cup (250 mL) thickly sliced mushrooms**
½	**cup (125 mL) light cream**
1	**tablespoon (15 mL) chopped fresh parsley**
2	**teaspoons (10 mL) Dijon mustard**
1½	**teaspoons (7 mL) lemon juice**

Pound chicken breasts until about ¼-inch (5 mm) thick. Combine flour, salt and pepper on piece of wax paper. Dredge chicken in flour mixture.

In large heavy frypan, heat oil over medium heat. Add chicken and saute for about 7 minutes or until no longer pink inside, turning once. Transfer to serving platter and keep warm.

Add butter to frypan and increase heat to high; heat until butter is bubbly and hot. Add onion and mushrooms; saute for about 5 minutes or until lightly browned. Reduce heat to low. Add cream, parsley, mustard and lemon juice; cook until mixture comes to a boil, stirring constantly. Drain any accumulated juices from chicken into cream mixture; stir.

Pour sauce over chicken. ⏱

WHAT IS DIJON MUSTARD?

A genuine Dijon mustard must be made in Dijon, France, which has been famous for its mustard since the 1300s.

A Dijon-type mustard can be made anywhere by combining brown or black mustard seeds (no white allowed) with wine, wine vinegar and verjuice (juice from unripe grapes), and grinding the seeds.

Dijon mustard is pale, greyish yellow. Its clean, sharp flavor can range from mild to hot.

Peanutty Chicken
Makes 4 servings

Any devotee of Szechuan food knows that peanuts and chicken are a natural combination, preferably with a fair whack of hot chilies somewhere in the mix. This recipe, inspired by Lorraine Barquest's entry in our Six O'Clock Solutions contest, gets its heat from hot pepper flakes. Add steamed rice and stir-fried snow peas or Chinese greens for a satisfying meal.

1	tablespoon (15 mL) peanut oil
2	whole boneless chicken breasts, skinned and halved
	Chopped peanuts
	Cilantro sprigs

Peanut sauce

2	teaspoons (10 mL) peanut oil
1	shallot, chopped fine
2	garlic cloves, chopped fine
½	cup (125 mL) light coconut milk
¼	teaspoon (1 mL) dried crushed hot red pepper
¼	cup (50 mL) smooth peanut butter
1	tablespoon (15 mL) lime juice
2	teaspoons (10 mL) soy sauce
1	teaspoon (5 mL) grated fresh ginger

In large heavy frypan, heat 1 tablespoon (15 mL) oil over medium heat. Add chicken; cook, covered, for 8 to 10 minutes or until no longer pink inside, turning once. Transfer chicken to serving platter and keep warm.

Meanwhile, prepare sauce: In small heavy saucepan, heat oil over medium heat. Add shallot and garlic; saute 3 minutes or until tender. Add coconut milk and dried red pepper; bring to a boil. Remove pan from heat and whisk in peanut butter. Return to heat and bring to a simmer, stirring constantly. Stir in lime juice, soy sauce and ginger.

Pour some of the peanut sauce over chicken. Serve remaining sauce separately. Garnish chicken with peanuts and cilantro sprigs. ◷

STIR-FRIED GREENS

When you're planning to stir-fry a green vegetable, cut it and wash it first, but don't dry off the water that clings to the leaves. Then chop some ginger or garlic or both (I use ginger and garlic with stronger greens, ginger on its own for Shanghai bok choy and baby bok choy).

Heat the wok on high, add oil and when the oil is hot, add the ginger and garlic and cook for a minute or two. Just before the garlic starts turning golden, sprinkle salt into the pan, then add the greens and whatever water still clings to them.

Stir and fry until the greens are glistening with oil, then put the lid on, turn the heat to medium and cook for another minute or two — until the stalks are tender-crisp.

Chicken Strips

Makes 4 servings

Who can explain the universal appeal of finger food? All we know for sure is that chicken tastes better to children when it's cut into rectangles they can dip into a sauce. So when you're tired of trying to expand culinary horizons of your offspring, and just want them to eat something with food value, dammit, give this recipe a try.

2	**whole boneless chicken breasts, skinned and halved**
⅓	**cup (75 mL) grated parmesan cheese**
½	**cup (125 mL) fine dry bread crumbs**
1	**teaspoon (5 mL) dried thyme**
1	**teaspoon (5 mL) dried basil**
	Pinch dried crushed hot red pepper
	Pinch each salt and pepper
½	**cup (125 mL) plain low-fat yogurt**
1	**small garlic clove, crushed**

Pound chicken breasts until about ¼-inch (5 mm) thick. Cut into strips, about ½-inch (1 cm) wide and 3 inches (7 cm) long.

In pie plate, combine cheese, bread crumbs, thyme, basil, dried red pepper, salt and pepper. In small bowl, combine yogurt and garlic.

Dip chicken in yogurt, then in crumb mixture until well coated; shake off loose crumbs. Place on baking sheet.

Bake at 425 F (220 C) for 15 minutes or until chicken is no longer pink inside. ⏲

STOP BURGER DRIPS

Here's another tip for feeding youngsters: If you're serving them hamburgers, look for hamburger-style pita breads. They're thicker than a regular pita, but smaller in diameter — just the right size for a hamburger patty. Slip the burger in and your child can edge closer to achieving a drip-free hamburger.

Chicken Focaccia Burgers
Makes 4 servings

Barbara Stickle uses her commuting time to dream up quick dinners to make for her husband and three-year-old son. She entered this inspiration — sauteed chicken breasts, garnished with onions cooked in balsamic vinegar and sandwiched between slices of toasted focaccia bread — in our Six O'Clock Solutions contest, and won first place in the poultry category.

"A great change from run-of-the-mill burgers," Stickle wrote in her entry, "and it appeals to the younger members of the family." There's an extra appeal for a busy cook: all you need to add is a salad, and dinner's complete.

1	tablespoon (15 mL) olive oil
2	cups (500 mL) sliced red onion
2	tablespoons (30 mL) balsamic vinegar
2	whole boneless chicken breasts, skinned and halved
	Olive oil
	Salt and pepper
2	small (about 6-inch or 15-cm) focaccia (see note)
	Light mayonnaise
	Dijon mustard
	Thinly sliced tomato

In large heavy frypan, heat 1 tablespoon (15 mL) oil over medium heat. Add onion and saute for 5 minutes, stirring occasionally. Reduce to low heat; stir in vinegar and cook for 5 minutes. Remove from pan and keep warm.

Meanwhile, pound chicken breasts to ¼-inch (5 mm) thickness. Brush both sides with oil and sprinkle with salt and pepper.

When onions are finished cooking, saute chicken over medium-high heat for 6 minutes or until no longer pink inside, turning once.

Cut each focaccia in half, then slice each piece in half horizontally. Place on baking sheet, cut side up, and broil for 1 to 2 minutes or until lightly toasted.

On each bottom piece, spread mayonnaise and/or mustard and a quarter of the onion mixture. Top with chicken breast and sliced tomato; cover with top piece of focaccia.

Note: If desired, a large, 12-inch (30 cm) focaccia could be used. Cut in quarters and then slice in half horizontally. ⏱

WHAT IS FOCACCIA BREAD?

When you see a flat bread (usually less than two inches thick), its dimpled surface dotted with salt crystals and fragrant with olive oil, you've found focaccia.

The root of focaccia's name comes from focus, Latin for fire. Originally focaccia was unleavened; modern focaccia usually contains flour, yeast, olive oil, salt and water.

Now that focaccia has become widely popular, many supermarkets carry it, although you'll likely get the best quality from a specialty shop or Italian bakery. If you're nowhere near a baker who sells focaccia, Quick Pizza Dough on page 169 makes a wonderful substitute. Roll the dough a little thicker than you might for a pizza. Before you bake it, brush the dough with olive oil, sprinkle with coarse salt and press your knuckles into the surface to give it the required dimples.

Chicken Tortilla Pizzas

Makes 4 servings

Individual portion packs are popular because, once in a while, we all yearn to have our own separate dinners. Here's one you can create yourself: four mini-pizzas, topped with sauteed chicken, a tomato-mushroom sauce and a mix of cheddar and monterey jack cheese.

Irene Hayton of North Vancouver, who entered this recipe in our Six O'Clock Solutions contest, uses ready-made tortillas to make an instant pizza base. All you need to add is a green salad, or, if you're feeding children, a fresh vegetable plate with a choice of quick low-fat dips. (See pages 79 and 82.)

1	(213-mL) can tomato sauce
1	teaspoon (5 mL) dried basil
1	teaspoon (5 mL) dried oregano
1	garlic clove, crushed
1	cup (250 mL) grated light cheddar cheese
1	cup (250 mL) grated light monterey jack cheese
2	whole boneless chicken breasts, skinned and cut into ½-inch (1 cm) pieces
1	tablespoon (15 mL) water or chicken stock
12	mushrooms, sliced
4	(7-inch or 18-cm) whole-wheat tortillas
4	green onions, chopped
2	medium tomatoes, diced

Preheat oven broiler.

In small bowl, combine tomato sauce, basil, oregano and garlic; set aside. Combine cheddar and monterey jack cheese; set aside.

In non-stick frypan, saute chicken for 2 minutes, adding water to prevent sticking. Add mushrooms and saute for 4 minutes. Remove from heat.

Place tortillas on 2 baking sheets; broil for about 1 minute on each side (watch carefully to make sure they don't burn).

Preheat oven to 400 F (200 C).

For each pizza, spread tortilla with some of the tomato sauce mixture; top with a quarter of the chicken mixture, green onions and tomatoes. Sprinkle with ½ cup (125 mL) cheese mixture.

Bake for 10 minutes or until cheese melts. ○

LOADING THE DICE

When a recipe in this cookbook asks you to dice an ingredient, we mean cut it into tiny cubes, a quarter to an eighth of an inch in size.

Spicy Chicken and Bell Pepper Stir-Fry

Makes 4 servings

HOW TO STORE GINGER

Wrap ginger tightly in plastic and store it in the fridge. It will keep several days. For longer storage, peel ginger, wrap in aluminum foil and freeze. When you need ginger, grate off the amount you need without thawing it.

Or peel ginger and immerse it in a jar of dry sherry. It will keep indefinitely in the fridge. The sherry has little impact on the ginger taste, but the ginger flavors the sherry. You can re-use the sherry for storing more ginger or add it as a secret ingredient to stir-fries and fruit salads.

One of the prettiest sights a produce stand has to offer is ranks of ripe bell peppers — red, orange and yellow — lined up side-by-side, crying out to be eaten. Take home one of each color, add a cup of snow peas, chicken breasts and Chinese seasonings: the result is a vibrantly colored one-dish meal with deep, slightly spicy undertones. All you really need to add is steamed rice, but you might like to take the ragged edges off pre-dinner hunger by setting out a bowl of salty-sweet Japanese rice crackers.

½	cup (125 mL) orange juice
2	tablespoons (30 mL) soy sauce
1	tablespoon (15 mL) hoisin sauce
1	tablespoon (15 mL) sesame oil
1	teaspoon (5 mL) sugar
1	teaspoon (5 mL) hot chili paste
1	tablespoon (15 mL) cornstarch
2	tablespoons (30 mL) vegetable oil
1	tablespoon (15 mL) grated fresh ginger
2	garlic cloves, chopped fine
2	whole boneless chicken breasts, skinned and cut into ¼-inch (5 mm) strips
1	cup (250 mL) snow peas, trimmed and cut diagonally in half
½	large red bell pepper, cut into ¼-inch (5 mm) strips
½	large orange bell pepper, cut into ¼-inch (5 mm) strips
½	large yellow bell pepper, cut into ¼-inch (5 mm) strips

In small bowl, combine orange juice, soy sauce, hoisin sauce, sesame oil, sugar, chili paste and cornstarch; set aside.

In wok or large heavy frypan, heat oil over high heat. Add ginger and garlic; stir-fry for 30 seconds. Add chicken; stir-fry for 2 minutes. Add snow peas and peppers; stir-fry for 2 minutes.

Whisk orange juice mixture. Add to wok, stirring constantly, and cook for 2 minutes or until sauce is slightly thickened. ⟲

Stir-Fried Chicken with Broccoli

Makes 4 servings

You may be surprised to find a tablespoon of Thai fish sauce (nam pla) in this otherwise Chinese recipe. Food pages Pacific Rim writer Stephen Wong, who brought the recipe into The Vancouver Sun's test kitchen, says the fish sauce has a more subtle salty flavor than soy sauce alone would provide. All you need to add is steamed rice.

1 **pound (500 g) boneless chicken breasts, skinned and cut into thin strips**

Marinade

1 **tablespoon (15 mL) soy sauce**
1 **tablespoon (15 mL) cornstarch**
1 **teaspoon (5 mL) sugar**
1 **tablespoon (15 mL) water**
1 **tablespoon (15 mL) vegetable oil**

Vegetable mixture

3 **tablespoons (45 mL) vegetable oil, divided**
1 **medium carrot, peeled and sliced thin**
4 **cups (1 L) broccoli flowerets**
1 **tablespoon (15 mL) fish sauce**
½ **teaspoon (2 mL) sugar**
1 **large garlic clove, chopped fine**
¼ **cup (50 mL) water**
1½ **teaspoons (7 mL) sesame oil**
1 **medium onion, sliced thin**
5 **(¼-inch or 5-mm thick) slices peeled fresh ginger**
1 **tablespoon (15 mL) dry sherry**
½ **teaspoon (2 mL) white pepper**
Salt

Marinade: In medium bowl, combine soy sauce, cornstarch, sugar, water and oil. Add chicken and stir to coat. Let marinate for 15 minutes.

Vegetable mixture: Heat wok over medium-high heat; add 1 tablespoon (15 mL) vegetable oil. Add carrot and stir-fry for 30 seconds. Add broccoli and stir-fry for 1 minute. Stir in fish sauce, sugar, garlic and water; cover and cook for 5 minutes or until vegetables are just tender. Add sesame oil and toss to mix. Remove vegetables and keep warm.

Add remaining 2 tablespoons (30 mL) vegetable oil to wok. Add

FISH SAUCE

You might not think that the liquid run-off from barrels of fermenting salted fish would turn out to be a culinary treasure. But fish sauce (nam pla in Thailand and nuoc nam in Vietnam) is one of Southeast Asia's most popular flavorings, used as a table sauce as well as an ingredient in almost every savory dish. In the past, Europe loved fish sauce, too: it's an almost exact equivalent of garum, the preferred condiment of ancient Rome.

Uncooked, this thin, watery sauce has a powerful fish smell. The scent fades on cooking; fish sauce accentuates other flavors. Fish sauce lasts, unrefrigerated, indefinitely. Buy it at Asian markets and some supermarkets.

onion and ginger; stir-fry for 15 seconds. Add chicken with marinade; stir-fry for 1 minute. Stir in sherry and cook 1 minute. Add broccoli mixture and stir-fry for about 1 minute or until heated through. Add pepper and salt to taste. Transfer to serving platter and serve immediately. ○

WHAT IS COUSCOUS?

Think of couscous as pasta in the shape of tiny pearls: it's made from the same durum wheat semolina as good quality pastas. (Semolina refers to a grind that is fine, but coarser than flour.)

Couscous is also the characteristic dish of the Maghreb, the North African countries of Morocco, Tunisia and Algeria. In that case, it's a stew of meat, vegetables, chickpeas and raisins, cooked in the bottom of a special dish called a couscousier, while the couscous grains steam in the top.

For a quick side dish buy packaged, pre-cooked couscous. Place equal amounts of couscous and boiling water in a saucepan and add a dash of salt. Cover tightly, let sit for five minutes, then fluff with a fork.

Major Grey's Chicken Stir-Fry

Makes 4 servings

France Powell of Prince Rupert says she's most creative when the fridge is virtually empty and dinnertime is fast approaching. The chicken, bell pepper and chutney stir-fry she entered in our Six O'Clock Solutions contest confirms it. Powell serves it on a bed of couscous.

- ¾ **pound (350 g) boneless chicken breasts, skinned and cut into thin strips**
- ¼ **cup (50 mL) soy sauce**
- 2 **medium onions**
- 3 **medium red or yellow bell peppers**
- 3 **tablespoons (45 mL) vegetable oil, divided**
- ¼ **cup (50 mL) mango chutney**
  Salt and pepper

Put chicken and soy sauce in small bowl; stir to coat well. Set aside. Slice onions and peppers.

In wok or large heavy frypan, heat 1 tablespoon (15 mL) oil over medium-high heat. Add onions and stir-fry for 3 to 4 minutes or until golden. Remove from wok and set aside.

Add 1 tablespoon (15 mL) oil to wok. Add peppers and stir-fry for about 3 minutes or until tender-crisp. Remove from wok and set aside.

Increase heat to high and add remaining 1 tablespoon (15 mL) oil to wok. Using slotted spoon, remove chicken from soy sauce; reserve soy sauce. Add chicken to wok and stir-fry, in 2 batches, for 2 minutes or until no longer pink inside.

Return onions, peppers and chicken to wok. Add chutney and remaining soy sauce; simmer for 2 minutes, stirring frequently. Add salt and pepper to taste. ○

SIX CLOCK

Thai Stir-Fry with Chicken, Cilantro and Coconut Milk

Makes 4 servings

Sometimes you look at a list of ingredients and decide right away that you don't have time. That can be a shame: if the recipe is for a one-dish meal, it might be a quick cook's friend in disguise. This one, graced with the subtle tastes of Thai food, was inspired by a recipe Agnes Kadowaki of Vancouver entered in our Six O'Clock Solutions contest. Add rice and a cold cucumber salad for a satisfying meal.

4	tablespoons (60 mL) vegetable oil, divided
1	medium onion, chopped coarse
4	garlic cloves, chopped fine
1	pound (500 g) boneless chicken breasts, skinned and cut into thin strips
3	cups (750 mL) broccoli flowerets
1	red bell pepper, cut into bite-size pieces
½	cup (125 mL) chopped fresh cilantro
⅔	cup (150 mL) coconut milk

Brown sauce

2	tablespoons (30 mL) soy sauce
1	tablespoon (15 mL) oyster sauce
2	teaspoons (10 mL) brown sugar
1½	teaspoons (7 mL) grated fresh ginger
½	teaspoon (2 mL) hot chili paste
½	teaspoon (2 mL) sesame oil

Brown sauce: In small bowl, combine soy sauce, oyster sauce, brown sugar, ginger, chili paste and sesame oil; set aside.

In wok or large heavy frypan, heat 2 tablespoons (30 mL) vegetable oil over medium-high heat. Add onion and garlic; stir-fry for about 3 minutes or until tender. Increase heat to high and add chicken; stir-fry for about 3 minutes or until chicken is no longer pink inside. Remove from wok and set aside.

Heat remaining 2 tablespoons (30 mL) oil in wok. Add broccoli and red pepper; stir-fry for 2 minutes. Return chicken mixture. Add cilantro and brown sauce; stir-fry for 30 seconds. Add coconut milk and stir until heated through. ⏀

COLD CUCUMBER SALAD

Slice a medium cucumber (peeled if necessary) and lay it out on a plate. Sprinkle with half a teaspoon (2 mL) of ground roasted cumin, a squeeze of lime juice and salt and pepper to taste.

Chicken and Rotini with Dill and Pecan Pesto

Makes 4 servings

WHICH PASTA? WHAT SAUCE?

The general rule is to match a light sauce to a light pasta. Oil-based and tomato-based sauces go well with long thin pastas such as spaghetti, linguine and vermicelli.

For cream and cheese sauces pick either the thicker string pastas, such as fettuccine, or short, stubby pastas: farfalle (bow-ties), fusilli (corkscrews) or pennette (small quills).

Hearty meat, bean or mushroom sauces work best with large tubular pastas like penne or ziti.

Shells and twists that pick up plenty of sauce shine in pasta salads.

If it's summer and you happen to have a good supply of fresh dill, make this pasta using a third of a cup of dill and a half-cup of parsley. If, as is somewhat more likely, a winter day finds you with no nearby source of fresh herbs and a longing for a superb pasta dinner, use dried dill. You'll still get wonderful results. And because the pasta includes steamed vegetables, all you need to add is a substantial loaf of bread.

4	cups (1 L) rotini
1	tablespoon (15 mL) vegetable oil
2	whole boneless chicken breasts, skinned and cut into 1-inch (2.5 cm) pieces
2	cups (500 mL) steamed vegetables (sliced carrots, cubed squash or broccoli flowerets)

Dill pesto

½	cup (125 mL) pecan pieces
2	teaspoons (10 mL) dried dill weed
1	cup (250 mL) fresh parsley
1	garlic clove
½	cup (125 mL) grated parmesan cheese
½	cup (125 mL) vegetable oil
	Salt and pepper

Cook rotini in large amount of boiling salted water until tender; drain and return to pot.

Meanwhile, prepare pesto: In blender or food processor, combine pecans, dill, parsley, garlic and cheese; process for 1 minute or until finely chopped. With motor running, slowly add ½ cup (125 mL) oil; process for an additional 30 seconds. Add salt and pepper to taste.

In large heavy frypan, heat 1 tablespoon (15 mL) oil over medium-high heat. Add chicken and saute for about 4 minutes or until no longer pink inside.

Add pesto to pasta; toss. Gently stir in chicken and steamed vegetables. ⊘

Pan-Seared Chicken Pasta with Wilted Spinach

Makes 4 servings

Chef Michael Wilks of Da Pasta Bar brought this simple-to-make pasta to The Sun's test kitchen, and demonstrated that quick-and-easy cooking can, with the right ingredients, be company fare. The most time-consuming part of the preparation is washing the spinach: buy triple-washed if you can find it; bagged spinach is second best, but faster than starting from muddy bundles. With spinach in the main dish, look for a salad with a twist: orange and Belgian endive would work nicely.

¾   pound (350 g) fusilli lunghi (long curly pasta)
1   pound (500 g) boneless chicken breasts, skinned and
     cut into ¼-inch (5 mm) strips
     Salt and pepper
2   tablespoons (30 mL) extra virgin olive oil, divided
8   garlic cloves
2   cups (500 mL) sliced button mushrooms
1   cup (250 mL) sliced, stemmed shiitake mushrooms
1   teaspoon (5 mL) chopped fresh rosemary
1   cup (250 mL) chicken stock
½   cup (125 mL) dry white wine
8   cups (2 L) packed spinach leaves (about 2 bunches)
2   tablespoons (30 mL) cold butter,
     cut into ¼-inch (5 mm) dice
     Shaved parmesan cheese
     Freshly cracked pepper

Cook fusilli lunghi in large amount of boiling salted water until tender; drain and return to pot.

Lightly sprinkle chicken with salt and pepper. In large heavy frypan, heat 1 tablespoon (15 mL) oil over medium-high heat. Add chicken and saute for 2 to 3 minutes or until golden and no longer pink inside. Remove from pan and set aside.

Add remaining 1 tablespoon (15 mL) oil to frypan and heat over medium-low heat. Add garlic cloves and saute for 5 minutes or until golden, stirring occasionally. Add button and shiitake mushrooms; increase heat to high and saute for about 4 minutes or until light golden. Add rosemary, stock and wine; bring to a boil, stirring

ORANGE AND BELGIAN ENDIVE SALAD

When there's a lot of green in dinner already, you need a salad that won't look redundant.

Buy a shoot of Belgian endive for each person you're going to feed, more if they're small (the endives, not the people). Separate the leaves from the shoots, lay them out artistically on a plate. Add peeled, sliced orange, thin slices of fennel (and a few of the feathery bits for garnish), Italian black olives, thin and delicate red onion rings, oil, vinegar and plenty of black pepper.

and scraping browned bits from bottom of pan. Boil for 6 minutes or until reduced by half. Add salt and pepper to taste.

Add spinach, butter, chicken and mushroom mixture to pasta; toss. Serve with parmesan cheese and cracked pepper. ○

Speedy Spirals with Chicken, Tomatoes and Black Olives

Makes 4 servings

What's a teaspoon of anchovy paste doing in this otherwise straightforward recipe for a chicken-based pasta? It's performing anchovy magic, adding a satisfying, salty earthiness to the sauce, without a trace of fishy taste. If you're desperately short of time, make the sauce using pre-sliced California black olives. Or achieve a quantum leap in flavor by choosing the ripe Italian-style black olives that come in jars. All you need to add: a green salad and a loaf of Italian bread.

4	cups (1 L) rotini
¾	pound (350 g) boneless chicken breasts, skinned and cut into 1-inch (2.5 cm) pieces
3	tablespoons (45 mL) flour
5	tablespoons (75 mL) olive oil, divided
1	cup (250 mL) sliced ripe olives
2	medium tomatoes, chopped
1	garlic clove, crushed
½	teaspoon (2 mL) dried thyme
1	teaspoon (5 mL) anchovy paste

Cook rotini in large amount of boiling salted water until tender; drain and return to pot.

Dredge chicken in flour. In large heavy frypan, heat 2 tablespoons (30 mL) oil over medium-high heat. Add chicken and saute until golden brown. Add remaining 3 tablespoons (45 mL) oil, olives, tomatoes, garlic, thyme and anchovy paste; cook for 4 minutes or until chicken is no longer pink inside.

Add chicken sauce to pasta and toss. ○

WHAT IS ANCHOVY PASTE?

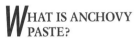

When a recipe calls for just a taste of anchovy, don't open a tin. Instead, use anchovy paste in a tube. Screw the lid back on and the paste — a combination of anchovies, vinegar, spices and water — will keep indefinitely in the fridge.

Chicken Spaghettini with Broccoli, Pine Nuts and Sun-Dried Tomatoes

Makes 4 servings

Sometimes the border between a family meal and a meal for company is blurred. You might first make this pasta, for example, as a quick mid-week dinner with friends, depending on the pine nuts, sun-dried tomatoes and fresh basil to give it the desired sense of something special. But once you know how quick and easy it is to prepare, and watch the way a nutritional heavyweight like broccoli gets devoured, you'll be tempted to make it for everyday family dinners, too.

Add a loaf of crusty Italian bread and finish with a spinach-and-mushroom salad after the pasta.

¾	**pound (350 g) spaghettini**
3	**cups (750 mL) broccoli flowerets**
⅓	**cup (75 mL) olive oil**
¾	**pound (350 g) boneless chicken thighs or breasts, skinned and cut into thin strips**
2	**tablespoons (30 mL) crushed garlic cloves**
⅛	**teaspoon (0.5 mL) dried crushed hot red pepper**
¾	**cup (175 mL) drained sun-dried tomatoes (packed in oil), sliced thin**
½	**cup (125 mL) grated parmesan cheese**
2	**tablespoons (30 mL) chopped fresh basil Salt and pepper**
⅓	**cup (75 mL) toasted pine nuts (see note)**

Cook spaghettini in large amount of boiling salted water until tender, adding broccoli 2 minutes before end of cooking time. Drain pasta and broccoli; return to pot.

Meanwhile, heat oil in large heavy frypan over medium-high heat. Add chicken, garlic and dried red pepper; saute for 2 minutes. Add sun-dried tomatoes and saute for 1 minute or until chicken is no longer pink inside.

Add chicken mixture to pasta and broccoli; toss. Add cheese, basil and salt and pepper to taste; toss. Serve sprinkled with pine nuts.

Note: To toast pine nuts, put in frypan over medium heat for 3 to 5 minutes or until golden, stirring frequently. ○

WHAT ARE PINE NUTS?

The edible seeds of a dozen or so of the world's 90-odd varieties of pine tree come complete with an elaborate protective device: the pine cone. Because seeds have to be removed from cones by hand, pine nuts are always expensive.

Protect your investment by buying in small quantities and storing the nuts in airtight containers. They'll keep three months in the refrigerator, nine in the freezer.

Very little heat separates a roasted pine nut from a charred pine nut. If you use a cast-iron pan to roast the nuts, empty them into a bowl as soon as they're done. There's enough residual heat in the pan to push them over the edge.

Radiatore Pasta with Chicken, Asparagus and Snow Peas

Makes 4 to 5 servings

No, they aren't miniature replicas of the steam-heat radiators that clunk and hiss in elderly buildings. Radiatore look more like the kind of radiator that cools your car's engine. If you can't find them, any short stubby pasta will work just fine.

This is a one-dish meal that demands nothing more than a loaf of good bread if time is tight. If you'd like to use it as the centrepiece of a more lavish meal, serve vegetable antipasto on Italian bread as an appetizer, and when the pasta's been eaten, a salad.

4	cups (1 L) radiatore
1	pound (500 g) asparagus, trimmed and cut diagonally into 1½-inch (4 cm) pieces
½	pound (250 g) snow peas, trimmed
4	tablespoons (60 mL) olive oil, divided
1	pound (500 g) boneless chicken breasts, skinned and cut into ¼-inch (5 mm) strips
1	small onion, sliced thin
2	cups (500 mL) sliced mushrooms
1	teaspoon (5 mL) finely chopped fresh rosemary
⅛	teaspoon (0.5 mL) dried crushed hot red pepper
	Grated parmesan cheese

Cook radiatore in large amount of boiling salted water for 6 minutes. Add asparagus and boil 2 minutes. Add snow peas and boil another 2 minutes. Drain pasta and vegetables and return to pot; add 1 tablespoon (15 mL) oil and toss.

Meanwhile, heat remaining 3 tablespoons (45 mL) oil in frypan over medium-high heat. Add chicken and onion; saute for 2 minutes. Add mushrooms and saute for 3 minutes or until tender. Stir in rosemary and dried red pepper; saute for 30 seconds.

Add chicken mixture to pasta and vegetables; toss. Serve with parmesan cheese. ○

PEAR, ARUGULA AND BRIE SALAD

Wash and tear arugula and arrange on a small platter. Remove the rind from a wedge of brie or camembert, cut the cheese into thin slices and scatter over the arugula. Peel a pear, slice it and arrange the slices over the cheese and greens. For dressing, drizzle extra virgin olive oil and balsamic vinegar over the salad. Add salt and freshly ground pepper to taste.

Virtuous Turkey Soup with Tomatoes and Fresh Basil

Makes 4 servings

Cabbage is not one of the fun vegetables. Cherry tomatoes, little broccoli trees, french fries and even celery sticks stuffed with Velveeta pack way more entertainment value. But there are times when you crave more solid virtues. This soup, based on ground turkey with enough cabbage to offer significant amounts of protective antioxidants, is a model of nutritional rectitude. As long as you keep quiet about what a healthful supper you've made, most people will be captivated by the Italian charm of tomatoes, basil, orzo and parmesan, and never know why they feel so nourished. You don't really need anything more for dinner than a loaf of Italian bread and a salad.

1	tablespoon (15 mL) olive oil
1	pound (500 g) ground turkey
1	medium onion, chopped fine
2	garlic cloves, chopped fine
2	cups (500 mL) coarsely chopped green cabbage
6	cups (1.5 mL) chicken stock
1	(796-mL) can stewed tomatoes
½	cup (125 mL) orzo (rice-shaped pasta)
2	tablespoons (30 mL) chopped fresh basil
	Salt and pepper
	Grated parmesan cheese

In large heavy saucepan, heat oil over medium-high heat. Add turkey and saute for 3 to 4 minutes or until no longer pink, stirring frequently. With slotted spoon, remove turkey and set aside.

Add onion and garlic to saucepan; saute for 2 minutes. Add cabbage and saute 1 minute. Stir in stock and tomatoes; bring to a boil. Add orzo and boil gently for 15 minutes or until pasta is tender; stirring occasionally. Add basil and turkey; heat through. Add salt and pepper to taste. Serve sprinkled with parmesan cheese.

WHAT IS ORZO?

Orzo is the little pasta that secretly wants to be rice. Before it's cooked, it looks like grains of rice. After it's cooked, it looks like orzo, but will happily stand in for rice whenever it can: as a side dish, in soups and in salads. If it's not in your supermarket, check the nearest Italian deli.

Texan Outrage Turkey Chili
Makes 4 servings

Chili aficionados will tell you that real chili takes all day to make. They might intimate that its secrets rival those of the shroud of Turin. If they're from Texas, they will assure you that a bowl of red must never contain beans. But a cook's got to do what a cook's got to do: in this case, make a very fast, very good, low-fat dinner starting with turkey sausages and store-bought salsa. Set out corn chips and salsa to nibble while you're cooking. Once the chili is simmering, make a hefty salad; cabbage salad would work nicely. Add a substantial bread and dinner's ready.

1	tablespoon (15 mL) vegetable oil
1	medium onion, chopped
1	pound (500 g) turkey sausages, casings removed
⅔	cup (150 mL) mild or medium salsa
¼	cup (50 mL) water
1	(540-mL) can kidney beans, undrained
1	(341-mL) can whole kernel corn, drained
1	teaspoon (5 mL) chili powder

In large heavy frypan, heat oil over medium-high heat. Add onion and saute for 3 minutes or until tender. Add sausage and saute for 5 to 7 minutes or until cooked, stirring to break up sausage; drain off liquid.

Stir in salsa, water, kidney beans with liquid, corn and chili powder; bring to a boil. Reduce heat and simmer, uncovered, for 5 minutes, stirring occasionally. Ladle into bowls. ⏲

Salad

2	cups (500 mL) finely shredded green cabbage
1	carrot, grated
1	unpeeled apple, cored and chopped
½	cup (125 mL) raisins
2	green onions, chopped

Yogurt dressing

6	tablespoons (90 mL) plain low-fat yogurt
1	tablespoon (15 mL) light mayonnaise
1	teaspoon (5 mL) liquid honey
	Salt and pepper

Salad: In bowl, combine all salad ingredients.

Dressing: In small bowl, combine yogurt, mayonnaise and honey; mix well. Add salt and pepper to taste.

Add dressing to salad and stir to mix well. Makes 4 servings.

Pronto Penne with Turkey Sausage

Makes 4 servings

Making a recipe based on turkey sausages taken out of their casings and cooked in a tomato sauce is like jumping the gun in a race: by the time the event has officially started, you've covered a lot of ground. Why? The seasoning's already in the meat.

While the sauce simmers, prepare a vegetable or green salad. Choose something that will stand up to the spices in the pasta sauce and sausages; steamed broccoli or a spinach-and-mushroom salad would do well.

1	tablespoon (15 mL) vegetable oil
1	medium onion, chopped
1	garlic clove, chopped fine
1	pound (500 g) turkey sausages, casings removed
4	cups (1 L) penne
1	(796-mL) can diced tomatoes
½	cup (125 mL) chicken stock
⅛	teaspoon (0.5 mL) dried crushed hot red pepper
¼	teaspoon (1 mL) salt
¼	teaspoon (1 mL) pepper
1	green bell pepper, chopped
	Grated parmesan cheese

In large heavy frypan, heat oil over medium-high heat. Add onion and garlic; saute for 3 minutes or until onion is tender. Add sausage and saute for 5 to 7 minutes or until cooked, stirring to break up sausage; drain off liquid.

Cook penne in large amount of boiling salted water until tender; drain and return to pot.

Meanwhile, stir tomatoes, stock, dried red pepper, salt and pepper into sausage mixture; bring to a boil. Reduce heat and simmer for 10 minutes, stirring occasionally. Add green pepper and simmer for 5 minutes.

Add sauce to penne and toss. Serve with parmesan cheese. ☾

FRESH OFF THE GRATE

Whenever a recipe in this cookbook calls for grated parmesan cheese, we mean cheese that's been freshly grated from a block just before it's used.

Take the extra moment to grate fresh cheese because it tastes better. When parmesan is grated long before it's eaten, it loses its round, nutty taste and turns sharp.

Tex-Mex Turkey Lasagne
Makes 8 servings

Large, inexpensive, child-pleasing and fast: this is the recipe to haul out the next time the kids invite their friends over for dinner. Corn tortillas stand in for lasagne noodles; between the tortillas there's a creamy layer based on low-fat cottage cheese and two layers of ground turkey in a spicy tomato sauce. A big panful bakes in just 20 minutes.

1	tablespoon (15 mL) vegetable oil
2	garlic cloves, chopped fine
1	pound (500 g) ground turkey
1	(341-mL) can whole kernel corn, drained
1	(398-mL) can tomato sauce
1	cup (250 mL) medium salsa
1	tablespoon (15 mL) chili powder
1½	teaspoons (7 mL) ground cumin
	Salt
1	(500-g) carton low-fat cottage cheese
2	large eggs, lightly beaten
¼	cup (50 mL) grated parmesan cheese
1	teaspoon (5 mL) dried oregano
12	corn tortillas
1	cup (250 mL) grated cheddar cheese

In large heavy frypan, heat oil over medium-high heat. Add garlic and saute for 30 seconds. Add turkey and saute for 3 minutes or until no longer pink; drain off liquid. Add corn, tomato sauce, salsa, chili powder and cumin; simmer for 3 minutes, stirring frequently. Add salt to taste.

In bowl, combine cottage cheese, eggs, parmesan cheese and oregano; mix well.

Arrange 6 tortillas on bottom and up sides of lightly greased 13x9x2-inch (33x23x5 cm) baking dish, overlapping as necessary. Cover with half the turkey mixture; spoon cottage cheese mixture over top. Arrange remaining 6 tortillas over cottage cheese mixture, overlapping as necessary. Top with remaining turkey mixture.

Bake at 375 F (190 C) for about 20 minutes or until hot and bubbly. Remove from oven. Sprinkle with cheddar cheese and return to oven for 1 minute or until cheese melts. ⏱

CREAMY HERB DIP

Once you have the lasagne in the oven, cut up raw vegetables and serve them with this creamy dip. They'll be more popular than salad.

¾	cup (175 mL) plain low-fat yogurt
¾	cup (175 mL) light mayonnaise
1½	teaspoons (7 mL) lemon juice
1	teaspoon (5 ml) honey
1	small garlic clove, crushed
1	tablespoon (15 mL) finely chopped fresh parsley
¼	teaspoon (1 mL) fines herbes
	Salt and pepper to taste

Combine all ingredients. Cover and refrigerate until serving time. Makes 1½ cups (375 mL).

Turkey Fajitas

Makes 4 servings

Fajitas are one-dish, hand-held meals wrapped in soft flour tortillas. They make a democratic sort of supper if you lay the cooked ingredients out on a platter and invite everyone to build his or her own perfect fajita. In this case, the filling is strips of turkey cutlet and sauteed red peppers, lettuce, tomatoes and whatever voltage of salsa you prefer.

8	(8-inch or 20-cm) flour tortillas
2	tablespoons (30 mL) vegetable oil, divided
1	medium onion, sliced thin
1	garlic clove, chopped fine
1	red bell pepper, cut into thin strips
1	pound (500 g) turkey cutlets, cut into thin strips
½	teaspoon (2 mL) ground cumin
¼	teaspoon (1 mL) ground coriander
¼	teaspoon (1 mL) salt
¼	teaspoon (1 mL) pepper
⅛	teaspoon (0.5 mL) dried crushed hot red pepper
1	tablespoon (15 mL) lime juice
½	cup (125 mL) mild or medium salsa
2	cups (500 mL) shredded lettuce
1	tomato, chopped
	Light sour cream or extra-thick plain yogurt

Stack and wrap tortillas in foil. Bake at 350 F (180 C) for 5 minutes or until heated through.

Meanwhile, heat 1 tablespoon (15 mL) oil in frypan over medium-high heat. Add onion and garlic; saute for 2 minutes. Add bell pepper and saute for 2 minutes or until vegetables are tender; remove from pan and set aside.

Add remaining 1 tablespoon (15 mL) oil to frypan. Add turkey, cumin, coriander, salt, pepper and dried red pepper; saute for 4 minutes or until turkey is no longer pink inside. Sprinkle with lime juice. Return onion mixture to frypan; stir and heat through.

Put about 1 tablespoon (15 mL) salsa in the centre of each tortilla. Top with ¼ cup (50 mL) lettuce, an eighth of both the tomato and the turkey mixture. Fold bottom of each tortilla (side closest to you) up over filling; then fold the sides in, overlapping. Top with a dollop of sour cream or yogurt. ↻

ABOUT VEGETABLE OIL

Nutritionists currently recommend oils with a high level of mono-unsaturated fat and a low level of saturated fat as the most healthful choice.

The top three? Canola, olive oil and soy oil, in that order. Use olive oil when you want more flavor — in salad dressings, for example — and canola or soy for baking.

Revisionist Turkey Stroganoff

Makes 4 servings

The first stroganoff, the one 19th century Russian diplomat Count Paul Stroganoff gave his name to, consisted of thin slices of beef tenderloin, onions and mushrooms, sauteed quickly in butter and combined with a sour cream sauce.

But stroganoff has turned out to be a pliable word. In this one, for example, ground turkey replaces beef, and yogurt stands in for sour cream. (That high, humming sound you hear is the count, spinning in his grave.) The result is a dinner that's relatively low in fat, and fast enough to put together after work.

6	**cups (1.5 L) broad noodles**
1	**tablespoon (15 mL) vegetable oil**
1	**pound (500 g) ground turkey**
¼	**cup (50 mL) finely chopped onion**
1	**garlic clove, chopped fine**
2	**cups (500 mL) sliced mushrooms**
1	**small red bell pepper, chopped**
½	**cup (125 mL) chicken stock**
⅓	**cup (75 mL) plain yogurt**
2	**teaspoons (10 mL) flour**
1	**tablespoon (15 mL) dry white wine**
1	**teaspoon (5 mL) Worcestershire sauce**
	Salt and pepper
1	**tablespoon (15 mL) finely chopped fresh parsley**

Cook noodles in large amount of boiling salted water until tender; drain.

Meanwhile, heat oil in large heavy frypan over medium-high heat. Add turkey, onion and garlic; saute for 3 minutes or until turkey is no longer pink. Add mushrooms and red pepper; saute for 3 minutes. Add stock and bring to a boil.

In small bowl, combine yogurt, flour, wine and Worcestershire sauce; mix until smooth. Stir into turkey mixture, stirring constantly until thickened. Add salt and pepper to taste.

Serve over hot noodles. Sprinkle with parsley. ⟲

GROUND TURKEY ALERT

Ground turkey spoils fast. Either use it on the day you buy it, or tuck it into the freezer to use later in the week.

Fat-Fightin' Turkey Burgers

Makes 4 servings

If you're trying to trim fat from your family's diet, changing from ground beef burgers to turkey burgers is a step in the right direction – as long as you check with your butcher to make sure the ground turkey doesn't include any fatty skin.

You could serve these patties on a plate, dressed up with a salad, and have a sit-down dinner. It's more fun to set out a tray of raw vegetables with a low-fat dip, and offer whole-wheat buns, a plate of tomatoes and lettuce, and all the relish, mustard and ketchup anyone's heart could desire. Just be sure to leave the mayonnaise in the fridge.

1	pound (500 g) ground turkey
¼	cup (50 mL) finely chopped onion
¼	cup (50 mL) plain low-fat yogurt
2	tablespoons (30 mL) fine dry bread crumbs
2	tablespoons (30 mL) grated parmesan cheese
1	tablespoon (15 mL) chili sauce
1	tablespoon (15 mL) chopped fresh basil
1	teaspoon (5 mL) chopped fresh oregano
½	teaspoon (2 mL) salt
¼	teaspoon (1 mL) pepper

In bowl, combine turkey, onion, yogurt, bread crumbs, cheese, chili sauce, basil, oregano, salt and pepper. Shape into 4 patties and place on lightly greased broiler pan. Broil for about 12 minutes or until cooked, turning once. ○

LOW FAT

CHUTNEY DIP FOR RAW VEGETABLES

1	cup (250 mL) plain low-fat yogurt
1	green onion, chopped
3	tablespoons (45 mL) chopped mango chutney
1	teaspoon (5 mL) curry powder

Combine all ingredients. Cover and refrigerate until serving time. Makes about 1¼ cups (300 mL).

Turkey Burgers with Sun-Dried Tomatoes and Fresh Herbs

Makes 4 servings

Just because dinner comes in the shape of a hamburger patty doesn't mean you need see a pair of golden arches in your mind's eye. Turkey burgers flavored with sun-dried tomatoes and fresh herbs are great tucked into a bun with the standard tomato, lettuce and onion. But they're just as comfortable on a plate with a serving of parsley-sprinkled pasta and steamed snow peas. Set out the burger condiments while the patties cook, but hide the ketchup.

1	pound (500 g) ground turkey
1	tablespoon (15 mL) fine dry bread crumbs
1	tablespoon (15 mL) water
2	tablespoons (30 mL) finely chopped, drained sun-dried tomatoes (packed in oil)
1	green onion, chopped fine
2	teaspoons (10 mL) chopped fresh oregano
1	teaspoon (5 mL) chopped fresh thyme
½	teaspoon (2 mL) salt
⅛	teaspoon (0.5 mL) pepper

In bowl, combine turkey, bread crumbs, water, sun-dried tomatoes, green onion, oregano, thyme, salt and pepper. Shape into 4 patties and place on lightly greased broiler pan. Broil for about 12 minutes or until cooked, turning once. ◷

NO-STICK BURGER TIP

Dip your hands in ice water before you shape each patty. You'll save time because the meat won't stick to your hands and the patties will be easier to handle.

Turkey with Sage Cranberry Sauce

Makes 4 servings

Turkey dinner, which may be the greatest North American contribution to world cuisine, is the antithesis of a quick meal. When you'd like the taste of turkey, sage and cranberries, but you don't have time for stuffing, trussing and roasting, try this alternative: turkey cutlets with a red wine, cranberry and sage sauce. Steamed rice and brussels sprouts cooked with baby carrots can be ready to meet the turkey on the table in less than half an hour.

1	**pound (500 g) turkey breast cutlets**
	Salt and pepper
2	**tablespoons (30 mL) butter, divided**
1	**tablespoon (15 mL) vegetable oil**
2	**tablespoons (30 mL) finely chopped shallots**
2	**tablespoons (30 mL) dry red wine**
²/₃	**cup (150 mL) whole berry cranberry sauce**
¹/₃	**cup (75 mL) chicken stock**
2	**teaspoons (10 mL) red wine vinegar**
1	**tablespoon (15 mL) chopped fresh sage**

If necessary, pound turkey cutlets until ¼-inch (5 mm) thick. Lightly sprinkle with salt and pepper.

In large heavy frypan, heat 1 tablespoon (15 mL) butter and oil over medium-high heat. Add cutlets and saute for 4 minutes or until no longer pink inside, turning once. Transfer to serving platter and keep warm.

Add remaining 1 tablespoon (15 mL) butter to frypan and heat. Add shallots and saute for 1 minute. Add red wine, cranberry sauce, stock, vinegar and sage; cook for 4 minutes or until slightly thickened, stirring constantly. Pour over cutlets. ◔

THE BEST BRUSSELS SPROUTS

Trim the tough outer leaves from 1½ pounds (750 g) of sprouts. Cut a small cross in the stem end of each sprout to speed cooking.

Stovetop: *In heavy saucepan, melt 1 tablespoon (15 mL) butter, add a finely chopped clove of garlic and the sprouts. Toss the sprouts over high heat to coat with the butter. Grind on salt and pepper to taste. Add ¼ cup (50 mL) of chicken or vegetable stock, cover, reduce heat to medium, and cook until tender. Check frequently to make sure the sprouts aren't scorching. Add more stock if needed.*

Microwave: *In a microwaveable casserole, melt 1 tablespoon (15 mL) butter. Add a finely chopped clove of garlic and the sprouts. Toss the sprouts to coat with butter. Add salt and pepper to taste and ¼ cup (50 mL) chicken or vegetable stock. Microwave at high for six to seven minutes, let stand for three minutes.*

Turkey with Papaya Ginger Sauce

Makes 4 servings

Faster and far less expensive than a trip to Maui, these turkey cutlets get their sunny disposition from ginger marmalade, lime juice and slices of papaya. They're especially good during summer heat waves and in the lingering days of winter, when any ray of sunshine is welcome.

In the summer, serve them with rice and grilled red peppers. In the winter, change the peppers for broccoli, or, if you're longing for spring, steamed asparagus.

1	**pound (500 g) turkey breast cutlets**
	Salt and pepper
1	**tablespoon (15 mL) butter**
1	**tablespoon (15 mL) vegetable oil**
1	**garlic clove, chopped fine**
⅓	**cup (75 mL) chicken stock**
¼	**cup (50 mL) ginger marmalade**
1	**tablespoon (15 mL) lime juice**
1	**small papaya, peeled and cut into slices about 2½ inches (6 cm) long**
1	**green onion, chopped**

If necessary, pound turkey cutlets until ¼-inch (5 mm) thick. Sprinkle lightly with salt and pepper.

In large heavy frypan, heat butter and oil over medium-high heat. Add cutlets and saute for 4 minutes or until no longer pink inside, turning once. Transfer to serving platter and keep warm.

Add garlic to frypan and saute for 30 seconds. Add stock and boil for about 2 minutes or until slightly reduced, stirring and scraping browned bits from bottom of pan. Drain any juices from turkey cutlets into frypan. Stir in marmalade and lime juice; simmer for 1 minute. Add papaya and green onion; cook for 2 minutes or until papaya is heated through, stirring frequently. Spoon over cutlets. ⏱

SOLO AND SUNRISE PAPAYAS

Hawaii grows two strains of small papayas called Solos, so named because at an average weight of one pound, they're a good size for one person to eat. One strain is sold as Solo (its full name is Solo Waimanalo), the other as Sunrise.

The easiest way to tell them apart from the outside is the pink sticker and higher price attached to the Sunrise papaya.

On the inside, Solo's flesh is yellow-orange. Sunrise's flesh is a glorious salmon pink, and at its best, has a taste and texture even more voluptuous than Solo's.

Turkey with Fruit Chutney

Makes 4 servings

People who make fruit chutneys do more than just bottle summer, they bottle time. All a short-order cook has to do to achieve a potent blend of sweet, tart and hot tastes is take the lid off. Chutney, combined with a modest amount of light cream and some quickly cooked turkey cutlets, gives maximum flavor in minimum time.

If you make your own fruit chutneys, experiment to see which one works best. We used mango. The lemon juice is optional: add it if your chutney is on the sweet side. Steamed green beans and either boiled new potatoes or pasta would round out a simple, relaxing supper.

1	pound (500 g) turkey breast cutlets
	Salt and pepper
1	tablespoon (15 mL) butter
1	tablespoon (15 mL) vegetable oil
⅓	cup (75 mL) light cream
3	tablespoons (45 mL) fruit chutney
½	teaspoon (2 mL) lemon juice, optional

If necessary, pound turkey cutlets until ¼-inch (5 mm) thick. Sprinkle lightly with salt and pepper.

In large heavy frypan, heat butter and oil over medium-high heat. Add cutlets and saute for 4 minutes or until no longer pink inside, turning once. Transfer cutlets to serving platter and keep warm.

Add cream to frypan and stir to remove browned bits from bottom of pan. Stir in chutney and lemon juice. Add salt and pepper to taste. Pour over cutlets. ⏱

WHAT IS CHUTNEY?

In India, a chutney is as likely to be raw as cooked, as long as it's highly spiced, which is what chatni *means.*

British colonials modified the spelling and narrowed the meaning: for us a chutney is a long-cooked mixture of fruit, vinegar, sugar and spices.

Limes, mangoes and apples are the traditional fruits to choose, but tomatoes, plums, cranberries, cherries and all citrus fruits make delicious chutney.

Lemon Sage Turkey

Makes 4 servings

Turkey cutlets cook in a flash. So even when they're part of a half-hour dinner plan, they still have time to sit on the kitchen counter, soaking up flavor from a marinade — in this case, lemon and sage. Couscous with currants is almost as quick to prepare as the cutlets. Add steamed carrots and cabbage for a satisfying mid-week meal, or turn it in a more celebratory direction with braised baby artichokes and a wild greens salad.

1	pound (500 g) turkey breast cutlets
1½	teaspoons (7 mL) grated lemon zest
2	tablespoons (30 mL) lemon juice
½	teaspoon (2 mL) dried sage
⅛	teaspoon (0.5 mL) salt
⅛	teaspoon (0.5 mL) pepper
3	tablespoons (45 mL) vegetable oil, divided
½	cup (125 mL) fine dry bread crumbs
	Lemon slices

If necessary, pound turkey cutlets until ¼-inch (5 mm) thick. In shallow dish large enough to hold turkey cutlets in a single layer, whisk together lemon zest and juice, sage, salt, pepper and 1 tablespoon (15 mL) oil. Add cutlets, turning to coat. Cover and let marinate for 20 minutes.

Remove cutlets from marinade and dredge in bread crumbs, shaking off excess crumbs.

In large non-stick frypan, heat remaining 2 tablespoons (30 mL) oil over medium-high heat. Add cutlets and saute for 4 minutes or until no longer pink inside, turning once. Serve garnished with lemon slices. ⏲

BRAISED BABY ARTICHOKES

Trim off the tough outer leaves and cut each artichoke in half. Rub the cut surface with lemon juice to keep it from discoloring.

In a heavy bottomed pan, heat olive oil and several cloves of crushed garlic. Add the artichokes, toss to coat with oil, then cook them, cut side down, until slightly browned.

Squeeze the juice of a lemon over the artichokes, put the lid on the pan and continue to cook at low heat for 10 to 15 minutes or until tender. Season with salt and pepper.

Buy approximately two pounds to serve four.

Turkey Sausages with Red Lentils

Makes 4 servings

Gerard Hivon of Victoria had two sources of inspiration for his entry in our Six O'Clock Solutions contest: vacations in the south of France and the need to cook lower-fat food.

The result, a homey lentil and turkey sausage dish, fragrant with rosemary, won testers' raves. Hivon suggests adding steamed greens or a salad to make a complete meal, and, of course, a good loaf of bread. Fresh fruit, served with a yogurt sauce for dipping, would make a pleasant dessert.

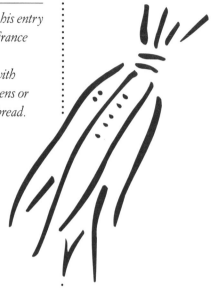

1	teaspoon (5 mL) olive oil
12	small turkey sausages
1	large onion, diced fine
1	medium carrot, diced fine
1	celery stalk, diced fine
1	teaspoon (5 mL) chopped fresh rosemary
1	cup (250 mL) red lentils
1½	cups (375 mL) chicken or turkey stock
	Salt and pepper

In 10-inch (25 cm) heavy frypan, heat oil over medium heat. Add sausages and saute for about 8 minutes or until brown; remove from pan and set aside.

Add onion, carrot, celery and rosemary; saute for about 8 minutes or until vegetables are tender-crisp.

Add lentils and stock. Place sausages on top; cover and simmer for about 10 to 12 minutes or until liquid is absorbed and lentils are tender. Remove sausages. Season lentils with salt and pepper to taste. Transfer lentils to serving platter and top with sausages. ○

CARDAMOM-YOGURT FRUIT SAUCE

½	cup (125 mL) plain low-fat yogurt
½	cup (125 mL) orange juice
⅓	cup (75 mL) mashed ripe banana
⅛	teaspoon (0.5 mL) cardamom

In blender or food processor, blend all ingredients until smooth. Makes about 1½ cups (375 mL).

Pizza with Turkey Sausage and Yellow Bell Pepper

Makes 4 to 6 servings

Some like it hot: they're the ones who will be buying spicy Italian turkey sausage and doubling the amount of dried crushed hot red peppers in the tomato sauce. But it's up to you. Mild sausage and, if you like, no hot peppers at all, will give you a mellow pizza with no volcanic surprises. Either way, turkey sausage and reduced-fat white cheddar cheese make this a prudent pizza. For nutritional bonus points, serve with a spinach salad dressed with a buttermilk vinaigrette.

1	pound (500 g) turkey sausages, casings removed
1	cup (250 mL) canned crushed tomatoes
1/4	teaspoon (1 mL) dried crushed hot red pepper
2	tablespoons (30 mL) chopped fresh basil
2	teaspoons (10 mL) chopped fresh thyme
1	small red onion
2	(12-inch or 30-cm) unbaked pizza crusts (Quick Pizza Dough recipe, page 169) or Italian-style bread shells
1	medium yellow bell pepper, cut into thin strips about 2 inches (5 cm) long
1	cup (250 mL) grated (light) white cheddar cheese
	Pepper
	Chopped fresh parsley

In large non-stick frypan, cook sausage over medium-high heat for about 4 minutes or until cooked, breaking up with a spatula. With slotted spoon, remove sausage to paper towel lined plate.

In small bowl, combine crushed tomatoes, dried red pepper, basil and thyme; set aside. Cut onion in half lengthwise, then cut each half crosswise into very thin slices.

For each pizza, spread half the tomato mixture over unbaked crust or bread shell leaving ½-inch (1 cm) border. Top with half the sausage, yellow pepper and onion. Sprinkle with half the cheese.

If using home-made dough, bake at 500 F (260 C) for 8 minutes, then slide pizzas from pans directly on to oven rack; bake an additional 1 to 2 minutes or until bottoms of crusts are crisp and golden. (On bread shells, bake at 450 F or 230 C for 10 minutes.) Sprinkle with pepper and parsley. ⟳

BUTTERMILK VINAIGRETTE WITH GARLIC AND DILL

½	cup (125 mL) buttermilk
1	tablespoon (15 mL) white wine vinegar
1	teaspoon (5 mL) Dijon mustard
1	garlic clove, chopped fine
1	teaspoon (5 mL) chopped fresh dill
½	teaspoon (2 mL) liquid honey
	Salt and pepper

Mix first 6 ingredients in glass jar with a lid and shake to mix. Add salt and pepper to taste. Makes about ½ cup (125 mL).

Hot Duck Salad with Soy Sesame Vinaigrette

Makes 4 servings

The law of kitchen exotica runs something like this: Food you usually eat only in restaurants will create a gratifying air of celebration if served at home, no matter how simple the recipe. This recipe, which chef and writer Anne Milne brought into the test kitchen for a story on duck, is a perfect example. If you made it with chicken breasts instead, it would still be a pleasant salad, but it wouldn't pack the same casual glamor.

Set out a bowl of olives, some hummus and some grilled vegetables as an appetizer. In summer, serve corn on the cob as a separate course before the salad; in winter, add baked apples for dessert.

Soy sesame vinaigrette

1	teaspoon (5 mL) pickled ginger
1	garlic clove
2	tablespoons (30 mL) rice vinegar
1	teaspoon (5 mL) lime juice
¼	cup (50 mL) vegetable oil
2	tablespoons (30 mL) sesame oil
1	teaspoon (5 mL) frozen orange juice concentrate
2	tablespoons (30 mL) soy sauce
1	teaspoon (5 mL) liquid honey
	Pinch salt
1	teaspoon (5 mL) sesame seeds

Salad

8	cups (2 L) mixed salad greens
1	whole boneless duck breast (about 1 pound or 500 g total), skinned and cut into thin strips
	Salt and pepper
1	tablespoon (15 mL) vegetable oil
1	teaspoon (5 mL) sesame oil
1	small red bell pepper, julienned
½	pound (250 g) mushrooms, sliced thin (button or shiitake or combination)
3	green onions, cut into 1-inch (2.5 cm) pieces
1	teaspoon (5 mL) sesame seeds

Vinaigrette: In food processor, puree ginger and garlic. With machine running, gradually add vinegar and lime juice. Slowly

WHERE TO BUY DUCK BREASTS

Most butchers stock fresh whole ducks, and will happily section them for you. Many also sell duck breasts, usually frozen — the best choice if you don't want to buy a whole duck and use the legs in another recipe.

Call ahead to make sure your butcher has duck breasts in stock. With a day or two's notice, most butchers will happily order them for you.

For barbecued duck (see recipe on next page), a Chinese butcher will be your best source. If your daily rounds don't take you past one, stop in at a restaurant with barbecued duck on the menu and ask for half a duck.

pour in vegetable and sesame oils, orange juice concentrate, soy sauce, honey and salt. Transfer to small bowl. Stir in sesame seeds; set aside.

Salad: Divide greens among 4 plates; set aside.

Lightly sprinkle duck with salt and pepper. In heavy frypan, heat vegetable and sesame oils over high heat. Add duck; stir-fry for 3 minutes. Add red pepper and mushrooms; stir-fry for 2 minutes or until vegetables are tender. Divide mixture among plates with greens. Sprinkle with green onions and sesame seeds. Drizzle salads with vinaigrette. ○

Barbecued Duck Pizza

Makes 4 to 6 servings

Super chef Wolfgang Puck of Los Angeles is believed to be the first person to put barbecued duck on a pizza. He was followed not long after by Duncan Lee of New Westminster, who contributed a barbecued duck pizza to our previous cookbook, Five-Star Food. *This time around, we've added shiitake mushrooms, and refined the method. Round out the meal with a butter lettuce and orange salad.*

2	**(12-inch or 30-cm) unbaked pizza crusts (Quick Pizza Dough recipe, page 169) or Italian-style bread shells**
1½	**teaspoons (6 mL) sesame oil**
6	**tablespoons (90 mL) hoisin sauce**
1	**pound (500 g) barbecued duck, boned and cut into small pieces**
2	**cups (500 mL) thinly sliced stemmed shiitake mushrooms**
½	**cup (125 mL) chopped green onions**

For each pizza, brush unbaked crust or bread shell lightly with ½ teaspoon (2 mL) sesame oil. Spread with 3 tablespoons (45 mL) hoisin sauce. Top with half the duck and mushrooms. Drizzle with ¼ teaspoon (1 mL) sesame oil.

If using home-made dough, bake at 500 F (260 C) for 8 minutes, then slide pizzas from pans directly on to oven rack; bake an additional 1 to 2 minutes or until bottom of crusts are crisp and golden. (On bread shells, bake at 450 F or 230 C for 10 minutes.)

Sprinkle each pizza with ¼ cup (125 mL) green onions. ○

WHAT IS HOISIN SAUCE?

Yet another of the soybean's clever disguises, hoisin sauce — also called Peking sauce because it's a necessary condiment for Peking duck — is a thick, sweet, reddish-brown sauce made from soybeans, garlic, chili peppers and spices.

Store hoisin sauce in the fridge once it's opened. It keeps indefinitely. If you buy it in a tin can, transfer it to a non-metal container before you store it.

CHAPTER THREE

SEAFOOD

The first rule of making satisfying meals in a half-hour or less is to buy good quality food and keep the cooking simple.

You couldn't find a better place to apply that principle than the seafood market. Think of sushi and sashimi — caught, cut and eaten, no cooking involved. The worst thing you can do to seafood, in fact, is overcook it.

The second worst thing is to confine yourself to one or two kinds of fish. Clams and mussels take no more time or effort to cook than any anonymous white fillet. Salmon is glorious, but so is halibut. And a clutch of silver trout, especially if you have a frypan big enough to cook all of them at once, can turn a half-hour meal into a culinary triumph.

In this chapter you'll find 40 dinners, from shellfish dishes for entertaining to can-of-tuna meals for busy weekdays. Try them out and you'll discover that fish is nature's convenience food.

Chop-Chop Cioppino

Makes 4 to 6 servings

Soup-for-dinner season runs from fall through spring. But any unseasonably cold, wet day calls for a dinner that's simple and comforting. The cook in a hurry could hardly ask for a better meal plan than one based on soup: add a salad and a loaf of good bread, and you're ready to feed the family in record time.

Chop-Chop Cioppino (pronounced chuh-PEE-noh), a streamlined version of the famous fish, shellfish and tomato stew that San Francisco's Italian immigrants are credited with creating, would also make a dandy little weeknight company dinner. The most important requirement: a good market, where you can get raw prawns and clams in their shells, along with a pound of cod or halibut fillets, fresh fennel and, if you don't make your own, prepared chicken stock.

2	tablespoons (30 mL) olive oil
1	small fennel bulb, chopped
1	small onion, chopped
3	garlic cloves, chopped fine
3	anchovy fillets
1	pound (500 g) cod or halibut fillets
12	raw prawns (in shell)
12	clams (in shell)
1	(540-mL) can tomatoes (undrained), chopped
3½	cups (875 mL) chicken stock
	Salt and pepper

In large saucepan, heat oil over medium heat. Add fennel, onion, garlic and anchovy fillets; saute for 10 minutes or until vegetables are light golden.

Meanwhile, cut cod fillets into 1½-inch (4 cm) pieces. Shell and devein prawns. Scrub clam shells; set aside.

Add tomatoes and stock to fennel mixture. Bring to a boil and add cod; reduce heat and simmer for 2 minutes. Add prawns and clams; simmer for 3 to 5 minutes or until prawns, clams and cod are cooked. Discard any clams that don't open. Add salt and pepper to taste. ○

WHAT IS FENNEL?

If I ruled the world, or even just the world's produce departments, Florence fennel would be sold in every grocery store and stocked in every vegetable crisper.

Fennel looks a bit like a cross between celery and dill: green stalks emerging from a fat, white bulb topped with feathery, dark-green fronds. Crisp, but not stringy, with a sweet, delicate licorice flavor, the bulb is good raw or cooked.

Cut the stocks off an inch or two above the bulb and discard them, or use them in making stock. The dark green foliage can be chopped and used as an anise-flavored herb.

Fennel makes an instant appetizer cut into strips, lightly salted, then set out with bread and a bowl of small, mild black olives.

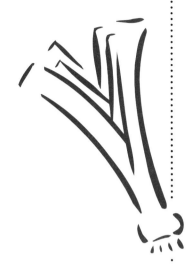

Creamy Cod Soup with Leeks and Green Onions

Makes 4 servings

A cod soup, enriched with light cream and brightened with fresh herbs, is simple, warming and, as most soups are, profoundly calming on a winter's evening.

Add a spinach-and-mushroom salad and some hearty bread and you have a balanced and pretty meal.

2	tablespoons (30 mL) vegetable oil
3	medium carrots, diced
2	leeks, sliced
2	celery stalks, chopped
1	red bell pepper, chopped
2	cups (500 mL) chicken stock
1½	cups (375 mL) clam nectar
1	pound (500 g) cod fillets, cut into 1-inch (2.5 cm) pieces
1	tablespoon (15 mL) chopped fresh basil
1	tablespoon (15 mL) chopped fresh oregano
¾	cup (175 mL) light cream
	Salt and pepper
	Chopped green onions

In large heavy saucepan, heat oil over medium-high heat. Add carrots; saute for 2 minutes. Add leeks, celery and red pepper; saute for 4 minutes. Add stock and clam nectar; bring to a boil. Reduce heat and simmer for 5 minutes. Add cod, basil and oregano; simmer for about 5 minutes or until fish flakes easily when tested with a fork. Stir in cream and heat through. Add salt and pepper to taste. Serve sprinkled with green onions. ⏲

OREGANO: FRESH VS. DRY

Under the hot sun of southern Europe, oregano grows pungent and strong. Raised in cooler northern climates, it fades, and begins to resemble its shy little cousin, sweet marjoram.

It makes sense to use fresh, locally grown oregano only when it won't be subjected to prolonged heat.

When you want to flavor a long-simmering pasta sauce, reach for dried oregano, preferably imported from somewhere hot.

Seafood Chowder with Pasta Shells

Makes 6 servings

Pasta in broth is somehow even more comforting a meal than pasta all by itself. And a pasta and seafood soup takes comfort's hand and climbs into the realm of luxury. This is the sort of meal the Silver Palate Cookbook *classified as a "Sunday night soup," meant to "make the transition from the weekend to the work week a little easier to swallow." A bonus: it's a pantry dish if you stock canned crab and shrimp as well as clams and chicken broth. All you need to add is a salad, crusty rolls and a simple dessert like baked pears.*

1½	cups (375 mL) small pasta shells
1	tablespoon (15 mL) olive oil
1	red or green bell pepper, cut into thin strips
3	celery stalks, sliced
½	cup (125 mL) chopped green onions
2	garlic cloves, chopped fine
1	teaspoon (5 mL) dried marjoram
3	(284-mL) cans chicken broth
1	(142-g) can baby clams
1	cup (250 mL) dry white wine
¼	pound (125 g) cooked shrimp
½	pound (250 g) cooked crab meat
1	tablespoon (15 mL) lemon juice
	Chopped fresh parsley

Cook pasta in large amount of boiling salted water until tender. Drain well and rinse thoroughly with cold water; set aside.

Meanwhile, heat oil in large saucepan over medium heat. Add red pepper, celery, green onions, garlic and marjoram; saute for 5 minutes.

Dilute chicken broth with juice drained from canned clams. Add water to make 5 cups (1.25 L) of liquid. Add to vegetables and simmer for 10 minutes.

Add wine, shrimp, crab meat, clams and pasta; heat through. Just before serving, stir in lemon juice. Serve sprinkled with parsley. ○

BAKED PEARS

Set the oven at 375 F (190 C) as soon as you get into the kitchen. Halve and core four bartlett pears. Place them skin side down in a baking dish and splash with a little lemon juice. Sprinkle each half lightly with cinnamon and brown sugar, dot with butter and slip them into the oven. They'll be cooked just before you sit down to dinner; they can cool while you eat the main course.

Clam and Cauliflower Chowder

Makes 4 servings

Most clam chowders are really a clam and potato stew. This one puts cauliflower in the place of potatoes, with one big advantage: you don't have to peel the vegetable. Stock the canned clams and clam nectar in your pantry and you can make this soup with only an express-lane trip to the supermarket.

Soup dinners demand a salad and good bread. For a homey dessert, why not finish with baked apples?

2	**(142-g) cans baby clams**
2	**tablespoons (30 mL) butter**
1	**medium onion, chopped**
2	**celery stalks, chopped**
1	**garlic clove, crushed**
1	**(398-mL) can clam nectar**
½	**cup (125 mL) dry white wine**
⅛	**teaspoon (0.5 mL) cayenne pepper**
½	**teaspoon (2 mL) dried thyme**
1	**small cauliflower, cut into small flowerets**
½	**cup (125 mL) light cream**
	Salt and pepper
1	**tablespoon (15 mL) chopped fresh parsley**

Drain clams, reserving liquid.

In large heavy saucepan, melt butter over medium heat. Add onion, celery and garlic; saute until vegetables are tender-crisp.

Gradually stir in reserved clam liquid, clam nectar and wine. Add cayenne pepper and thyme. Add cauliflower; bring to a boil. Reduce heat and simmer for 5 minutes or until cauliflower is tender-crisp.

Stir cream and clams into chowder; heat through. Add salt and pepper to taste. Just before serving, stir in parsley. ○

BAKED APPLES

If you have an hour from the time you start making dinner until the time you expect to be eating dessert, then you have plenty of time to make baked apples.

Turn the oven on to 375 F (190 C), wash the apples and core them to within a half-inch (1 cm) of the bottom. Fill the cavity with a mixture of brown sugar and cinnamon, roughly two teaspoons (10 mL) sugar and a quarter teaspoon (1 mL) of cinnamon per apple. Peel the top 1½ inches (4 cm). Put the apples in a pan, add enough boiling water to a depth of a half-inch (1 cm). Cover the apples and forget about them. They'll be ready in 40 to 60 minutes.

Even if the idea of eating baked apples only swims into your brain when the main course is already on the table, the microwave oven will let you have them for dessert.

Follow the same directions to prepare the apples. Put them in a microwaveable dish and cover with the lid or with plastic wrap. Cooking times will depend on your oven. As a rough guide, one apple will cook in three minutes, four apples in five minutes. In each case, let the apples rest five minutes after cooking. The sugar and cinnamon mixture will boil up over the apples. Spoon it back into the cavity or top the apples with a dab of vanilla ice cream and pour the sauce over the ice cream.

Dolly Watts' Salmon Soup or Haw'gwil Jem

Makes 5 servings

Through her catering company, Just Like Grandma's Bannock, Inc., Dolly Watts has become a one-woman culinary revolution, reinventing the first food of the West Coast. She brought this stew into The Vancouver Sun's test kitchen, explaining that before the arrival of metal cooking pots, cooks would pour cold water into a cedar box or tightly woven basket, add heated rocks and then the salmon. The result was a slow boil — in Gitksan, haw'gwil jem.

Despite what looks like a too-simple list of ingredients, our tasters gave Watts' stew five stars. Because it's a lighter-than-usual stew, make sure the rest of the meal is hearty. One suggestion: a spinach salad with mushrooms and toasted hazelnuts. Bannock is, of course, the bread of choice, and perhaps one day we'll be able to pick it up at the supermarket. In the meantime, a crusty whole-wheat loaf will have to do.

1	pound (500 g) salmon fillet (skin on)
6	cups (1.5 L) fish stock or water
5	medium potatoes, peeled and cubed
2	bunches wild onions or 1 large onion, chopped fine
	Salt and pepper

Cut salmon into 1-inch (2.5 cm) cubes.

In large saucepan, combine stock, potatoes and onions. Bring to a boil and boil for 5 minutes or until vegetables are just tender.

Add salmon, reduce heat to medium-low and simmer for 10 minutes or until fish flakes easily when tested with a fork. Add salt and pepper to taste. ⏱

Grilled Salmon and Pecan Salad

Makes 4 servings

Too hot for a full meal? Too hungry to eat just salad for dinner? Main-dish salads were invented for such occasions. Try this one on a warm summer evening when dinner needs to be both uncomplicated and delicious.

THE SALMON PEOPLE

The mythologies of the West Coast tell us that in the time when the myths took place, salmon looked like people, talked like people and often lived with people, taking human wives and husbands.

Now salmon live apart from people in underwater villages, and only shamans can still see them in human form.

But every year, the salmon choose to enter myth time again. Of their own accord, they swim into the rivers to offer themselves as food, casting off their bodies like so many glittering coats. As long as their bones are treated with respect, the salmon can reincarnate in human form under water.

Add a loaf of olive bread or a whole-wheat baguette and a plate of sliced ripe tomatoes with fresh mozzarella (known as bocconcini) drizzled with olive oil and balsamic vinegar, and generously sprinkled with chopped basil.

4	salmon fillets (skinless), about 6 ounces (170 g) each

Marinade

3	tablespoons (45 mL) lemon juice
2	tablespoons (30 mL) olive oil
2	large garlic cloves, crushed

Salad

8	cups (2 L) mixed torn greens
½	cup (125 mL) pecans, chopped coarse
¼	cup (50 mL) hazelnut oil
2	tablespoons (30 mL) apple cider vinegar
3	tablespoons (45 mL) chopped fresh basil
½	teaspoon (2 mL) salt
½	teaspoon (2 mL) pepper

Marinade: In shallow glass baking dish large enough to hold salmon fillets in single layer, whisk together lemon juice, olive oil and garlic.

Place fillets in marinade and turn to coat evenly; let stand for 5 minutes, turning twice.

Salad: In large bowl, combine greens and pecans. In small bowl, whisk together hazelnut oil, vinegar, basil, salt and pepper; set vinaigrette aside.

Place fillets in well-greased, hinged, wire rack holder; reserve marinade. Place on barbecue grill over medium-high heat for about 10 minutes per inch (2.5 cm) of thickness or until fish flakes easily when tested with a fork, turning once and basting frequently with marinade.

Meanwhile, toss greens with vinaigrette. Taste and adjust seasoning. Divide greens among 4 plates. Cut each fillet in half. Place 2 salmon pieces, one slightly overlapping the other, on top of the greens. ○

WHAT ARE BOCCONCINI?

Those little squashed balls of cheese you see in Italian delis, sometimes marinating in oil and herbs, more often covered with water, are mozzarella in its fresh form. The word bocconcini refers to the shape.

Like all mozzarella, bocconcini used to be made only from water buffalo milk. This is no longer true, since the demand for mozzarella has outstripped the buffalo milk supply. North American versions are almost invariably made from cow's milk.

Because they're a fresh cheese, bocconcini don't improve with storage. For the best flavor, use within a few days of purchase.

Salmon Fillets with Mango

Makes 4 servings

Sometimes it seems that ultimate human happiness resides in having all the mangoes you could possibly want to eat. Once you've had them raw and made mango soup and mango ice cream, here's another idea: slices of mango served with salmon steaks baked in a soy, lime and ginger sauce. Keep the rest of the meal simple. White rice and steamed or stir-fried snow peas will provide little oases of calm to refresh your senses. Then you can taste again just how well the exotic sweet-tart flavor of the mango plays off against the richness of the fish.

4	salmon fillets (skin on), about 6 ounces (170 g) each
3	tablespoons (45 mL) dry sherry
1	teaspoon (5 mL) grated lime zest
2	tablespoons (30 mL) lime juice
1	tablespoon (15 mL) soy sauce
2	teaspoons (10 mL) vegetable oil
3	tablespoons (45 mL) chopped green onion
1½	teaspoons (7 mL) grated fresh ginger
1	garlic clove, chopped fine
1	ripe mango, peeled and cut into wedges

Place salmon fillets, skin side down, in greased 13x9-inch (33x23 cm) baking dish.

In small bowl, whisk together sherry, lime zest and juice, soy sauce, oil, green onion, ginger and garlic; pour over fillets.

Bake, uncovered, at 450 F (230 C) for about 10 minutes per inch (2.5 cm) of thickness or until fish flakes easily when tested with a fork. Serve with mango wedges. ⏲

Buying Mangoes

A mango is ripe when its flesh yields to gentle pressure. Choose plump mangoes; avoid fruit with shrivelled skin or bruises.

It's okay to buy mangoes before they're ripe. Let your mangoes ripen at room temperature, out of direct sunshine.

Don't put a mango in the fridge for more than an hour, just before eating. Mangoes stored in the fridge will lose flavor and may blacken around the stem.

Salmon Fillets with Lime and Fresh Herbs

Makes 4 servings

If you grow herbs in the summer, this could easily become your favorite way to cook salmon. It's as changeable as the garden: any harmonious half-cup of herbs will do; the ones we've suggested are just a guideline.

For a mildly Tex-Mex meal, add steamed rice with a half-cup of diced red and yellow bell pepper sprinkled on top of the rice for the last five minutes of cooking, and a green salad with chunks of avocado. Corn on the cob would make a fine first course, especially if you provide a spice grinder full of roasted cumin along with the salt, pepper and butter.

4	salmon fillets (skinless), about 6 ounces (170 g) each
	Salt and pepper
	Herb sprigs
	Lime wedges

Marinade

1	teaspoon (5 mL) grated lime zest
⅓	cup (75 mL) lime juice
2	tablespoons (30 mL) olive oil
3	tablespoons (45 mL) chopped fresh Thai or sweet basil
2	tablespoons (30 mL) chopped fresh chives
2	tablespoons (30 mL) chopped fresh cilantro
1	tablespoon (15 mL) chopped fresh lemon thyme
2	garlic cloves, crushed
2	serrano peppers, seeded and chopped fine

Marinade: In shallow glass baking dish large enough to hold salmon fillets in single layer, whisk together lime zest and juice, oil, basil, chives, cilantro, thyme, garlic and serrano peppers.

Place fillets in marinade and turn to coat evenly; let stand for 5 minutes, turning several times.

Place fillets on greased broiler pan and broil for about 10 minutes per inch (2.5 cm) of thickness or until fish flakes easily when tested with a fork, turning once and basting frequently with marinade.

Transfer fillets to serving platter and sprinkle with salt and pepper. Garnish with herb sprigs and lime wedges. ⟳

Almost Instant
Broiled Salmon Steaks

Makes 4 servings

Some quick dinner plans are like mini-marathons: dinner can be on the table in 30 minutes, but only if the cook chops as fast as a seasoned pro and never stops moving. Others, like this gently seasoned, mildly Asian recipe, give you plenty of time to talk to the people you're about to feed.

As long as you keep fresh ginger in your vegetable crisper, all you need to buy is salmon and something green to stir-fry. My first choice: delicate, pale green Shanghai bok choy, cooked with just salt, oil and ginger.

¼	**cup (50 mL) vegetable oil**
3	**tablespoons (45 mL) soy sauce**
3	**tablespoons (45 mL) lemon juice**
1	**garlic clove, chopped fine**
¾	**teaspoon (4 mL) grated fresh ginger**
⅛	**teaspoon (0.5 mL) pepper**
4	**salmon steaks, about 6 ounces (170 g) each**

In shallow dish large enough to hold salmon steaks in single layer, combine oil, soy sauce, lemon juice, garlic, ginger and pepper. Add salmon steaks and turn to coat well; let stand for 15 minutes, turning steaks frequently.

Remove steaks from marinade and place on greased broiler pan; reserve marinade. Broil for about 10 minutes per inch (2.5 cm) of thickness or until fish flakes easily when tested with a fork, turning once and basting frequently with marinade. ⏱

WHAT'S BROILING?

Broiling brings intense heat directly to the surface of whatever you're cooking. That means the surface browns and the flavors intensify. It also means you run the risk of a dinner that's charred on the outside and raw on the inside.

For best results, preheat your broiler and set the pan so the food sits from four to six inches away from the heat.

A proper broiler pan has a perforated surface that lets melted fat drain away. Use one: you'll avoid oven fires caused when hot fat spits toward the flame.

Broiled Salmon Steaks with Blueberries

Makes 4 servings

Tanis MacMillan of Merville, B.C., entered this recipe in our Six O'Clock Solutions contest. Tasters loved it, but competition was fiercer in this category than in any other, and two other dishes pulled ahead. In our eyes, this salmon and blueberry dish is still a winner, and far too good not to share. MacMillan suggests serving her salmon with rice and a leafy green salad.

4	salmon steaks, about 6 ounces (170 g) each
2	tablespoons (30 mL) olive oil
	Salt and pepper

Sauce

1	tablespoon (15 mL) olive oil
1	small onion, chopped fine
1	garlic clove, chopped fine
2	cups (500 mL) fresh or frozen blueberries
¼	cup (50 mL) water
2	tablespoons (30 mL) apple cider vinegar
1	tablespoon (15 mL) Dijon mustard
¼	cup (50 mL) brown sugar
1	teaspoon (5 mL) ground coriander
½	teaspoon (2 mL) ground marjoram
½	teaspoon (2 mL) ground thyme

Sauce: In heavy medium saucepan, heat 1 tablespoon (15 mL) oil over medium-high heat. Add onion and garlic; saute for 3 minutes or until tender. Add blueberries, water, vinegar, mustard, sugar, coriander, marjoram and thyme; bring to a boil. Reduce heat and simmer for 10 to 15 minutes or until slightly thickened, stirring frequently.

Meanwhile, brush salmon steaks with 2 tablespoons (30 mL) oil and sprinkle lightly with salt and pepper. Place on greased broiler pan. (Steaks will take about 10 minutes per inch or 2.5 cm of thickness to cook.) Broil steaks until almost cooked, turning once. Brush steaks generously with blueberry sauce and broil for 1 minute; turn, brush generously with sauce and broil 1 minute (watch carefully to prevent burning). Serve with remaining sauce on the side. ☉

*S*ALMON AVAILABILITY

You can get farmed fish all year long. Look for fresh, wild-caught salmon from July through October.

The peak season for all B.C. wild species is July and August. Spring, coho, sockeye and pink are gone by the end of September. The season for chum, a less desirable eating fish, continues through October.

Barbecued Salmon Steaks with Peach and Berry Salsa
Makes 4 servings

Salsas are an excuse to put together riotous flavors — in this case raspberries and peaches, jolted with jalapeno peppers, fresh mint and cilantro — and see how they taste when they all hit your tongue at once. Don't be put off by what looks like a long list of ingredients: it goes together quickly, and the salmon is simplicity itself to cook.

With the salmon, serve boiled nugget potatoes and a green salad. Since the grill's already sizzling, you might like to cook a few slabs of red pepper and one or two leeks to slice and add to the salad.

4	salmon steaks, about 6 ounces (170 g) each
	Salt and pepper

Marinade

2	tablespoons (30 mL) olive oil
2	tablespoons (30 mL) balsamic vinegar
2	large garlic cloves, crushed

Salsa

2	peaches (peeled) or nectarines, sliced thin
½	cup (125 mL) finely diced English cucumber
½	cup (125 mL) thinly sliced red onion
1	teaspoon (5 mL) finely chopped jalapeno pepper
1	tablespoon (15 mL) chopped fresh cilantro
1	tablespoon (15 mL) chopped fresh mint
2	teaspoons (10 mL) raspberry vinegar
1	teaspoon (5 mL) sugar
	Salt and pepper
1	cup (250 mL) raspberries

Marinade: In shallow glass baking dish large enough to hold salmon steaks in single layer, whisk together oil, balsamic vinegar and garlic.

Add steaks to marinade and turn to coat evenly; let stand for 5 minutes, turning several times.

Meanwhile, prepare salsa: In bowl, combine peaches, cucumber, onion, jalapeno pepper, cilantro, mint, raspberry vinegar, sugar and salt and pepper to taste. Gently stir in raspberries; set aside.

Place steaks on greased barbecue grill over medium-high heat and cook for about 10 minutes per inch (2.5 cm) of thickness or

Hot Grill Tips

If you don't want your food to stick, make sure the grill is screaming hot before you start cooking.

For best results with sweet barbecue sauces, brush them on toward the end of cooking. Add them too early and they'll burn instead of caramelizing.

until fish flakes easily when tested with a fork, turning once and basting frequently with marinade.

Transfer steaks to serving platter and sprinkle lightly with salt and pepper. Top with some of the salsa. Pass remaining salsa separately. ○

Broiled Salmon Steaks with Herbed Almond Butter

Makes 4 servings

A dab of butter, studded with almonds and dill, melting into the top of a broiled salmon steak: it's the kind entree you might find in a genteel hotel dining room. Maintain the mood by serving orzo (a rice-shaped pasta) with parsley and a touch of melted butter, and steamed baby carrots. Steamed asparagus as a first course would make this a more formal dinner; a wild greens salad served after the main course would give the meal a nudge toward contemporary cooking. Serve Double Oranges for a simple yet elegant finish.

4	**salmon steaks, about 6 ounces (170 g) each**
	Vegetable oil
	Salt and pepper

Herbed almond butter

1	**tablespoon (15 mL) slivered almonds, toasted (see note)**
¼	**cup (50 mL) butter, at room temperature**
1	**small garlic clove, chopped fine**
1	**tablespoon (15 mL) chopped fresh dill**
1½	**teaspoons (7 mL) lemon juice**
¼	**teaspoon (1 mL) salt**
	Pinch paprika

Almond butter: Chop almonds and combine with butter, garlic, dill, lemon juice, salt and paprika. Chill butter until ready to use.

Lightly brush salmon steaks with oil and sprinkle with salt and pepper. Place on greased broiler pan. Broil for about 10 minutes per inch (2.5 cm) of thickness or until fish flakes easily when tested with a fork, turning once. Top each steak with about 1 tablespoon (15 mL) almond butter.

Note: To toast almonds, place on baking sheet and bake at 350 F (180 C) for 5 to 7 minutes or until golden. ○

Maple Roast Sesame Salmon Steaks

Makes 4 servings

Maple syrup meets soy sauce, sesame oil and Szechuan peppercorns; Pacific salmon takes on a sesame seed crust. The results are so harmonious that anyone who makes this recipe ought to get a grant for promoting multiculturalism. Bonus points if you serve baklava for dessert.

If you want to give dinner a push in the direction of North America, add nugget potatoes and steamed green beans. Emphasize the other side of the marriage with steamed rice and stir-fried greens.

4	salmon steaks, about 6 ounces (170 g) each
3	tablespoons (45 mL) sesame seeds
2	tablespoons (30 mL) vegetable oil
2	green onions
	Salt and pepper

Marinade

2	tablespoons (30 mL) maple syrup
1	tablespoon (15 mL) soy sauce
1	tablespoon (15 mL) sesame oil
2	large garlic cloves, crushed
1	tablespoon (15 mL) grated fresh ginger
¼	teaspoon (1 mL) freshly ground Szechuan or black peppercorns

Marinade: In shallow glass baking dish large enough to hold salmon steaks in single layer, whisk together maple syrup, soy sauce, sesame oil, garlic, ginger and ground peppercorns.

Place steaks in marinade and turn to coat evenly; let stand for 5 minutes, turning several times.

Put sesame seeds on large plate. Remove steaks from marinade and coat both sides with seeds.

In heavy, ovenproof 12-inch (30 cm) frypan, heat vegetable oil over high heat. Add steaks and cook 1 minute on each side. Place frypan in 450 F (230 C) oven and roast for 8 to 10 minutes or until fish flakes when tested with a fork.

Meanwhile, diagonally slice green onions into 1-inch (2.5 cm) pieces. Transfer steaks to serving platter. Sprinkle with salt and pepper to taste and green onions. ○

WHAT ARE SZECHUAN PEPPERCORNS?

The dried berry of a small prickly ash tree, Szechuan peppercorns aren't related to black pepper in any way except their peppery taste.

The red-brown berries, about a sixth of an inch long, taste of lemon and spice. They're an essential part of five-spice powder, along with star anise, cloves, fennel and cassia.

For best flavor, roast and grind Szechuan peppercorns just before using.

WHAT IS RAITA?

When you need to cool the sting of hot chilies, this yogurt-based East Indian dish is more effective by far than water or beer. A cross between a salad and a relish, raita often contains roasted cumin seeds and chopped fresh herbs, especially cilantro. After that, all bets are off. There are potato, eggplant, spinach and mint raitas, as well as the more commonly encountered cucumber raita, so feel free to experiment. You'll get the most voluptuous results if you use either whole-milk yogurt or extra-thick yogurt.

Jalapeno Salmon Cakes

Makes 4 servings

In the days when canned salmon signified elegance and refinement, salmon cakes were one of the happier meals to come out of the pantry. A can of salmon, mixed with the ever-present leftover mashed potatoes, an egg and some bread crumbs to help hold it all together, was an easy meal, with a slap-dash sort of glamor to it. Today, most of us think of school lunches when we see a can of salmon. But if you add garlic, jalapeno and roasted cumin, salmon cakes can still be a meal to look forward to — especially if you top them with a raita.

For best results, cook the cakes in a non-stick pan or a non-stick electric frypan.

Raita

1	cup (250 mL) plain low-fat yogurt
½	cup (125 mL) grated English cucumber
½	teaspoon (2 mL) salt

Salmon cakes

1	teaspoon (5 mL) cumin seeds
2	(213-g) cans salmon, drained and flaked
2	jalapeno peppers, seeded and chopped fine
1	large onion, chopped fine
2	garlic cloves, chopped fine
1	large egg, lightly beaten
¼	cup (50 mL) light mayonnaise
¼	teaspoon (1 mL) salt
¼	teaspoon (1 mL) pepper
½	cup (125 mL) yellow cornmeal
1	teaspoon (5 mL) vegetable oil

Raita: In bowl, combine yogurt, cucumber and salt; set aside.

Salmon cakes: In large non-stick frypan, roast cumin seeds over medium-high heat for 1 to 2 minutes or until fragrant, shaking pan and stirring frequently. Grind in mortar with pestle.

In medium bowl, combine ground cumin seeds, salmon, jalapeno peppers, onion, garlic, egg, mayonnaise, salt and pepper; shape into 8 patties.

Put cornmeal on large plate; coat salmon cakes lightly with cornmeal.

In large non-stick frypan, heat oil over medium heat. Add salmon cakes and cook for 10 to 14 minutes or until golden, turning once. Serve with raita. ⏱

Summer Sole with Fresh Tomatoes

Makes 4 servings

This is a recipe for hot days, when cooks have no time for fussing and tomatoes are at their best. Sole with tomatoes and fresh herbs demands only that you place fillets in a baking dish and sprinkle on a salsa-like mixture of tomatoes, shallots, jalapeno pepper and herbs before firing the fish into the oven. Add boiled new potatoes and stir-fried snow peas to complete the meal.

4	sole fillets, about 6 ounces (170 g) each
	Salt and pepper
3	tablespoons (45 mL) olive oil
2	medium tomatoes, seeded and chopped
2	shallots, chopped fine
1	jalapeno pepper, seeded and chopped fine
1	large garlic clove, chopped fine
2	tablespoons (30 mL) finely chopped fresh basil
2	teaspoons (10 mL) finely chopped fresh oregano

Place sole fillets in greased baking dish large enough to hold fillets in single layer. Sprinkle lightly with salt and pepper.

In small bowl, combine oil, tomatoes, shallots, jalapeno pepper, garlic, basil and oregano; spoon evenly over fillets. Bake at 400 F (200 C) for about 8 minutes or until fish flakes easily when tested with a fork. Add salt and pepper to taste.

WHAT ARE SHALLOTS?

Shallots look like tiny red onions, at least until you cut one open and find that it's formed in cloves, like garlic. More subtle and delicate in flavor than onions, shallots also have a reputation for being easier to digest. Like leeks, they're not at their best raw.

Stored in a cool, dry, well-ventilated place, they'll keep for up to a month. If you can't find shallots, use regular cooking onions: the flavor won't be as subtle, but they'll do.

Cod with Fresh Salsa and Lime Sauce

Makes 4 servings

Prepared fresh salsa, humming with cilantro, is one of the great boons of the modern supermarket. Jazz it up even more, and you have Vancouver Sun reader Donna Shier's prize-winning recipe for cod baked in a fiery salsa-and-lime sauce.

You can, of course, substitute any white flaky fish for the cod; Shier first tried the recipe with dogfish. She prefers her salsa on the scorching end of the scale, but if you know you don't like chilies that bite back, substitute mild salsa for the medium suggested here.

Mexican-inspired fish calls out for rice, especially rice with diced red or yellow pepper sprinkled over the top five minutes before it's finished cooking, then stirred in before serving. Follow the fish with a green salad topped with slices of avocado and a few chopped black olives. Nothing could beat a ripe mango for dessert; if it's not mango season, serve a fat-free mango fruit ice.

1	**pound (500 g) cod fillets, cut into serving-size pieces**
1	**cup (250 mL) fresh medium salsa**
¼	**cup (50 mL) butter, melted**
3	**tablespoons (45 mL) lime juice**
2	**garlic cloves, crushed**

Place cod fillets in 11x7-inch (28x18 cm) greased baking dish. Combine salsa, butter, lime juice and garlic; pour over fish. Bake at 425 F (220 C) for about 10 minutes or until fish flakes easily when tested with a fork. ⏲

WHAT IS DOGFISH?

The biggest dogfish grow to just over four feet, which is small for a shark. They're abundant in all seas, usually found close to their main source of food: herring and smelt.

Most of the North American catch goes to Europe, where dogfish fillets are prized for fish and chips. Until very lately, we used dogfish only as a source of fish meal and oil. Because it has a high fat content and quickly turns rancid, dogfish is usually sold frozen.

For best results, marinate thawed fillets overnight in a solution of two teaspoons lemon juice or a tablespoon of vinegar in a quart of water for each pound of fish. Without this precaution, small amounts of urea in the flesh can give off a smell of ammonia when it's cooked.

Cod with Wine and Sun-Dried Tomatoes

Makes 4 servings

Sun-dried tomatoes used to be a little-known Italian specialty; now they're infiltrating any number of recipes with no other apparent ties to Italy. This baked cod is an example. All it does is take advantage of the sun-dried tomato's concentrated burst of flavor to make a fast and satisfying main course. Cheating? Of course.

Add pasta (spinach fettuccine would add a welcome patch of green to the plate) and a side dish of steamed or microwaved butternut squash.

1	pound (500 g) cod fillets, cut into serving-size pieces
1	tablespoon (15 mL) vegetable oil
2	garlic cloves, chopped fine
½	teaspoon (2 mL) salt
¼	teaspoon (1 mL) pepper
½	teaspoon (2 mL) dried thyme
⅓	cup (75 mL) dry white wine
6	sun-dried tomatoes (packed in oil), drained and cut into thin strips
1	small lemon, sliced thin

Brush cod fillets with oil and sprinkle with garlic. Sprinkle with salt, pepper and thyme.

Place fillets in 11x7-inch (28x18 cm) baking dish and add wine. Top with sun-dried tomatoes and lemon slices. Cover with foil and bake at 375 F (190 C) for 20 minutes or until fish flakes easily when tested with a fork. ⏲

WHAT ARE SUN-DRIED TOMATOES?

Sun-dried tomatoes are roma tomatoes that have been split open and dried so the flavor intensifies. In Italy's Calabria region, where they originated, they dried in the sun. These days processors use dehydrators.

When we call for sun-dried tomatoes in this book we normally mean the ones packed in oil. They're sold in delis and many supermarkets, usually in small, clear plastic tubs.

You can economize by buying dried tomatoes, often sold in plastic bags in supermarkets, and reconstituting them by soaking in boiling water for about five minutes. Depending on the recipe, you may want to add extra oil.

Don't be tempted to buy sun-dried tomatoes in jars from supermarket shelves. They're a shadow of their unprocessed selves.

Cod with Capers

Makes 4 servings

WHAT ARE CAPERS?

True capers are the unopened flower bud of the caper bush, which grows wild all around the Mediterranean. Capers are sold pickled in strongly salted wine vinegar. Good capers are olive green and firm to the touch; the smaller the caper, the better the flavor.

False capers are unripe nasturtium seeds, which, when pickled in salted vinegar, taste similar to capers.

Once you've opened a jar of capers, keep it in the fridge and make sure there's enough liquid in the bottle to cover the capers. When capers are exposed to air, their taste turns nasty.

After a jangly day, you don't need challenges at dinner. When you're looking for comfort, stability and the illusion that at least some things stay the same, try making a dish so old that in slightly modified forms it's been around longer than Mrs. Beeton.

To maintain a calm, traditional mood, serve your cod with julienned carrots, steamed and then tossed in a small amount of butter and sprinkled with parsley. Add rice, or if it's the right time of year, tiny new potatoes.

6	tablespoons (90 mL) dry bread crumbs
2	tablespoons (30 mL) grated parmesan cheese
1	pound (500 g) cod fillets, cut into serving-size pieces
	Pepper
3	tablespoons (45 mL) butter, divided
1	tablespoon (15 mL) vegetable oil
1	tablespoon (15 mL) lemon juice
2	teaspoons (10 mL) chopped fresh parsley
2	teaspoons (10 mL) drained capers

Combine bread crumbs and cheese on plate. Sprinkle cod fillets lightly with pepper, then dredge in bread crumb mixture.

In heavy frypan, heat 1 tablespoon (15 mL) butter and oil over medium heat. Add fillets and saute for 8 to 10 minutes or until fish flakes easily when tested with a fork, turning once. Transfer to serving platter and keep warm. Discard any crumbs remaining in frypan.

Add remaining 2 tablespoons (30 mL) butter to frypan and heat for 1 minute. Remove frypan from heat and stir in lemon juice, parsley and capers; spoon over fillets. ○

Cod with Fresh Tomato and Tomatillo Sauce

Makes 4 servings

In the last few years, the giant, cresting wave of Mexican food has carried tomatillos (pronounced tohm-ah-TEE-oh) into our produce departments. These pretty little green berries with the papery husks not only add a tart note to cod fillets, they charm any dinner guest who hasn't spent a lot of time in Mexican markets.

¾	**cup (175 mL) flour**
⅓	**cup (75 mL) grated parmesan cheese**
½	**cup (125 mL) milk**
1	**pound (500 g) cod fillets, cut into serving-size pieces**
	Salt and pepper
4	**tablespoons (60 mL) vegetable oil, divided**
1	**shallot, chopped fine**
1	**jalapeno pepper, chopped fine**
1	**garlic clove, chopped fine**
4	**tomatillos, husked, rinsed and chopped**
2	**medium tomatoes, chopped**
2	**tablespoons (30 mL) chopped fresh basil**
1½	**teaspoons (7 mL) lime juice**

Combine flour and parmesan cheese on plate. Put milk in shallow dish. Lightly sprinkle cod fillets with salt and pepper; dip in flour mixture to coat lightly. Dip in milk and then in flour mixture again.

In large heavy frypan, heat 3 tablespoons (45 mL) oil over medium heat. Add fillets and saute for 8 to 10 minutes or until fish flakes easily when tested with a fork, turning once. Transfer fillets to serving platter.

Meanwhile, heat remaining 1 tablespoon (15 mL) oil in small heavy frypan over medium heat. Add shallot, jalapeno pepper and garlic; saute for 1 minute. Add tomatillos and cook for 1 minute, stirring frequently. Add tomatoes and basil; heat through. Stir in lime juice. Spoon over fillets. ⏲

YOU SAY TOMATO, I SAY TOMATILLO

Despite its name, the little fruit that's sometimes called a Mexican green tomato is a closer relative of the Cape Gooseberry, which has the same papery husk.

Tomatillos are worth buying whenever you see good firm fruit with dry, tight-fitting husks. They'll keep for up to a month in a paper bag in the refrigerator, and make great additions to guacamole and salads as well as salsas.

Spicy Broiled Cod

Makes 4 servings

HOW TO ROAST CUMIN

You can buy ground cumin by the jar, but the spice will pack more of a flavor punch if you buy the seeds, roast them and grind them yourself. A raw cumin seed is a bundle of trapped possibilities. If you really want to smell and taste the spice, you have to heat it before you add it to other food.

To roast, use a heavy frypan over medium-high heat. Add whole seeds and roast for one to two minutes, shaking the pan frequently. The seeds should darken, but if they're black, they're burned. Use a mortar and pestle (or a clean coffee grinder) to grind them.

There are evenings when culinary invention seems a hollow joke, when even reading a recipe demands more energy than you have. Spicy broiled cod is a formula meant for such times: not only is it the soul of simplicity, but if you make it once or twice, you'll no longer need to look at the recipe. Add steamed broccoli, some rice or pasta, then sit back at the dinner table, cool, unharassed and smug. You've just made a very good, very low-fat dinner, and you can be proud of yourself.

1	tablespoon (15 mL) ground cumin
1½	teaspoons (7 mL) chili powder
½	teaspoon (2 mL) cayenne pepper
1	teaspoon (5 mL) finely chopped garlic
1	pound (500 g) cod fillets, cut into serving-size pieces
	Olive oil
	Lime slices

Combine cumin, chili powder, cayenne pepper and garlic.

Brush cod fillets lightly with oil. Sprinkle both sides of fillets with spice mixture. Place on greased broiler pan and broil for about 10 minutes per inch (2.5 cm) of thickness or until fish flakes easily when tested with a fork.

Transfer fillets to serving platter and garnish with lime slices. ○

Fast Mexican Snapper

Makes 4 servings

If you really wanted to make Huachinango a la Veracruzana, you'd start with a whole red snapper, add a long list of spices, and bake the fish for almost an hour. For something closer to instant gratification, try this pared-down version: snapper fillets cooked in a tomato sauce flavored with garlic, lime and jalapeno.

If it's summer, start the meal with corn on the cob and present the fish with rice and a green salad. If the corn's past its peak, try frozen kernels, jazzed up with a half-cup of diced sweet red pepper, a pat of butter and a grinding of roasted cumin as an extra side dish.

2	cups (500 mL) chopped tomatoes
⅓	cup (75 mL) chopped green onions
3	tablespoons (45 mL) lime juice
1	jalapeno pepper, seeded and chopped
1	tablespoon (15 mL) chopped fresh parsley
1	garlic clove, crushed
	Salt and pepper
1	pound (500 g) red snapper fillets

In large heavy frypan, combine tomatoes, green onions, lime juice, jalapeno pepper, parsley, garlic and salt and pepper to taste; stir well and bring to a boil. Reduce heat and simmer, uncovered, for 10 minutes.

Add snapper fillets to sauce, cover and cook for about 10 minutes or until fish flakes easily when tested with a fork.

Transfer fillets to serving platter. Using a slotted spoon, remove tomato mixture and place on top of fillets. ○

CHILI BURNS

Pepper sprays are a weapon because capsaicin, the active ingredient in chili peppers, burns.

That's why chili experts suggest you wear rubber gloves while chopping hot peppers in your kitchen. (New Mexico State University's alternative tip: a thin coating of solid fat on the fingers.)

Even a relatively mild jalapeno can do damage if its juices find their way under your fingernails, or, worse by far, into your eyes.

If you've gone ahead without gloves, and your fingers start to burn, try rinsing them with a weak bleach solution, then washing them again.

If you wear contact lenses, don't take chances. Use gloves.

Steamed Sea Bass with Black Bean Sauce

Makes 4 servings

Out of 900 entries in our Six O'Clock Solutions contest, this one rose to the top, winning Vancouver Sun reader Catherine Liang of Ocean Park a trip for two to San Francisco.

Why did this pared-down modern version of a Chinese classic win? Great flavor is a given. But Brenda Thompson and Ruth Phelan, the Sun home economists who made the recipe for three separate rounds of tastings, loved it for other reasons: it's low-fat and it's as easy a dinner as you can make.

Prepared black bean garlic sauce — Liang prefers Lee Kum Kee brand — cuts the preparation time to a few minutes. Steamed rice and stir-fried green vegetables are a natural choice for rounding out the meal.

1¼	**pounds (625 g) sea bass fillets (about 1½-inches or 4-cm thick)**
3	**tablespoons (45 mL) black bean garlic sauce**
1	**small piece fresh ginger (about ½-inch or 1-cm long), julienned**
1	**green onion, cut into 2-inch (5 cm) pieces**
½	**teaspoon (2 mL) peanut oil**
	Fresh cilantro leaves

Place steam rack in wok or large frypan. Fill wok with water to about 1 inch (2.5 cm) below rack. Cover and bring water to a boil.

Meanwhile, rinse and pat dry sea bass fillets. Place in single layer in 10-inch (25 cm) pie plate. Spread black bean garlic sauce over top and sides of fillets. Top with ginger and green onion; drizzle with oil.

Place pie plate on rack in wok; cover and steam for 12 minutes or until fish flakes easily when tested with a fork. Remove from steamer and garnish with cilantro. ◑

IMPROVING A STEAMER

If you don't own a steamer, don't despair. It's easy to improvise with a roasting rack placed in a wok or in any large frypan with a lid. Electric frypans make great temporary steamers, and give you more room on the stovetop to stir-fry vegetables.

Halibut with Fresh Rosemary and Pine Nuts

Makes 4 servings

Being in possession of four pristine halibut steaks, glistening with freshness, is reason enough to hold a celebratory dinner. This recipe establishes a modestly Italian mood: you coat the steaks with fresh rosemary, bread crumbs, parmesan cheese and pine nuts, then fry them quickly in olive oil.

You could add rice or boiled new potatoes, but it would be hard to improve on rice-shaped orzo pasta, tossed with a little olive oil and a few tablespoons of finely chopped parsley. Asparagus in the spring, the freshest of green beans in the summer, or broccoli in the fall would be my choice for greening the plate: lightly steamed, then flashed in a frypan with a few cloves of crushed garlic and a little olive oil.

2	tablespoons (30 mL) lemon juice
3	tablespoons (45 mL) olive oil, divided
1	teaspoon (5 mL) finely chopped fresh rosemary
¼	teaspoon (1 mL) salt
	Pinch pepper
4	halibut steaks, about 6 ounces (170 g) each
½	cup (125 mL) fine dry bread crumbs
¼	cup (50 mL) finely chopped pine nuts
¼	cup (50 mL) grated parmesan cheese

In small bowl, combine lemon juice, 1 tablespoon (15 mL) oil, rosemary, salt and pepper; mix well. Pour into shallow dish large enough to hold halibut steaks in single layer. Add steaks, turning to coat both sides.

Combine bread crumbs, pine nuts and parmesan cheese on plate. Dip steaks into crumb mixture, coating both sides; press crumb mixture on to fish.

In large heavy frypan, heat remaining 2 tablespoons (30 mL) oil over medium-high heat. Add steaks and saute for about 10 minutes per inch (2.5 cm) of thickness or until fish flakes easily when tested with a fork, turning once. ○

HOLY FLOUNDER!

In Medieval Europe, every flatfish was called a butt. "Halibut" means holy flounder, supposedly because, as an especially valued fish, it was only eaten on church holy days.

Atlantic halibut, Hippoglossus hippoglossus, *is the largest of the flatfish. Pacific halibut is usually considered to be a separate species,* Hippoglossus stenolepis.

GREAT FOR ENTERTAINING

Halibut on Fettuccine with Chili-Sesame Sauce

Makes 4 servings

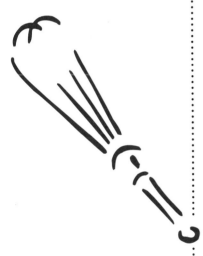

A long list of ingredients in a recipe sometimes means trouble for the cook in a hurry. The exception: when the ingredients are all part of a high-intensity sauce and go together as quickly as you can measure them.

This is a hearty dish for a cold night. All you need to add is a green vegetable, either steamed and given a squeeze of lemon, or stir-fried with a bit of ginger and a good grinding of salt.

⅓	**cup (75 mL) light soy sauce**
⅓	**cup (75 mL) tahini (sesame seed paste)**
⅓	**cup (75 mL) brown sugar**
2	**tablespoons (30 mL) vegetable oil**
4	**teaspoons (20 mL) red wine vinegar**
½	**teaspoon (2 mL) dried crushed hot red pepper**
½	**teaspoon (2 mL) sesame oil**
½	**pound (250 g) fettuccine**
½	**cup (125 mL) chopped green onions**
3	**cups (750 mL) water**
2	**tablespoons (30 mL) lemon juice**
4	**halibut steaks, about 6 ounces (170 g) each**
2	**teaspoons (10 mL) chopped fresh cilantro**
1	**teaspoon (5 mL) roasted sesame seeds**

In small bowl, whisk together soy sauce, tahini, sugar, vegetable oil, vinegar, dried red pepper and sesame oil until well blended. Pour into small saucepan and warm over low heat.

Cook fettuccine in large amount of boiling salted water until tender; drain and return to pot. Add green onions and ½ cup (125 mL) of the warm soy sauce mixture to pasta; toss and keep warm. Reserve remaining soy sauce mixture.

Meanwhile, bring 3 cups (750 mL) water and the lemon juice to a boil in large frypan. Add halibut steaks; reduce heat and simmer, covered, for about 10 minutes per inch (2.5 cm) of thickness or until fish flakes easily when tested with a fork. Gently remove steaks.

Divide pasta amont 4 plates; then top each with a halibut steak. Spoon remaining warm soy sauce mixture over steaks. Sprinkle with cilantro and sesame seeds. ⏀

Halibut with Strawberry, Lime and Mint Salsa

Makes 4 servings

Halibut with strawberries is a summery combination. When you can pick your own berries and cut the mint from your herb garden, life is good indeed. But this isn't a one-season meal. In mid-winter, when you need a cheerful, festive dinner that's startlingly fast, turn to frozen strawberries and fresh herbs from the grocery store.

Make the salsa as soon as you step into the kitchen, so the flavors have as long as possible to blend. Then start cooking the rice, pasta or potatoes. Set out crisp East Indian wafers, called pappadams, for pre-dinner nibbling.

2	cups (500 mL) diced strawberries
¼	cup (50 mL) finely chopped red onion
1	tablespoon (15 mL) chopped fresh mint
1	tablespoon (15 mL) balsamic vinegar
1	tablespoon (15 mL) lime juice
¼	teaspoon (1 mL) brown sugar or to taste
	Salt and pepper
4	halibut steaks, about 6 ounces (170 g) each
	Olive oil
	Mint sprigs

In bowl, combine strawberries, onion, chopped mint, vinegar, lime juice, sugar and pinch of salt and pepper; set salsa aside.

Brush halibut steaks with oil and sprinkle lightly with salt and pepper. Place in baking dish large enough to hold steaks in single layer. Bake at 450 F (230 C) for about 10 minutes per inch (2.5 cm) of thickness or until fish flakes easily when tested with a fork.

Place steaks on serving platter. Spoon salsa over top and garnish with mint sprigs. ↻

WHAT ARE PAPPADAMS?

Almost everyone likes these crisp wafers, which is why they're a standard appetizer in most East Indian restaurants. Pappadams are made from a lentil dough that has been rolled out and dried. Buy either spicy or plain pappadams (also called papars) at East Indian groceries and some supermarkets.

To cook pappadams: heat a half-inch of vegetable oil in a medium frypan. When the oil is hot, but not smoking, drop a pappadam into the oil.

It should puff up immediately. If it doesn't, the oil isn't hot enough. Use tongs to flatten the pappadam (it will curl in the hot oil). Don't overcook; the pappadam should not turn brown. Drain on paper towels.

EXTRA FAST

Trout with Herb Butter

Makes 4 servings

FREEZING CHIVES

When your garden is bursting with chives, save some for the winter. Chop them with scissors and drop them into a plastic freezer container or a freezer bag. The chives will freeze but you can still measure them out with a spoon.

Should you find yourself in a well-equipped summer cabin near a fruitful trout stream, this recipe will stand you in good stead. In the more likely possibility you're stopping by the fish counter on your way home from work, remember: no cod fillet in the world will ever look as good as a little speckled fish, cooked whole in the pan.

For all their glamor, trout are quick and easy to cook. Coated on the inside with herb butter, and drizzled with a little more just before serving, they come to the table moist and fragrant. Eat them with boiled new-crop potatoes, topped with chopped chives, and quickly steamed baby carrots.

4	**fresh trout, about ½ pound (250 g) each**
¼	**cup (50 mL) butter, at room temperature**
1	**shallot, chopped fine**
2	**teaspoons (10 mL) finely chopped, drained sun-dried tomatoes (packed in oil)**
1	**tablespoon (15 mL) finely chopped fresh basil**
1	**teaspoon (5 mL) lemon juice**
	Pinch cayenne pepper
1	**tablespoon (15 mL) butter**
1	**tablespoon (15 mL) vegetable oil**
	Lemon wedges

If desired, cut head and tail off each trout. Combine ¼ cup (50 mL) butter, shallot, sun-dried tomatoes, basil, lemon juice and cayenne pepper; blend well. Spread about 1 teaspoon (5 mL) of butter mixture inside each trout; place remaining butter mixture in small saucepan.

In large heavy frypan, heat 1 tablespoon (15 mL) butter and oil over medium-high heat. Add trout and saute for about 8 minutes or until fish flakes easily when tested with a fork, turning once.

Meanwhile, place butter mixture over low heat until melted.

Place trout on serving plates. Garnish with lemon wedges and drizzle with warm butter mixture. ◴

Seafood with Green Curry and Lemon Grass

Makes 4 servings

To anyone who has cooked Thai food, the idea of a quick Thai dinner seems hysterically funny. But the complexities of taste in this dish, adapted from Thailand The Beautiful Cookbook, *come from prepared curry paste, so the only time-consuming task is shopping.*

Make this recipe once, and you'll have the fish sauce and curry paste on hand. Stock coconut milk and canned bamboo shoots on your staples shelf, and you need only visit a good seafood market and a produce store that sells herbs. (If you can't find Thai basil, don't fret; chopped sweet basil will do in a pinch.) Lemon grass will keep in the freezer, wrapped in foil, for several months. The rest of dinner is simple: rice and stir-fried green vegetables.

2	**tablespoons (30 mL) vegetable oil**
¼	**pound (125 g) prawns or shrimp, shelled and deveined**
¼	**pound (125 g) scallops**
¼	**pound (125 g) mussels, cleaned**
¼	**pound (125 g) fish fillets, cut into ½-inch (1 cm) thick slices**
3	**to 4 tablespoons (45 to 60 mL) green curry paste**
¼	**cup (50 mL) coconut milk**
2	**tablespoons (30 mL) fish sauce**
1	**teaspoon (5 mL) sugar**
2	**tablespoons (30 mL) canned sliced bamboo shoots**
1	**stalk lemon grass, cut into 1-inch (2.5 cm) pieces**
½	**small green bell pepper, cut into thin strips**
⅓	**cup (75 mL) packed fresh Thai basil leaves**

In large heavy saucepan, heat oil over medium-high heat. Add prawns, scallops and mussels; saute for 2 minutes.

Add fish fillets, curry paste, coconut milk, fish sauce, sugar, bamboo shoots, lemon grass, green pepper and basil. Cover and cook for about 3 minutes or until fish is opaque. Discard any mussels that do not open. Transfer to serving platter. ⏱

WHAT IS LEMON GRASS?

At first glance, it resembles a scallion past its prime: a long, grey-green stock with a slightly bulbous white end. But scallions are never as stiff and woody as the tropical grass that gives Thai and Vietnamese soups their tart, lemon-like flavor.

Cut off and discard the tops, leaving the lower six inches for use. Then peel off the dry outer layers of the bulb until you reach the moist, tender core.

The best way to store fresh lemon grass is wrapped in foil in the freezer. Freezing makes it tender and easier to cut. If you can't find lemon grass, try substituting lemon peel with a tiny amount of fresh grated ginger.

Scallops in Strawberry, Balsamic Vinegar and Pepper Sauce

Makes 4 servings

Scallops are both quick and elegant. Dressed with a sauce made from fresh strawberries and balsamic vinegar, they give a time-pressed cook a dazzling seasonal dinner for company.

Chef Ken Bogas, of Mangiamo!, who invented this recipe for us in the middle of berry season, has two pieces of advice: buy the biggest scallops you can find; and try a pinot noir with dinner, because the predominant fruit tastes in this red wine are raspberry and strawberry. Serve rice sprinkled with slices of toasted almond and steamed green beans on the side. Make salad a separate course and finish with a dessert as simple as chocolate-dipped apricots.

1½	**pounds (750 g) large scallops**
1	**tablespoon (15 mL) vegetable oil**
	Salt
2	**cups (500 mL) strawberries, halved**
¼	**cup (50 mL) butter, cut into small pieces**
2	**tablespoons (30 mL) balsamic vinegar**
2	**teaspoons (10 mL) cracked black pepper**

Pat scallops with paper towels to remove as much moisture as possible.

In large heavy frypan, heat oil over high heat. Add scallops and sprinkle lightly with salt; saute for about 6 minutes or until cooked, turning once.

Put strawberries, butter, vinegar and pepper in another frypan. Place over high heat just until butter melts, stirring constantly; remove from heat.

Spoon an equal portion of strawberry sauce on each of 4 plates; top each with an equal portion of scallops. ◐

CHOCOLATE-DIPPED DRIED APRICOTS

Falling-off-a-log simple, tart apricots dipped in chocolate have the best pleasure-to-time-spent ratio of any sweet treat I know.

Melt a half-pound (250 g) of good quality semi-sweet Belgian chocolate in a small bowl in the microwave oven. (Use medium power; chocolate will burn if you try to melt it at full power.)

Line a cookie sheet with wax paper. Dip dried apricots into the melted chocolate and lay them out on the wax paper. Refrigerate. Once the chocolate has hardened, pack the apricots into a tin and store in the refrigerator.

Sizzling Prawns with Ginger

Makes 4 servings

This is a riotously colorful dish: red and yellow bell peppers, green serrano pepper and cilantro, and pink-and-white prawns. Nibble on some Indonesian shrimp crackers while you prepare steamed rice and a simple vegetable stir-fry for a satisfying dinner. What could look prettier than bok choy, with its contrasting green and white stalks?

3	tablespoons (45 mL) vegetable oil
1	medium onion, chopped
1¼	pounds (625 g) prawn tails, shelled and deveined
1	small red bell pepper, julienned
1	small yellow bell pepper, julienned
1	serrano pepper, seeded and chopped fine
5	garlic cloves, chopped fine
1	tablespoon (15 mL) finely chopped fresh ginger
3	tablespoons (45 mL) soy sauce
2	tablespoons (30 mL) dry sherry
¼	cup (50 mL) chopped fresh cilantro

In large wok, heat oil over high heat. Add onion; stir-fry for 1 minute. Add prawns, red and yellow bell peppers, serrano pepper, garlic and ginger; stir-fry for 3 minutes. Add soy sauce and sherry; cook for 1 minute, stirring constantly. Stir in cilantro. ⟳

WHAT ARE SHRIMP CRACKERS?

Indonesian shrimp crackers come in two forms: big, curved puffs, ready to eat straight out of the bag; and thin, flat, oblong flakes that aren't edible until you pop them into hot oil. In a second or two, they swell to three or four times their original size. (Use a wok to cut down on the amount of oil you need.)

Pre-cooked crackers are more convenient, but never taste quite as fresh and shrimpy as the ones you fry yourself. Look for the words krupuk udang *on the label and for Dutch or Indonesian brands. Avoid multi-hued Chinese shrimp crackers.*

Clams Provençal

Makes 4 servings

Clams Provençal makes for a companionable dinner: one big dish in the centre of the table with plenty of bread for mopping up the sauce. A sourdough, French or Italian loaf will give you the truest taste of the wine/pepper/parsley/clam-liquor sauce. Serve a bruschetta (see adjacent recipe) to nibble on before dinner and a hefty salad as a separate course following the clams.

5	pounds (2.25 kg) clams (in shell)
2	tablespoons (30 mL) olive oil
1	medium onion, sliced thin
1	fennel bulb, chopped fine
5	garlic cloves, chopped fine
¼	teaspoon (1 mL) dried crushed hot red pepper
¾	cup (175 mL) dry white wine
4	plum tomatoes, seeded and diced
¼	cup (50 mL) chopped fresh basil
	Salt and pepper
¼	cup (50 mL) chopped fresh parsley

Scrub clams well under cold running water, discarding any that remain open.

In large heavy pot, heat oil over medium-high heat. Add onion, fennel, garlic and dried red pepper; saute for 3 minutes.

Increase heat to high. Add wine and bring to a boil. Add tomatoes, basil and clams; cover and steam for about 5 minutes or until clam shells open, occasionally giving the pan a vigorous shake. Discard any clams that do not open.

Add salt and pepper to taste. Transfer clams to a large serving platter or individual bowls. Spoon some of the tomato mixture over clams and sprinkle with parsley. ⏲

BRUSCHETTA WITH TOMATOES AND BOCCONCINI

4	slices Italian bread
	Olive oil
2	garlic cloves, crushed
1	cup (250 mL) chopped tomato
4	teaspoons (20 mL) finely chopped fresh basil
	Salt and pepper
4	thin slices bocconcini

Toast bread slices. Brush lightly with olive oil and rub with crushed garlic. In this order, top each slice of bread with: 1/4 cup (50 mL) tomato, 1 teaspoon (5 mL) basil, salt and pepper to taste and a slice of bocconcini. Broil for 3 to 5 minutes or until the cheese bubbles.

Linguine with Clam and Black Olive Sauce

Makes 4 servings

Anyone who has a clutch of recipes for favorite meals from the pantry achieves a profound serenity that the what's-for-dinner? demons cannot ruffle. All you need fresh from the grocery is a loaf of bread and the makings for a green salad.

¾	**pound (350 g) linguine**
1	**tablespoon (15 mL) olive oil**
1	**medium onion, chopped**
2	**garlic cloves, chopped fine**
1	**(142-g) can baby clams**
½	**cup (125 mL) dry white wine, chicken stock or fish stock**
1	**tablespoon (15 mL) butter**
½	**cup (125 mL) sliced, pitted black olives**
2	**tablespoons (30 mL) chopped fresh basil or parsley, divided**
	Salt and pepper

Cook linguine in large amount of boiling salted water until tender; drain and return to pot.

Meanwhile, heat oil in large frypan over medium heat. Add onion and garlic; saute for 3 to 5 minutes or until tender. Drain clams, reserving juice. Add juice and wine to frypan. Increase heat to high and bring to a boil; cook for about 3 minutes or until liquid is reduced by half. Stir in butter, olives, 1 tablespoon (15 mL) basil and clams; heat through.

Add clam sauce to pasta and toss. Add salt and pepper to taste. Transfer pasta to serving platter. Sprinkle with remaining 1 tablespoon (15 mL) basil. ♉

TYPES OF OLIVES

When you're trying to decide which olive to use in a recipe, the best rule of thumb is to use one you like on its own.

All olives are bitter before they're cured. The biggest differences in taste come from the curing method.

Lye-cured, or Spanish-style olives, are picked young, soaked in lye, then rinsed and fermented in brine for six months to a year. They're generally mild, and you often find them stuffed with pimentos, jalapenos or almonds.

Dry-cured olives are layered with salt until they become wrinkled and chewy. They have a concentrated, earthy taste.

Brine-cured olives rely entirely on brine for curing. They're the most varied of the three groups, ranging from the strong, vinegar-tasting Greek kalamata, which is slit so even more brine can penetrate, to the mellow, nutty tasting French niçoise olives.

Seashell Pasta with Prawns, Feta and Red Peppers

Makes 4 servings

Dates stuffed with cream cheese are the essence of simple luxury, especially if you use large, fleshy medjool dates and flavor the cream cheese with orange liqueur.

Count on roughly a teaspoon (5 mL) of cream cheese per date; a half-cup (125 mL) ought to stuff 24 medjools. How much liqueur you beat into the cream cheese is a matter of taste. For a mild orange flavor, two teaspoons (10 mL) is plenty.

Cut a slit in each date and take out the pit. Then, using a small spoon, fill the dates with the cream cheese mixture. Refrigerate them, covered with plastic wrap, until serving.

If you're looking for a dish that's as pretty as it is fast, try this distinctly nautical pink-white-and-green pasta. The feta melts into a creamy sauce, the shells catch the sauce, the prawns sit like little pink nuggets among the shells: it's pasta for company.

As soon as anyone hungry shows up, set out a tray of raw vegetables and a little bowl of Italian-style black olives and a baguette. After the pasta, serve a salad of mixed greens. Finish with a dessert of dates and cream cheese.

4	**cups (1 L) large (1-inch or 2.5-cm) pasta shells**
1	**tablespoon (15 mL) olive oil, divided**
1	**pound (500 g) shelled raw prawns**
2	**garlic cloves, crushed**
2	**red bell peppers, chopped**
½	**cup (125 mL) dry white wine, chicken stock or fish stock**
1	**cup (250 mL) crumbled feta cheese**
⅓	**cup (75 mL) chopped green onions**
½	**cup (125 mL) chopped fresh basil, divided**
	Salt and pepper

Cook pasta in large amount of boiling salted water until tender; drain and return to pot.

Meanwhile, heat 1 teaspoon (5 mL) oil in medium frypan over medium-high heat. Add prawns and saute for 3 minutes or until pink. Remove and set aside.

Add remaining 2 teaspoons (10 mL) oil to frypan. Add garlic and red peppers; saute for 3 minutes. Add wine and bring to a boil; cook for 3 minutes or until reduced by half. Add cheese and stir until melted. Stir in green onions, 6 tablespoons (90 mL) basil and cooked prawns; heat through.

Add prawn sauce to pasta and toss. Add salt and pepper to taste. Transfer to serving platter. Sprinkle with remaining basil. ○

In-Your-Face Mussels with Parsley Pesto and Fettuccine

Makes 4 servings

When writing this book, I set aside Wednesday nights for recipe-testing dinner parties: lots of food, no guarantees. This extraordinary pasta dish — one of the winners — got its name from an enthusiastic guest. Olives, capers, red wine vinegar and masses of parsley combine to make a dark and pungent paste that coats the mussels and demands to be licked off the shells.

Most delis stock vegetable antipasto ready-made in tomato sauce. Set some out, with a whole-wheat baguette, to take the edge off pre-dinner hunger. Follow the mussels with a salad.

¾	**pound (350 g) fettuccine**
½	**cup (125 mL) fresh bread crumbs (from day-old bread)**
2	**tablespoons (30 mL) red wine vinegar**
3	**tablespoons (45 mL) water**
1¾	**cups (425 mL) chopped fresh parsley, divided**
1	**tablespoon (15 mL) drained capers**
¼	**cup (50 mL) Italian black olives, pitted**
2	**garlic cloves**
¼	**cup (50 mL) olive oil**
½	**cup (125 mL) dry white wine**
2	**garlic cloves, crushed**
36	**mussels, cleaned**
	Salt and pepper

Cook fettuccine in large amount of boiling salted water until tender; drain.

Meanwhile, soak bread crumbs in vinegar and water for 1 minute.

In food processor, combine 1½ cups (375 mL) parsley, capers, olives, 2 garlic cloves, oil and soaked bread crumbs. Process until smooth; set aside.

In large saucepan, bring wine and crushed garlic to a boil. Stir in mussels, cover and cook for 3 to 4 minutes or until mussels open. Discard any mussels that do not open. Add parsley puree and heat through. Add pasta and salt and pepper to taste; toss. Transfer to serving platter. Sprinkle with remaining ¼ cup (50 mL) parsley. ☾

MUSSEL-MANIA

Buy privacy-seeking mussels: they should either be shut tight in their shells or ready to snap shut when you tap them. Avoid broken shells, and mussels that feel very much heavier than the others (probably full of sand) or ones that are too light and loose.

Store mussels in the refrigerator for no more than a day or two before cooking. Just before you're ready to eat them, wash mussels in cold water, scraping any barnacles off with a small knife.

If your mussels still have beards, or, more correctly, byssal threads attached, rejoice. They're more likely to be alive and healthy than mussels that have been mechanically de-byssed. Remove the threads by grasping them close to the shell and tugging. The best tool: small blunt-nosed pliers.

PASTA? MAKE MINE DRY

Unless you while away placid hours making your own fresh pasta, most of the time you're better off using dried.

Good imported dried pasta is less expensive than fresh pasta. Made from hard durum wheat, it contains less fat and more complex carbohydrates than fresh pastas made with refined flour and eggs.

Dry pasta keeps almost indefinitely, so it's easy to stock the pantry. Fresh pasta should be used within a few days, or frozen and used within a month.

The one advantage if you're really pressed for time: depending on its thickness, fresh pasta cooks in two to four minutes. Dry pasta requires between seven and 14 minutes, depending on the size and brand. (See guide, page 180.)

Down-Home Spaghetti with Tuna-Tomato Sauce

Makes 4 servings

We all have our own versions of comfort food. The common characteristics? Homey, nourishing, economical, unchallenging and best of all, already in the pantry.

The makings for spaghetti with a tuna and tomato sauce are standard fixtures on most cupboard shelves. Add a head of lettuce and a good loaf of bread, and you've made dinner. You need only keep a slightly more lavish stock of Italian staples to have olives for nibbling before dinner and, if you like, marinated artichoke hearts and sun-dried tomatoes for the salad.

2	tablespoons (30 mL) vegetable oil
3	large garlic cloves, chopped fine
1	(796-mL) can diced tomatoes
3	tablespoons (45 mL) finely chopped fresh parsley
1	tablespoon (15 mL) finely chopped fresh oregano
1	(184-g) can chunk light tuna, drained
	Pinch dried crushed hot red pepper
¼	teaspoon (1 mL) salt
⅛	teaspoon (0.5 mL) pepper
¾	pound (350 g) spaghetti
2	teaspoons (10 mL) flour
1	tablespoon (15 mL) water
	Chopped fresh parsley
	Grated parmesan cheese

In heavy frypan, heat oil over medium-high heat. Add garlic and saute 30 seconds. Add tomatoes, 3 tablespoons (45 mL) parsley and oregano; reduce heat and simmer for 15 minutes. Add tuna, dried red pepper, salt and pepper.

Meanwhile, cook spaghetti in large amount of boiling salted water until tender; drain and return to pot.

Combine flour and water; stir well. Add a little hot tuna sauce to flour mixture; return to sauce and simmer for 1 minute or until slightly thickened, stirring constantly.

Add tuna sauce to pasta and toss. Sprinkle with parsley. Serve with parmesan cheese. ☾

Penne with Tuna, Lemon, Capers and Olives

Makes 4 servings

Everyone needs a psychic anchor, a secret bit of wisdom that guarantees you will never be without a good meal. In practice, that often means knowing a wonderful recipe based on pasta and a can of tuna.

Here, olives, capers, garlic, lemon and green onions take the tuna in a Mediterranean direction. Capers keep indefinitely in the fridge; olives come in cans for emergencies, and the least equipped of corner stores can usually cough up a lemon and a bunch of green onions if you don't have them on hand. Any short, stubby pasta will do, but penne is especially nice.

All you need to complete the meal is steamed broccoli with a bit of lemon juice or a green salad. If even that's a stretch, but you have green peas in the freezer, pop them into the microwave with a pinch of sugar.

4	cups (1 L) penne
2	tablespoons (30 mL) butter
2	tablespoons (30 mL) olive oil
4	large garlic cloves, chopped fine
1½	teaspoons (7 mL) finely grated lemon zest
¼	cup (50 mL) lemon juice
3	large green onions, chopped fine
2	tablespoons (30 mL) drained capers
10	kalamata olives, pitted and chopped
1	(184-g) can chunk light tuna, drained
	Salt and pepper
¼	cup (50 mL) finely chopped fresh parsley
	Grated parmesan cheese

LEMONS, WITH ZEST

Do you protectively cover your knuckles every time you read a recipe that calls for grated lemon zest? Fear no more. With a citrus zester in the kitchen (see illustration above), you'll never grate your knuckles again.

That's not the end of the benefits. Zest that's peeled off and then chopped with a cleaver won't clump together as grated zest will. Furthermore, you won't waste time trying to coax the zest off the grater.

Cook penne in large amount of boiling salted water until tender; drain and return to pot.

Meanwhile, heat butter and oil in small heavy frypan over medium heat. Add garlic and saute for 2 minutes. Add lemon zest, lemon juice, green onions, capers and olives; saute for 2 minutes.

Reduce heat to low. Add tuna and separate with a fork into large pieces; heat through, stirring gently to keep tuna in large chunks. Add salt and pepper to taste.

Add tuna mixture and parsley to pasta; toss. Serve with parmesan cheese. ◐

Kitchen Sink Rotini with Tuna and Pine Nuts

Makes 4 servings

This pasta manages to incorporate many of the test kitchen's favorite flavorings, from sun-dried tomatoes to parmesan cheese. Pick up a red pepper and some mushrooms during your weekly shopping, then, as long as your pantry shelves are stocked, you can turn out this pretty, intensely flavored pasta whenever the spirit strikes.

4	cups (1 L) rotini
3	tablespoons (45 mL) pine nuts
3	tablespoons (45 mL) oil drained from sun-dried tomatoes (packed in oil)
1	medium onion, chopped
1	red bell pepper, diced
1	cup (250 mL) sliced mushrooms
2	tablespoons (30 mL) chopped, drained sun-dried tomatoes (packed in oil)
2	tablespoons (30 mL) drained capers
2	(184-g) cans chunk light tuna, drained
	Salt and pepper
	Grated parmesan cheese

Cook rotini in large amount of boiling salted water until tender; drain and return to pot.

Meanwhile, toast pine nuts in large heavy frypan over medium heat for 2 minutes or until golden. Remove from pan and set aside.

In same frypan, heat oil over medium-high heat. Add onion, red pepper and mushrooms; saute for 5 minutes or until vegetables are tender-crisp. Stir in sun-dried tomatoes, capers and pine nuts.

Add vegetable mixture, tuna and salt and pepper to taste to pasta; toss. Serve with parmesan cheese. ⊘

Fettuccine with Lox, Horseradish and Chutzpah

Makes 4 servings

If you were trapped in your house by unexpected guests and all you had to feed them was four ounces of smoked salmon, you could do it with this pasta recipe. But that's by no means the best reason for making this fettuccine. Instead, make it to find out why lox and horseradish are as solid a pairing as peaches and cream or oysters and champagne. (For those unfamiliar with Yiddish, chutzpah isn't an ingredient, it's an attitude.)

If it's asparagus season, steam a piggishly large amount to serve as a first course with a drizzle of extra virgin olive oil, a squeeze of fresh lemon juice and some chopped fresh herbs. Or put together a pretty wild-greens salad to serve on its own after the pasta.

¾	**pound (350 g) fettuccine**
3	**tablespoons (45 mL) butter**
1	**tablespoon (15 mL) flour**
½	**cup (125 mL) dry white wine**
1	**cup (250 mL) light cream**
1	**tablespoon (15 mL) horseradish**
¼	**cup (50 mL) finely chopped fresh dill, divided**
¼	**teaspoon (1 mL) salt**
¼	**teaspoon (1 mL) pepper**
¼	**pound (125 g) sliced smoked salmon, cut into thin strips**

Cook fettuccine in large amount of boiling salted water until tender; drain and return to pot.

Meanwhile, melt butter in large frypan over medium heat. Sprinkle with flour and cook 1 minute, stirring constantly. Add wine and stir until blended. Gradually stir in cream; bring to a boil, stirring constantly. Cook for 3 minutes or until slightly thickened, stirring constantly. Add horseradish, 2 tablespoons (30 mL) dill, salt and pepper. Stir in smoked salmon.

Add sauce to pasta and toss. Taste and adjust seasoning. Transfer to serving platter. Sprinkle with remaining dill. ◯

HOLD YOUR HORSES

Horseradish is neither favored by horses nor a radish. So what gives?

The word "horse" used to be freely applied to any large coarse version of something else — as in horse chestnuts and horse laughs. Horseradishes, like their distant radish cousins, are edible roots. But while biting into a radish might sting, the tough, fiery root of Armoracia rusticana will bring tears to your eyes.

Prepared horseradish sauce loses strength as it ages. Open your jar and sniff. You ought to get a hot, pungent blast; if you don't, replace it.

Smoked Salmon and Red Pepper Frittata

Makes 4 servings

GRILLING VEGETABLES

With the exception of sprouts and tender greens, it's hard to think of a vegetable that doesn't take well to grilling.

As a general rule, if you'd eat the vegetable raw, then it can go on the barbecue with no more preparation than trimming and rubbing with olive oil. You'll get extra taste if you flavor the olive oil with crushed garlic or fresh herbs, or both.

When you want to grill vegetables you wouldn't dream of eating raw — potatoes, sweet potatoes, parsnips, beets — partially cook them before you put them on the barbecue. (Although most of us eat raw carrots, they fall in the pre-cook category, too.) The tougher vegetables have had enough pre-cooking when a fork penetrates with only a little resistance.

If you fall in love with grilled vegetables, it's worth investing in a perforated rack to place on top of the grill. You won't get the same pretty grill marks, but you'll lose fewer asparagus stalks and sugar peas to the flames.

Reaching for eggs is one of the quick cook's reflexes. If you've seen one too many omelets, then thank Kelly Saunders, who entered this recipe in our Six O'Clock Solutions contest. Her idea: eggs gussied up with smoked salmon and red pepper.

For four people, this is a light dinner. Add a chewy bread and a substantial salad — greens with grilled vegetables in the summer, with oranges and niçoise olives in the winter — to make it a sustaining meal.

1   tablespoon (15 mL) plus 1 teaspoon (5 mL) olive oil
1   medium red bell pepper, julienned
6   large eggs
2   tablespoons (30 mL) light cream
¼   pound (125 g) sliced smoked salmon, cut into ½-inch (1 cm) square pieces
1   green onion, chopped
⅛   teaspoon (0.5 mL) pepper
¼   cup (50 mL) grated parmesan cheese
    Salt

In 10-inch (25 cm) heavy ovenproof frypan, heat oil over medium heat. Add red pepper and saute for about 5 minutes or until tender.

Preheat broiler. In medium bowl, whisk eggs and cream until frothy. Whisk in salmon, green onion and pepper. Pour into frypan over red pepper and cook over medium heat for about 6 minutes or until bottom of frittata is just golden, lifting the edges of frittata and tilting pan occasionally to allow uncooked egg to run underneath.

Sprinkle with cheese and broil for 1 to 2 minutes or until top is puffy and golden. Slide on to serving platter and cut into wedges to serve. Season to taste with salt. ⊘

Smoked Salmon Pizza

Makes 4 to 6 servings

Pizzas are usually workaday meals: quick, inexpensive and acceptable to children. Smoked-salmon pizza is pizza for grownups and for modest special occasions, such as Friday night after a long, hard week. Naturally, the lox never sees the inside of the oven. Instead, you bake the shell, then top it with the classic friends of smoked salmon: cream cheese, capers, sliced onions, black pepper and a squeeze of lemon. Fresh thyme works well too, in the absence of capers.

Somehow the whole thing seems much more filling than the same ingredients made into smoked-salmon appetizers on bread. Add a wild greens salad and you have a satisfying light meal.

2	**(12-inch or 30-cm) unbaked pizza crusts (Quick Pizza Dough recipe, page 169) or Italian-style bread shells**
1	**small red onion**
²⁄₃	**cup (150 mL) light spreadable cream cheese**
6	**ounces (170 g) sliced smoked salmon, cut into bite-size pieces**
2	**tablespoons (30 mL) drained capers**
½	**lemon**
	Pepper
	Small pieces fresh dill

Using a fork, prick unbaked pizza crusts all over. Bake at 500 F (260 C) for 8 minutes, then slide crusts from pans directly on to oven rack; bake an additional 1 to 2 minutes or until bottoms of crusts are crisp and golden. (For bread shells, bake according to package instructions.)

Cut onion in half lengthwise, then cut each half crosswise into thin slices.

For each pizza, spread half the cream cheese evenly over hot baked pizza crust or bread shell, then quickly top with half the smoked salmon. Sprinkle with half the onion and capers. Squeeze a little lemon juice over pizza and sprinkle with pepper. Garnish with dill. Serve immediately. ☉

COLD-SMOKED BLISS

Hot-smoked salmon spends from six to 12 hours in the smokehouse at temperatures between 120 and 180 F, and comes out cooked as well as smoked.

Cold-smoked salmon spends from one day to three weeks in the smokehouse, but the temperature never goes above 90 F. Lox, the Jewish form of cold-smoked salmon, is soaked in brine before it's smoked, and "cooked" by the salt more than the heat.

Like sushi, seviche and other forms of fish unacquainted with high temperatures, lox maintains a delicate texture and fresh, pure taste. Cooking lox is a desecration. It should never be more than barely warmed, so add it to sauces when the cooking is finished.

Shrimp Pizza with Mustard, Goat Cheese, Dill and Caramelized Onions

Makes 4 to 6 servings

This is a knock-'em, sock-'em sort of pizza with strong tastes bouncing off each other. So don't bother starting with fresh shrimp, or spending the extra money for the hand-peeled variety. If you didn't make it to the fish market, you could even use canned shrimp without serious consequences. What's important here is the way the sweetness of caramelized onions plays off the bite of grainy mustard, the sharpness of goat cheese and the cleansing overlayer of dill. Add a green salad, and dinner's ready.

4	medium onions
3	tablespoons (45 mL) olive oil
¼	cup (50 mL) sweet whole-grain mustard
2	(12-inch or 30-cm) unbaked pizza crusts (Quick Pizza Dough recipe, page 169) or Italian-style bread shells
½	pound (250 g) cooked shrimp
½	cup (125 mL) coarsely chopped fresh dill
5	ounces (150 g) goat cheese, crumbled
	Pepper

Cut onions in half lengthwise, then cut each half crosswise into thin slices.

In large frypan, heat oil over medium-high heat. Add onions and saute for 3 minutes. Reduce heat to medium-low and continue cooking for 15 minutes or until onions are golden brown, stirring occasionally.

For each pizza, spread half the mustard evenly over unbaked pizza crust or bread shell. Top with half the caramelized onions, shrimp and dill, then half the goat cheese. Sprinkle lightly with pepper.

If using home-made dough, bake at 500 F (260 C) for 8 minutes, then slide pizzas from pans directly on to oven rack; bake an additional 1 to 2 minutes or until bottoms of crusts are crisp and golden. (On bread shells, bake at 450 F or 230 C for 10 minutes.) ⏱

GOAT CHEESE AND FETA

Back before the world of cheese-making turned international, only the Greeks made feta: a tangy, salty, sheep or goat's milk cheese. Meanwhile, the French used their goat's milk to make chevre, a soft, moist, creamy fresh cheese with a tart, but none the less luxurious taste.

Now there are chevres from California and Canadian fetas. They may be pure goat's milk, or may include cow's milk.

When a recipe in this book calls for goat cheese, we mean chevre. When it calls for feta, we mean feta.

CHAPTER FOUR

Vegetarian

Good cooks always know what season it is. They fill their dinner tables with ripe local food because it's the shortest route to the best taste. If you have any doubts, try making this chapter's recipe for Summer's End Pasta with ripe corn and field tomatoes late in August. When you have truly fresh food, the best policy is to get out of the way and let it speak for itself.

What do you do when it's winter and good produce is hard to find? Stock the shelves with dried beans (canned if you don't have time to cook and freeze them) and a good brand of canned tomatoes. Pull out sun-dried tomatoes and Italian-style olives. Turn to recipes such as Bean Soup with Kale and Multi-colored Pasta, and Winter Linguine with Cauliflower. Cook Mustardy Mushroom Stew and Chickpeas with Cumin and Ginger. Buy mandarin oranges as soon as they come into the stores and put a bowl of them out for dessert.

Every season has its pleasures. Slow down to taste them, and you'll find yourself happily lodged in the present moment, where time is at its most friendly.

Orzo and White Bean Soup with Double Tomatoes

Makes 4 servings

How much Italian flavor can you pull off a pantry shelf in less than half an hour? On its way to answering that question, this nourishing soup layers canned tomatoes and sun-dried tomatoes into the same broth, doubling the effect of winter sunshine.

Because the ingredients are so simple, each one counts for a lot, and none more so than the parmesan cheese you sprinkle on at the end. Grate it from a block of parmesan, or, better yet, if you have a small, hand-held grater, pass the cheese at the table. Even without a bottle of Italian wine, you'll be impressed with the results. Add a green salad and a loaf of bread for a satisfying meal.

1	tablespoon (15 mL) vegetable oil
1	medium onion, chopped
2	garlic cloves, chopped
1	(398-mL) can stewed tomatoes
4	cups (1 L) vegetable stock
2	tablespoons (30 mL) chopped, drained sun-dried tomatoes (packed in oil)
	Pinch dried crushed hot red pepper
½	cup (125 mL) orzo (rice-shaped pasta)
1	(540-mL) can white kidney beans, drained and rinsed
	Salt and pepper
	Grated parmesan cheese

In large heavy saucepan, heat oil over medium heat. Add onion and garlic; saute for 4 minutes or until onion is tender.

Add tomatoes, stock, sun-dried tomatoes and dried red pepper; bring to a boil. Add orzo and simmer about 12 minutes or until pasta is tender, stirring occasionally. Add beans and heat through. Add salt and pepper to taste. Serve sprinkled with cheese. ◌

STOCKING UP

When I can't buy fresh vegetable stock, and my frozen supply has run out, I use concentrated vegetable bouillon from a jar, reconstituted with hot water. Natural foods stores stock several brands; I use Nutri-Chef.

The last resort: vegetable soup cubes. Both Bovril and Knorr make them; both brands contain MSG.

Bean Soup with Kale and Multi-Colored Pasta

Makes 4 servings

Suppose you already know kale's more sober virtues — it's a nutritional powerhouse like fellow brassicas, broccoli, cauliflower and cabbage. It's also a hardy vegetable capable of giving us greens in mid-winter. You might even like the look of its extravagantly frilly, dark green leaves — and some that are creamy white or floridly purple — and appreciate its mild, cabbagey taste. But how do you incorporate kale into a quick meal that everyone will eat?

This soup is a good place to start. It's a sustaining broth of kale, navy beans, tomatoes and multicolored vegetable corkscrew pasta, jazzed up with basil, freshly grated parmesan and jalapeno pepper. A bonus: because the greens are already in your soup bowl, you don't need salad. Add a substantial loaf of bread, and dinner's made.

1	**tablespoon (15 mL) vegetable oil**
1	**medium onion, chopped**
1	**jalapeno pepper, chopped fine**
1	**garlic clove, chopped**
4	**cups (1 L) vegetable stock**
1	**(796-mL) can tomatoes (undrained), chopped**
1	**cup (250 mL) vegetable corkscrew pasta**
3	**cups (750 mL) coarsely chopped kale leaves**
1	**(398-mL) can navy beans, drained and rinsed**
2	**tablespoons (30 mL) chopped fresh basil**
	Salt and pepper
	Grated parmesan cheese

In large heavy saucepan, heat oil over medium heat. Add onion, jalapeno pepper and garlic; saute for about 2 minutes.

Add stock and tomatoes; increase heat to medium-high and bring to a boil. Add pasta and cook for 3 minutes. Stir in kale and cook for 2 minutes. Add beans and basil; cook for 2 minutes or until pasta is cooked. Add salt and pepper to taste. Serve sprinkled with parmesan cheese. ○

WHAT IS KALE?

Botanically, kale is a cabbage that doesn't form heads.

Gastronomically, it's a vegetable in the midst of an image change. Kale once sat at the turnip-cabbage-potato end of the vegetable class: inexpensive, easy to grow and much eaten. Then decades of iceberg lettuce intervened, and kale slipped out of produce markets.

Now it's back as one of the more dramatic and beautiful vegetables grown north of California in the winter. You'll find kale floating about in gourmet salad mixes and garnishing plates in expensive restaurants.

Nutritionally, that's good news. Kale offers substantial amounts of vitamins A and C, folic acid, calcium and iron.

Eat kale within a few days of buying it. As it ages, the flavor can become unpleasant.

Holy Moley Chili

Makes 6 servings

When you go so far as to leave the meat right out of your chili, you know you're a long way from Texas. But the bulgur that stands in for ground beef is the least of this chili's surprises. For one thing, it's the prettiest bowl of red I've ever seen. Inspired by the Red, Gold, Black and Green Chili in Moosewood Restaurant Cooks at Home, *it's speckled with yellow corn, green bell peppers and black beans. Best of all, a deep, low rumble of cocoa hums just below the taste of cumin and chilies in a modest homage to Mexican* mole *sauces.*

For the quickest, most minimal dinner, all you need to add is a loaf of bread. But carrot sticks taste especially good with chili, and a spinach-and-avocado salad would be a welcome sight once the chili's eaten.

WHAT IS BULGUR?

Take wheat kernels, steam, dry and crush them, and you'll end up with bulgur. (If all you do is crush the kernels, you'll have cracked wheat.)

Because it's partially cooked when you buy it, bulgur is one of the fastest grains to prepare.

In Holy Moley Chili, it's used to give texture to the dish. If you're serving bulgur on its own, in place of rice, here's how to prepare it: Measure one cup bulgur into a heavy saucepan. Add 1½ cups water and a dash of salt. Cover, bring to a boil, then reduce heat to low. Cook 15 minutes.

3	tablespoons (45 mL) vegetable oil
3	medium onions, chopped
1	tablespoon (15 mL) chili powder
1	tablespoon (15 mL) ground cumin
¼	teaspoon (1 mL) cayenne pepper
2	medium green bell peppers, chopped
3	garlic cloves, chopped fine
3	tablespoons (45 mL) unsweetened cocoa powder
1	(796-mL) can tomatoes (undrained), chopped
1	cup (250 mL) water
1	(398-mL) can red kidney beans, drained and rinsed
1	(398-mL) can black beans, drained and rinsed
2	cups (500 mL) fresh or frozen whole kernel corn
½	cup (125 mL) bulgur
	Salt and pepper
	Plain low-fat yogurt
	Chopped fresh cilantro

In large heavy saucepan, heat oil over medium heat. Add onions, chili powder, cumin and cayenne pepper; saute for 5 minutes or until onions are tender, stirring occasionally. Add green peppers and garlic; saute for 1 minute. Add cocoa, tomatoes and water; bring to a boil. Add kidney and black beans, corn and bulgur. Reduce heat to low and simmer, uncovered, for 15 minutes or until bulgur is cooked. Add salt and pepper to taste.

To serve, top with a dollop of yogurt and sprinkle with cilantro. ⏲

Quinoa Salad with Corn, Cucumber and Lime

Makes 4 servings

If eating were governed by logic, we'd eat a lot more quinoa (pronounced KEEN-wa) than we do. But it takes a long time to warm up to a new grain. That's why, six years after good-looking, good-tasting, highly nutritious quinoa started gaining popularity in North American markets, it remains an oddity.

Joseph Forest, a Vancouver chef who specializes in vegetarian cooking, brought this salad to the test kitchen as part of a story on meatless options in barbecue season. Try it and you may find yourself giving quinoa a place on your table. For a substantial supper, serve it with a loaf of crusty bread and a big platter of grilled vegetables, laid out on a bed of spinach or other dark green, and drizzled with olive oil and balsamic vinegar.

1¾	cups (425 mL) water
1	cup (250 mL) quinoa, rinsed
½	cup (125 mL) finely diced English cucumber
4	green onions, chopped fine
¼	cup (50 mL) finely chopped fresh cilantro
⅓	cup (75 mL) frozen whole kernel corn, thawed
3	tablespoons (45 mL) fresh lime juice
3	tablespoons (45 mL) vegetable oil
1	tablespoon (15 mL) sesame oil
1	teaspoon (5 mL) honey, optional
	Salt and pepper

In 1-quart (1 L) saucepan, bring water to a boil. Add quinoa to boiling water. Reduce heat, cover and simmer for 15 minutes or until grain is tender, stirring occasionally. Drain off excess water; let quinoa cool.

Add cucumber, green onions, cilantro and corn to quinoa; toss. Combine lime juice, vegetable oil, sesame oil, honey, and salt and pepper to taste. Add to quinoa mixture and stir with a fork. ↺

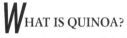

WHAT IS QUINOA?

The tiny golden seed the Incas revered as their "mother grain" has more protein (16.2 per cent) than any other cereal. And quinoa's protein occurs in an almost perfect balance of the amino acids that allow our bodies to break down and use protein in foods.

But this nutritional treasure hides in a bitter coat called saponin that protects the seeds from insects and birds.

Commercially available quinoa is washed before packaging. To make sure all of the saponin is gone, place uncooked quinoa in a large bowl, cover with cold water, swirl and drain well. Repeat rinsing and draining until water is clear.

SIX CLOCK

Summer Salad with White Beans and Avocado

Makes 4 servings

A million monkeys at a million typewriters would probably finish the works of William Shakespeare long before they exhausted the number of quick main-dish salads you can make from a can of beans. Clearly, this is just one suggestion. What makes it different is the contrast in flavors and textures — from the licorice crunch of florence fennel to the buttery smoothness of avocado. Be gentle when you mix in the avocados; when they're ripe, they easily turn to mush. Serve the salad on a bed of greens, with a dark grainy bread for a simple summer supper.

2	(398-mL) cans navy beans, drained and rinsed
½	cup (125 mL) finely chopped red onion
2	large garlic cloves, chopped fine
½	cup (125 mL) chopped fennel bulb
3	jalapeno peppers, seeded and chopped fine
1	large carrot, grated coarse
½	cup (125 mL) finely chopped fresh flat-leaf parsley
⅓	cup (75 mL) extra virgin olive oil
2	tablespoons (30 mL) white wine vinegar
2	tablespoons (30 mL) lemon juice
	Salt and pepper
2	avocados, peeled and cubed
6	cups (1.5 L) torn arugula or mixed salad greens
	Chopped fresh flat-leaf parsley for garnish

In large bowl, combine beans, onion, garlic, fennel, jalapeno peppers, carrot, ½ cup (125 mL) parsley, oil, vinegar, lemon juice, and salt and pepper to taste. Gently stir in avocados.

Divide greens among 4 plates. Mound bean salad on top of greens. Garnish with parsley. ○

WHAT IS ARUGULA?

Also called rocket, rucola, Mediterranean rocket, rocket salad and Italian cress, arugula (pronounced ah-ROOG-u-la) belongs in everyone's salad vocabulary.

Look for a long, narrow, dark green leaf that's a bit like a dandelion leaf, with deep, irregular indentations.

Arugula tastes nutty, like peanut butter with a nip of horseradish at the end. When it's fresh and young, it can stop you in your tracks with pleasure.

As the plant ages, the leaf grows more pungent, until finally it's too fiery to eat raw. (Saute overly peppery arugula with olive oil, garlic, salt and pepper and you'll tame the bite.)

Penne with Tomatoes, Basil and Goat Cheese

Makes 4 servings

In a pasta as simple as this one, each ingredient has to carry its own weight. Fresh basil, creamy goat cheese and ripe Italian olives (don't use kalamatas; they're too strong) each lends its own note. The result is a sophisticated tomato-sauce pasta with a residual goat cheese tang. A bonus: the sauce goes together so quickly that you needn't start cooking it until the pasta's in the water. That means you might have time to start the meal with Parmesan Poppy Seed Bread (see adjacent recipe). Finish dinner with a dark green salad.

4	cups (1 L) penne
1	tablespoon (15 mL) olive oil
1	medium onion, chopped
1	garlic clove, crushed
1	jalapeno pepper, seeded and chopped fine
1	(398-mL) can plum tomatoes
1/4	pound (125 g) soft goat cheese, cut into small pieces
3	tablespoons (45 mL) chopped fresh basil
2	tablespoons (30 mL) chopped black olives
	Salt and pepper
	Grated parmesan cheese

Cook penne in large amount of boiling salted water until tender; drain and return to pot.

Meanwhile, heat oil in large frypan over medium-high heat. Add onion, garlic and jalapeno pepper; saute for 3 minutes or until onion is tender. Add tomatoes, stirring to break them up. Reduce heat and simmer for about 4 minutes, stirring occasionally. Reduce heat and add goat cheese, basil and olives; stir until cheese melts.

Add sauce to pasta and toss. Add salt and pepper to taste. Sprinkle with parmesan cheese. ○

PARMESAN POPPY SEED BREAD

Cut four slices of Italian-style bread. Brush each slice with olive oil, sprinkle with a teaspoon (5 mL) of poppy seeds and a tablespoon (15 mL) of grated parmesan cheese. Broil until the cheese begins to turn golden.

Summer's End Pasta

Makes 4 servings

If you're reading this in January, you'll need eight months to make this recipe. On a late August afternoon, when the corn and tomatoes are at their peak, you can do it in 20 minutes — and you couldn't fix a better dinner if you cooked all day. Green onions, basil and a mix of red wine vinegar and balsamic vinegar all add to the flavor; slices of parmesan shaved from a block make it a very pretty pasta. All you need to add is green salad, a loaf of bread and a view of the late-summer twilight.

3	**cups (750 mL) rotini**
2	**teaspoons (10 mL) red wine vinegar**
2	**teaspoons (10 mL) balsamic vinegar**
3	**tablespoons (45 mL) olive oil or to taste**
2½	**cups (625 mL) chopped seeded tomatoes**
1	**cup (250 mL) cooked corn kernels**
¼	**cup (50 mL) chopped green onions**
¼	**cup (50 mL) chopped fresh basil**
	Salt and pepper
¼	**cup (50 mL) shaved parmesan cheese**

Cook rotini in large amount of boiling salted water until tender; drain and return to pot.

In large bowl, whisk together red and balsamic vinegars and oil. Stir in tomatoes, corn, green onions and basil.

Add hot pasta to tomato mixture and toss. Add salt and pepper to taste. Top with shaved parmesan. ♂

GETTING CORN OFF THE COB

For cooked corn kernels, blanch the husked cobs in boiling salted water for about three minutes. When the cobs are cool enough to handle, cut off the kernels.

The low-tech way to take corn off the cob is to grab the husked cob in one hand and a sharp kitchen knife in the other. Start about midway down the cob and slice off the kernels. When you've worked your way around the cob, turn it over and hold on to the cut part while you slice off the remaining kernels.

The high-tech way is to buy a specialized kitchen gadget that slides over the cob, slicing off the kernels as it goes. Kitchen shops sell them at prices ranging from under $5 to $15.

A rough guide: you'll get about a ½ cup of kernels from an ear of corn.

Bow-Tie Pasta with Broccoli, Cauliflower and Double-Tomato Sauce

Makes 4 servings

In our laws and on our plates, we define tomatoes as vegetables. But botanically, every tomato is a really a fruit, and none more so than the plump, vine-ripened tomatoes of summer. Like August peaches, they're at their best raw.

How do you make a satisfying quick dinner with uncooked tomatoes? Try this bow-tie pasta: its fresh tomato sauce, heavy on green onions and with the addition of sun-dried tomatoes, is as astonishing a burst of tomato flavor as you'll find. With the broccoli and cauliflower that's cooked with the pasta, this is close to a one-dish meal. Serve corn on the cob as a first course and set out a loaf of grainy bread with the pasta.

3	cups (750 mL) bow-tie pasta (farfalle)
1½	cups (375 mL) small broccoli flowerets
1½	cups (375 mL) small cauliflowerets
2½	cups (625 mL) finely chopped plum tomatoes (about 1 pound or 500 g)
½	cup (125 mL) chopped green onions
1	teaspoon (5 mL) dried basil
2	tablespoons (30 mL) vegetable oil
2	tablespoons (30 mL) chopped, drained sun-dried tomatoes (packed in oil)
1	garlic clove, chopped fine
	Salt and pepper
	Grated parmesan cheese

Cook pasta in large amount of boiling salted water until tender, adding broccoli and cauliflower 3 minutes before end of cooking time. Drain pasta and vegetables and return to pot.

Meanwhile, combine tomatoes, green onions, basil, oil, sun-dried tomatoes and garlic in large bowl.

Add hot pasta and vegetables to tomato mixture; toss. Add salt and pepper to taste. Serve with parmesan cheese. ☾

Winter Linguine with Cauliflower and Hot Pepper

Makes 4 servings

In the summer, eating vegetables as a main course is as easy as falling off a log. Little sighs of "eat me, eat me" rise from the produce bins and fresh food does everything but follow you home from the store.

In the winter it's not so easy. Here's a recipe for the months when even the imported tomatoes look chilly. It's a substantial pasta studded with snow-white cauliflower, crushed peppers for warmth and parsley to gladden the eye. A dark peasant loaf of rye or pumpernickel is a good foil for the pasta; add a winter salad of dark greens and navel oranges to give this square meal its fourth corner.

3	tablespoons (45 mL) vegetable oil, divided
3	tablespoons (45 mL) butter, divided
1	medium cauliflower, cut into small flowerets
¾	pound (350 g) linguine
1	large garlic clove, chopped fine
1	medium onion, sliced thin
1	(540-mL) can tomatoes, drained and chopped
¼	teaspoon (1 mL) dried crushed hot red pepper
	Salt and pepper
¼	cup (50 mL) chopped fresh parsley
¼	cup (50 mL) grated parmesan cheese
	Grated parmesan cheese

In large frypan, heat 2 tablespoons (30 mL) oil and 2 tablespoons (30 mL) butter over medium heat. Add cauliflower and saute for about 15 minutes or until lightly browned, stirring frequently. Remove cauliflower and set aside.

Meanwhile, cook linguine in large amount of boiling salted water until tender; drain and return to pot.

Heat remaining 1 tablespoon (15 mL) oil and 1 tablespoon (15 mL) butter in frypan over medium heat. Add garlic and onion; saute for about 5 minutes or until lightly browned and tender. Add tomatoes and cauliflower; add dried red pepper, and salt and pepper to taste. Simmer for 5 minutes.

Add cauliflower sauce, parsley and ¼ cup (50 mL) parmesan cheese to pasta; toss. Serve with parmesan cheese. ⟲

SHOPPING FOR CAULIFLOWER

Beware of cauliflower with brown spots or tell-tale knife marks where the brown has been cut away. Browning is a sign of age. Old cauliflower can taste and smell unpleasantly strong and cabbagey when cooked.

Spaghetti with Broccoli, Pepper and Tomato

Makes 4 servings

Broccoli is so well established as a good-for-you vegetable that buying it becomes a habit. Then it happens: the day arrives when you've eaten quite enough steamed broccoli and you're in no mood to eat any more of it raw. How do you make the little green flowers look new again?

This pasta puts lightly cooked broccoli together with fresh basil, tomatoes, red or yellow bell pepper and a reasonably assertive amount of crushed hot chili pepper. With all that vegetable virtue in the main course, there's no need for a salad. Instead, put out a bowl of hummus, a substantial loaf of bread and some olives to eat before dinner.

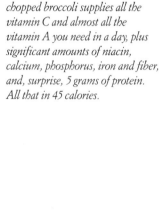

THE BROCCOLI BOOM

Broccoli shows up frequently in the recipes and in menu suggestions in this book, and for good reason.

Force a convention of nutritionists to name the top 10 foods and broccoli would be on everyone's list. One cup of chopped broccoli supplies all the vitamin C and almost all the vitamin A you need in a day, plus significant amounts of niacin, calcium, phosphorus, iron and fiber, and, surprise, 5 grams of protein. All that in 45 calories.

¾	**pound (350 g) spaghetti**
4	**cups (1 L) broccoli flowerets**
¼	**cup (50 mL) vegetable oil**
1	**garlic clove, chopped fine**
¼	**teaspoon (1 mL) dried crushed hot red pepper**
1	**yellow or red bell pepper, chopped coarse**
½	**small onion, chopped**
4	**large tomatoes, seeded and chopped coarse**
1	**tablespoon (15 mL) chopped fresh basil**
¼	**cup (50 mL) chopped fresh parsley**
	Salt and pepper
	Grated parmesan cheese

Cook spaghetti in large amount of boiling salted water until tender, adding broccoli 2 minutes before end of cooking time. Drain pasta and broccoli and return to pot.

Meanwhile, heat oil, garlic and dried red pepper in large heavy frypan over medium heat until hot, stirring constantly. Add bell pepper and onion; saute until tender-crisp. Add tomatoes and basil; cook for 3 minutes, stirring occasionally.

Add tomato sauce and parsley to pasta and broccoli; toss. Add salt and pepper to taste. Serve with parmesan cheese. ⏱

Garden Patch Pasta with Curls

Makes 4 servings

In its dried state, fusilli lunghi looks rather like pasta with a corkscrew perm. You don't have to use it, of course. Fettuccine, spaghetti or linguine would all do a competent job, except for one thing: they wouldn't capture the lighthearted quality of this garden-patch pasta.

With cauliflower, snow peas, cherry tomatoes and yellow zucchini in the sauce, you're not going to need a salad. Instead, set out a bowl of vegetable antipasto with some whole-wheat rolls for anyone who's unbearably hungry before dinner. Round out the meal with the sweetness of grilled fruit.

¾	**pound (350 g) fusilli lunghi (long curly pasta)**
2	**tablespoons (30 mL) vegetable oil**
1	**tablespoon (15 mL) butter**
2	**garlic cloves, chopped fine**
2	**cups (500 mL) small cauliflowerets**
1	**cup (250 mL) snow peas, trimmed and halved**
1	**medium yellow zucchini, sliced**
½	**cup (125 mL) light cream**
¼	**cup (50 mL) chopped fresh basil**
1	**tablespoon (15 mL) chopped fresh oregano**
1	**cup (250 mL) small cherry tomatoes, halved**
	Salt and pepper
½	**cup (125 mL) grated parmesan cheese**
	Chopped fresh parsley
	Grated parmesan cheese

Cook fusilli lunghi in large amount of boiling salted water until tender; drain and return to pot.

Meanwhile, heat oil and butter in large heavy frypan over medium heat. Add garlic and saute for 30 seconds. Increase heat to medium-high; add cauliflower and saute for 2 minutes. Add snow peas and saute for 1 minute. Add zucchini and saute for 1 minute. Add cream, basil and oregano; bring to a boil. Boil for 4 minutes. Reduce heat; add tomatoes and heat through. Add salt and pepper to taste.

Add vegetable sauce to pasta and toss. Stir in ½ cup (125 mL) parmesan cheese. Serve sprinkled with parsley and parmesan cheese. ↻

GRILLED FRUIT

If you've never tried fruit on the grill, you're in for a pleasant surprise. Heat caramelizes the sugar in the fruit and intensifies the flavor.

Larger, firmer fruit, such as halved bananas, pears, peaches or apricots, and slices of pineapple, can go directly on a hot greased grill. (For best results use a spray-on vegetable oil. Brush the fruit with melted butter, if you wish.) Cook for a few minutes on each side.

Cook smaller fruit, such as strawberries, on a fine-meshed vegetable grill or in an aluminum foil "tray" with holes punched in the bottom.

Serve grilled fruit with vanilla ice cream, coconut custard sauce or on its own, with a squeeze of lime juice.

OYSTER MUSHROOM AND ROSEMARY BRUSCHETTA

2   to 3 tablespoons (30 to 45 mL) olive oil

2   garlic cloves, chopped fine

3   cups (750 mL) coarsely chopped oyster mushrooms (or a mix of oyster and button)
    Coarse salt

2   teaspoons (10 mL) finely chopped, drained sun-dried tomatoes (packed in oil)

1   teaspoon (5 mL) finely chopped fresh rosemary

1   tablespoon (15 mL) lemon juice

4   to 6 slices bread
    Pepper

1   tablespoon (15 mL) finely chopped fresh parsley

In frypan, heat olive oil. Add garlic and saute 1 minute. Add mushrooms and stir. Grind salt to taste over mushrooms (it will help them release liquid) and saute until cooked. Stir in sun-dried tomatoes, rosemary and lemon juice.

Toast the bread; spread with mushroom mixture. Sprinkle with pepper to taste and parsley.

Penne with Broccoli, Mushrooms and Wilted Spinach
Makes 4 servings

Something wonderful happens to dark leafy greens when they're lightly cooked with garlic and just a bit of oil. They shrink, of course, to a quarter their unwilted volume, but more important, their flavor mellows and rounds. We call for spinach in this recipe because it's the most readily available, but you could substitute arugula, mizuna, chard or kale, getting a slightly different flavor each time. Start the meal with a bruschetta of oyster mushrooms and rosemary; finish with fresh fruit.

3   cups (750 mL) penne
4   cups (1 L) broccoli flowerets
3   tablespoons (45 mL) olive oil, divided
2   large garlic cloves, chopped fine
½   small red onion, sliced thin
1   teaspoon (5 mL) dried oregano, crumbled
½   teaspoon (2 mL) dried crushed hot red pepper
2   cups (500 mL) sliced mushrooms
2   medium tomatoes, chopped
4   cups (1 L) packed spinach, chopped coarse
½   teaspoon (2 mL) grated lemon zest
     Salt and pepper
¼   cup (50 mL) grated parmesan cheese, optional

Cook penne in large amount of boiling salted water until tender, adding broccoli 2 minutes before end of cooking time. Drain and return pasta and broccoli to pot.

Meanwhile, heat 1 tablespoon (15 mL) oil in large heavy frypan over medium-high heat. Add garlic, onion, oregano and dried red pepper; cook for 2 minutes or until onion is tender, stirring constantly. Reduce heat to medium and add mushrooms and tomatoes; cook for 5 minutes, stirring frequently. Stir in spinach and lemon zest. Cook, covered, for 1 minute.

Add vegetable mixture to pasta and broccoli; toss. Stir in remaining 2 tablespoons (30 mL) oil; toss to coat well. Add salt and pepper to taste. Transfer to serving platter and sprinkle with cheese. ○

Penne with White Beans and Tomatoes

Makes 4 servings

Tuscans were eating pasta e fagioli *long before anyone knew that by eating beans and grains together you could create the protein equivalent of a New York steak. They ate pasta with beans because they liked pasta with beans.*

So think of this recipe when you'd like an easy, economical, great-tasting Italian meal. Or pull it out when you don't have time to shop: apart from a green pepper, it's made from pantry staples. A glass of red wine to toast the Italians would be very nice, but all you really need to add is a green salad and a loaf of crusty bread.

1	tablespoon (15 mL) olive oil
1	medium onion, chopped
1	garlic clove, chopped fine
½	cup (125 mL) chopped green pepper
1	(540-mL) can tomatoes
1	teaspoon (5 mL) dried oregano
¼	teaspoon (1 mL) pepper
2	cups (500 mL) penne
1	(540-mL) can white kidney beans, drained and rinsed
⅓	cup (75 mL) grated parmesan cheese

In frypan, heat oil over medium heat. Add onion, garlic and green pepper; saute for 3 minutes. Stir in tomatoes, oregano and pepper; bring to a boil. Reduce heat and simmer, uncovered, for 10 minutes.

Meanwhile, cook penne in large amount of boiling salted water until tender; drain.

Stir beans and cheese into sauce; heat through. Serve over penne. ⏱

DE-GASSING THE BEAN

If you cook your own beans, you can get rid of 80 per cent of the gas-producing saccharides (simple sugars) by following these steps:

Once beans have soaked, discard the soaking water and rinse the beans, adding fresh water for cooking.

Then use a time-honored East Indian trick: add a pinch of ground asafetida to the cooking water. (This ground resin comes from the roots and stem of the asafetida plant, is sometimes sold under the name hing *and is available from spice shops and East Indian groceries.) Or follow the lead of Japanese cooks who achieve the same results by adding a piece of kombu, a dried seaweed. You'll find kombu in most health food stores. When the beans are well cooked, drain and rinse them. Pay no attention to writers who tell you to use reserved bean-cooking liquid in recipes. Use water instead.*

If you're using canned beans, drain and rinse them before using.

Spaghetti with Warm Tomato-Avocado Sauce

Makes 4 servings

WHAT AVOCADO IS THAT?

Between April and November, you're most likely to have your hand on a Hass avocado, the main commercial variety grown in California. Hass's shape tends toward round. The skin is bumpy and turns from green to black as the fruit ripens.

In the winter, you're more likely to find a Fuerte avocado. Also from California, smooth, green-skinned Fuerte has a shape that reminds you why these fruits were once called avocado pears. Fuerte is milder tasting than Hass.

When it's tomato time, and big, fat beefsteaks sit on your kitchen counter crying out to be used, enlist them for this pasta sauce. Lynn Foden of White Rock sent the recipe in to our Six O'Clock Solutions contest, and her pleasantly spicy vegan dish came close to winning.

Lime, cilantro and jalapeno pepper in the pasta sauce make corn chips and salsa a natural choice for teasing appetites before dinner. Fill in any empty corners with a loaf of grainy bread and a spinach, olive and red onion salad.

1	tablespoon (15 mL) olive oil
1	medium onion, chopped fine
2	garlic cloves, chopped fine
1	serrano pepper, seeded and chopped fine
4	medium tomatoes, cut into ½-inch (1 cm) cubes
¾	teaspoon (4 mL) salt
⅛	teaspoon (0.5 mL) pepper
½	cup (125 mL) chopped fresh cilantro
2	ripe medium avocados, peeled and cut into ¾-inch (2 cm) cubes
2	tablespoons (30 mL) lime juice
¾	pound (350 g) linguine (made without eggs)

In large heavy saucepan, heat oil over medium heat. Add onion, garlic and serrano pepper; saute for 4 to 5 minutes or until onion is tender.

Add tomatoes, salt and pepper; cook for 8 to 10 minutes or until sauce has thickened slightly, stirring frequently. Remove from heat and stir in cilantro, avocados and lime juice.

Meanwhile, cook linguine in large amount of boiling salted water until tender; drain and return to pot.

Add avocado sauce to pasta and toss. ○

Broccoli Mustard Fettuccine with Lemon

Makes 4 servings

Pasta. Tomatoes. Basil. Parmesan. Mustard.

Any seven-year-old could tell you which ingredient doesn't fit. That's why this pasta sauce comes as such a delightful surprise. The idea originated with The Greens Cookbook, *by Deborah Madison and Edward Espe Brown; we've made substantial changes, mostly in the direction of simplicity and less fat.*

¼	cup (50 mL) butter, at room temperature
2	tablespoons (30 mL) Dijon mustard
3	shallots, diced fine
2	garlic cloves, chopped fine
2	teaspoons (10 mL) balsamic vinegar or to taste
¼	cup (50 mL) chopped fresh parsley
4	drained sun-dried tomatoes (packed in oil), slivered
4	cups (1 L) broccoli flowerets, cut into small pieces
1¼	pounds (625 g) fresh fettuccine
	Zest of 1 lemon, slivered
	Salt and pepper
	Grated parmesan cheese

Bring large pot of salted water to a boil.

In bowl, combine butter, mustard, shallots, garlic, vinegar and parsley. In medium frypan over low heat, melt butter mixture. Stir in ½ cup (125 mL) of the boiling water and sun-dried tomatoes; keep warm.

Meanwhile, add broccoli to boiling water; cook for 1 minute. Using slotted spoon, transfer broccoli to butter mixture in frypan.

Add fettuccine to boiling water and cook for 4 minutes or until tender; drain and return to pot. Add broccoli mixture and lemon zest; toss. Add salt and pepper to taste. Transfer to serving platter and sprinkle with parmesan cheese. ⊘

ICE CUBE TRICKS

When you're zesting the lemon for the Broccoli Mustard Fettuccine, take a moment to juice it as well. The juice will freeze well in mini ice cube trays and possibly save you from discovering a dried up rindless lemon in the bottom of your fruit bowl a few days later.

Similarly, when a recipe calls for a tablespoon of tomato paste, take a moment to empty the tin. You can use the mini ice cube trays again, or simply measure the paste by tablespoons on to a wax-paper-lined cookie sheet, then put the cookie sheet in the freezer.

Once your "cookies" are hard, transfer them into a freezer container, for the next time you need a tablespoon of tomato paste.

Spaghetti Frittata with Broccoli, Goat Cheese and Sun-Dried Tomatoes

Makes 4 servings

True, this is an omelet cooked with the cheese and vegetables mixed into the eggs — the definition of a frittata. But spaghetti is one of the major ingredients, and that makes it rather like the baked noodle dish called kugel, traditionally served on the Jewish sabbath. Should we call this a frugel? Or perhaps a kuttata? I suspect it really doesn't matter: the basic ingredients are so homey and satisfying that cooks will welcome it into their repertoire. A loaf of bread and a green salad are all you need to add.

½	**pound (250 g) spaghetti, broken in half**
2	**cups (500 mL) broccoli flowerets (cut very small)**
2	**tablespoons (30 mL) vegetable oil**
1	**small onion, chopped**
1	**garlic clove, chopped fine**
3	**tablespoons (45 mL) chopped, drained sun-dried tomatoes (packed in oil)**
3	**ounces (75 g) soft goat cheese, cut into small pieces**
4	**large eggs, lightly beaten**
1	**teaspoon (5 mL) salt**
¼	**teaspoon (1 mL) pepper**
1	**tablespoon (15 mL) chopped fresh basil**
¼	**cup (50 mL) grated parmesan cheese**

Cook spaghetti in large amount of boiling salted water until tender, adding broccoli 2 minutes before end of cooking time. Drain and return spaghetti and broccoli to pot.

Meanwhile, heat oil in heavy ovenproof 10-inch (25 cm) frypan over medium heat. Add onion and garlic; saute for 4 minutes or until tender. Stir in sun-dried tomatoes.

Add goat cheese and onion mixture to hot spaghetti and broccoli; toss.

Lightly beat eggs with salt, pepper and basil. Add to pasta mixture; toss. Place in frypan and spread evenly with fork. Cook over medium heat for about 3 minutes. Sprinkle evenly with parmesan cheese and bake at 375 F (190 C) for 5 minutes or until eggs are cooked. ⊘

Southwestern Corn Cakes

Makes 4 servings

There's no reason why eating pancakes for supper should be a guilty pleasure. After all, they're no less adaptable than their little French cousins, the crepes, and crepes are welcomed on dinner tables everywhere. So don't restrict this recipe to brunches; use it whenever you feel like eating a homey, comforting meal with a southwestern mood.

Corn kernels, jalapeno and red bell pepper, and roasted cumin set the tone, making salsa and guacamole the obvious pancake toppings. Sour cream or extra-thick yogurt works, too; and you could add any of a galaxy of preserves, including tomato chutney and red pepper relish. A green salad on the side — try butter lettuce, radishes and green onions — makes a more substantial dinner.

2	cups (500 mL) frozen whole kernel corn, thawed
3	large eggs, beaten
2	tablespoons (30 mL) milk
1	tablespoon (15 mL) butter, melted
½	cup (125 mL) finely chopped onion
½	cup (125 mL) finely chopped red bell pepper
1	jalapeno pepper, seeded and chopped fine
1	cup (250 mL) all-purpose flour
1½	teaspoons (7 mL) baking powder
½	teaspoon (2 mL) salt
⅛	teaspoon (0.5 mL) pepper
½	teaspoon (2 mL) roasted cumin seeds, ground (see note)
	Salsa
	Guacamole

In large bowl, combine corn, eggs, milk, butter, onion, red pepper and jalapeno pepper.

In separate bowl, combine flour, baking powder, salt, pepper and cumin. Stir flour mixture into corn mixture.

Heat large non-stick frypan over medium heat. For each corn cake, spoon about ¼ cup (50 mL) batter on to frypan. Flatten cakes with back of spatula until 4 inches (10 cm) in diameter. Cook for 6 to 10 minutes or until golden, turning once. Repeat with remaining batter. Serve with salsa and guacamole. Makes 12 corn cakes.

Note: In heavy frypan, roast cumin seeds over medium-high heat for 1 to 2 minutes or until fragrant, shaking pan frequently. Grind in mortar with pestle. ☉

NON-STICK FRYPANS

One way to reduce fat in your diet is to use a non-stick pan: you can usually cut the amount of fat you need to saute food to a third of what's called for in most recipes.

If the mention of non-stick frypans brings back memories of a pan that flaked, scratched or just stopped working after only modest use, then it's time you had a fresh look at a kitchenware store. You can now buy a non-stick pan with a 20-year guarantee, and many can be used with metal cooking tools.

Durable non-stick frypans aren't inexpensive; they start at around $100. But if you're trying to cut fat, it's a good investment.

Speedy Cheese Enchiladas

Makes 4 servings

At first glance, the fact that salsa now outsells ketchup in North America sounds like an astonishing change in eating habits. In truth, very few people are dipping their french fries in salsa. Instead, more cooks are making meals like this one, in which a cooked salsa, commercial or home-made, adds a lot of flavor in very little time.

With the lettuce and tomato topping, you don't really need to add a salad. If you want to make this a more substantial meal, add steamed rice sprinkled with chopped fresh cilantro.

1½	**cups (375 mL) grated havarti cheese, divided**
1½	**cups (375 mL) mild or medium salsa, divided**
1	**cup (250 mL) ricotta cheese**
1	**medium red bell pepper, chopped**
2	**green onions, chopped**
¼	**cup (50 mL) chopped fresh cilantro**
1	**teaspoon (5 mL) ground cumin**
1	**garlic clove, chopped fine**
8	**(8-inch or 20-cm) flour tortillas**
	Toppings: shredded lettuce, ripe olive slices and chopped tomato

Combine 1 cup (250 mL) havarti cheese, ½ cup (125 mL) salsa, ricotta cheese, red pepper, green onions, cilantro, cumin and garlic; mix well.

Spoon about ⅓ cup (75 mL) cheese mixture down centre of each tortilla; roll up. Place seam side down in 13x9-inch (33x23 cm) baking dish. Spoon remaining 1 cup (250 mL) salsa evenly over enchiladas.

Bake at 375 F (190 C) for 15 minutes. Sprinkle with remaining ½ cup (125 mL) havarti cheese and bake for about 5 minutes. Top as desired. ⏁

WHAT IS CILANTRO? WHAT IS CORIANDER?

Cilantro and coriander are different stages in the life of one plant: Coriandrum sativum.

We use cilantro to describe its youthful phase: lacy, tender leaves with a hint of licorice in the taste. Cilantro is sometimes called Chinese parsley.

Once the plant produces seeds, we revert to the botanical name, coriander. Sweetly spicy, the seeds have a hint of orange in their taste.

Buy coriander seeds whole and roast them gently before grinding. Ground coriander loses flavor quickly.

Spinach and Broccoli Enchiladas

Makes 4 servings

George Bush went on record as not liking broccoli, and Popeye aside, there are few who have kind words for cooked spinach. But roll them up in a tortilla, add bottled salsa and lots of cheddar cheese, and suddenly everyone's applauding.

This is one of the more time-consuming recipes in the book: it will take between 35 and 45 minutes from a standing start. But, if you have the time, the taste makes it worth while. If you're feeding big appetites, add a green salad and steamed rice.

1	(300-g) package frozen chopped spinach, thawed (see note)
1	tablespoon (15 mL) vegetable oil
1	medium onion, chopped
2	garlic cloves, chopped fine
1½	cups (375 mL) grated old cheddar cheese, divided
1	cup (250 mL) ricotta cheese
1	cup (250 mL) finely chopped broccoli
1	cup (250 mL) mild or medium salsa, divided
1	teaspoon (5 mL) ground cumin
	Salt
8	(7-inch or 18-cm) flour tortillas
	Shredded lettuce, optional
	Sliced radishes, optional
	Salsa

Drain spinach and squeeze out excess moisture; set aside.

In large heavy frypan, heat oil over medium-high heat. Add onion and garlic; saute for about 3 minutes or until tender. Stir in spinach. Remove from heat and add ½ cup (125 mL) cheddar cheese, ricotta cheese, broccoli, ⅓ cup (75 mL) salsa, cumin and salt to taste.

Spoon ⅓ cup (75 mL) of the spinach mixture down centre of each tortilla; roll up. Place seam side down in lightly greased 11x7-inch (28x17 cm) shallow baking dish. Spoon remaining salsa evenly over enchiladas.

Cover with foil and bake at 350 F (180 C) for about 25 minutes or until heated through.

Sprinkle with remaining 1 cup (250 mL) cheddar cheese and

WHAT IS RICOTTA CHEESE?

Originally, ricotta was a byproduct of cheese-making, and in much of Italy, it still is. When milk has been heated and separated into curds and whey, the curds go on to become mozzarella and provolone. The whey, cooked once more, becomes ricotta (literally "recooked"): a soft, mild, white, fresh cheese — like cottage cheese, but smoother. In North America, ricotta is made from whey and whole or skim milk.

top with lettuce and radishes, if desired. Serve with salsa.

Note: Place spinach in bowl. Microwave at high for 2 to 3 minutes or until thawed, but not heated through. ⏱

Just in Quesadillas
Makes 4 servings

If Friday nights ever find you standing in the kitchen, hungry, dazed, disinclined to leave the house but incapable of doing anything complicated with food, this recipe could bail you out. As long as you keep standard Mexican ingredients in the fridge — fresh limes (or, in a pinch, bottled lime juice), jalapeno peppers, monterey jack cheese and tortillas — you can ease yourself into the weekend without even making a trip to the corner store. Salsa and guacamole go well with the quesadillas; steamed basmati rice will add heft to the meal.

1	**tablespoon (15 mL) olive oil**
1	**garlic clove, chopped fine**
1	**jalapeno pepper, seeded and chopped fine**
1	**(796-mL) can Italian stewed tomatoes, well drained and chopped**
1	**tablespoon (15 mL) lime juice**
8	**(8-inch or 20-cm) flour tortillas**
¼	**cup (50 mL) chopped fresh parsley**
2	**cups (500 mL) grated monterey jack cheese**
	Olive oil

In frypan, heat 1 tablespoon (15 mL) oil over medium-high heat. Add garlic and jalapeno pepper; saute 30 seconds. Add tomatoes and lime juice; bring to a boil. Reduce heat and simmer for 10 minutes. Let cool slightly.

Arrange tortillas in single layer on baking sheets. Spread about 3 tablespoons (45 mL) tomato mixture on each tortilla; sprinkle with parsley, then ¼ cup (50 mL) cheese. Fold in half and brush lightly with oil.

Bake at 425 F (220 C) for 10 minutes or until cheese has melted. ⏱

WHAT IS BASMATI RICE?

No one who has cooked basmati rice would be surprised to learn that basmati translates as "queen of fragrance." As India's most highly prized rice cooks, it perfumes your house.

The aroma and the nutty taste result from aging, which also reduces the rice's moisture content.

Buy basmati rice in ethnic stores and most supermarkets. It takes no more time to cook than other, less rewarding types of long-grain rice.

Black Bean Burritos

Makes 4 servings

When you're hungry and tired, and your inner cook is on strike, what you need is a 15-minute meal. This one is mine. In its most basic form, it's beans and cheese, wrapped in a flour tortilla and popped into the microwave for 90 seconds. You need fresh salsa on the side, but everything else is elaboration: wonderful if you have it, no problem if you don't. Guacamole is a natural addition and makes a more substantial meal; if there's life in the vegetable crisper, make a spinach salad.

1	teaspoon (5 mL) cumin seeds
4	(9-inch or 23-cm) flour tortillas
1½	cups (375 mL) dried black bean flakes
1	cup (250 mL) plus 2 tablespoons (30 mL) boiling water
1	cup (250 mL) grated light monterey jack cheese
1	cup (250 mL) grated jalapeno monterey jack cheese
1	red bell pepper, chopped
2	green onions, chopped
	Salsa
	Guacamole

In heavy frypan, roast cumin seeds over medium-high heat for 1 to 2 minutes or until fragrant, shaking pan frequently. Grind in mortar with pestle; set aside.

Stack tortillas and wrap in foil. Bake at 350 F (180 C) for 5 minutes or until heated through.

Meanwhile, put bean flakes in small bowl and add boiling water; stir and let stand 5 minutes. Stir in ground cumin. Combine the 2 monterey jack cheeses; set aside.

Spread each tortilla with ⅓ cup (75 mL) bean mixture, top with ½ cup (125 mL) cheese mixture and a quarter of the red pepper and green onions. Roll up tortillas and place seam side down on baking sheet. Cover with foil and bake at 350 F (180 C) for 8 minutes or until heated through. Serve with salsa and guacamole.

Microwave Instructions: To heat tortillas, stack and wrap in paper towel; microwave at high for 1 to 1½ minutes or until heated through.

To cook filled tortillas, place 1 tortilla seam side down on plate. Microwave, uncovered, at high for 80 seconds or until heated through. Repeat with remaining tortillas. ☉

ABOUT JALAPENO CHEESE

If you know you want cheese and spice together, you'll save time by buying monterey jack with jalapeno peppers already incorporated into the cheese.

The peppers are hot: you may want to mix grated, spiced monterey with mild monterey to get the right degree of heat.

Polenta with Black Bean Salsa

Makes 4 servings

Most quick cooks have given polenta a miss. True, you can make northern Italy's staple cornmeal mush in almost no time, but even if you stir in a quantity of cheese, mush for dinner is a hard sell. And shaped polenta, the kind you can grill, broil or fry, takes far too long to prepare from scratch. Now, tubes of ready-made polenta are available in supermarkets and delis (look for it in the specialty sections with olives and imported cheeses). All you do is slice it, heat it and top it with any sauce you'd use on pasta.

Naturally, once you have instant polenta on hand, it's hard to stop experimenting. Here's one happy discovery: grilled polenta with a colorful black bean, corn and red bell pepper salsa. Guacamole on the side adds a touch of velvet luxury; adding a mixed-greens salad makes it a satisfying meal.

½	**(1-kg or 2.2-pound) packaged roll of polenta, cut into ½-inch (1 cm) slices**
1	**(398-mL) can black beans, drained and rinsed**
1	**medium red bell pepper, seeded and diced**
½	**cup (125 mL) frozen whole kernel corn, thawed**
¼	**cup (50 mL) diced onion**
2	**garlic cloves, chopped fine**
½	**cup (125 mL) finely chopped fresh cilantro**
¼	**cup (50 mL) lime juice**
2	**tablespoons (30 mL) extra virgin olive oil**
	Salt and pepper

Place polenta slices on ungreased baking sheet and bake at 350 F (180 C) for 8 to 10 minutes or broil for 10 to 12 minutes, or until golden, turning once.

Meanwhile, combine beans, red pepper, corn, onion, garlic and cilantro in small bowl. Combine lime juice and oil; stir into bean mixture. Add salt and pepper to taste. Set aside.

For each serving, cut 2 slices of baked polenta in half; place on serving plate. Spoon some of the salsa over top. Serve remaining salsa separately. ⏀

JUICE IT

When a recipe in this book calls for lemon or lime juice, you'll get the best results if you squeeze the juice on the spot.

No matter what the label may claim, there's no mistaking bottled lemon or lime juice for the real thing. And because both lemons and limes keep in the vegetable crisper for up to 10 days, there's no reason to use anything else.

If you have more juice than the recipe calls for, freeze it in miniature ice cube trays: a lifesaver when you find yourself caught short.

Jamaican Black Beans with Pineapple-Pear Salsa

Makes 4 servings

Rice-and-beans was once an emblem of poverty, something you ate when you couldn't afford a nice marbled steak. Now that we're all urged to cut our fat consumption, rice-and-beans has become a sort of poster child for sensible eating. To feel more gratified than prudent, make a pineapple and pear salsa while you're waiting for the rice to cook. (Fresh pineapple is wonderful; canned will do in a pinch.) All you need to add is a green salad.

2	tablespoons (30 mL) olive oil
2	large onions, sliced thin
3	garlic cloves, chopped fine
2	tablespoons (30 mL) grated fresh ginger
2	teaspoons (10 mL) dried thyme
½	teaspoon (2 mL) ground allspice
2	(398-mL) cans black beans, drained and rinsed
1	teaspoon (5 mL) grated orange zest
2	cups (500 mL) orange juice
	Salt and pepper

Pineapple and pear salsa

1	(398-mL) can crushed pineapple, drained
1	small pear, peeled and chopped fine
2	tablespoons (30 mL) chopped fresh cilantro
1	green onion, chopped fine
4	teaspoons (20 mL) lime juice
	Salt

In large heavy saucepan, heat oil over medium heat. Add onions and saute for 8 minutes or until golden, stirring frequently. Add garlic, ginger, thyme and allspice; saute for 2 minutes, stirring constantly. Stir in beans, and orange zest and juice. Bring to a boil; reduce heat to medium-low and simmer for 10 minutes or until mixture thickens slightly, stirring occasionally.

Mash some of the beans with back of spoon for a slightly thicker consistency. Add salt and pepper to taste. Serve with pineapple and pear salsa.

Salsa: In medium bowl, combine pineapple, pear, cilantro, green onion, lime juice and salt to taste. Makes about 2 cups (500 mL). ○

PUMPING IRON

Food contains two kinds of iron: heme, found in meat, eggs and fish, and non-heme, found in plant foods.

Of the two, our bodies absorb heme iron more readily. But you can improve the absorption rate of non-heme iron by eating your iron-rich legumes, nuts, seeds and dark green vegetables at the same time as foods containing vitamin C.

Turns out this is easy. In many traditional recipes, the match is already made. Hummus, for example, combines chickpeas and lemon juice; Mexican bean dishes taste best with fresh tomato salsa. And you can always improve your odds by nibbling on raw broccoli or a slice of red bell pepper.

Chickpeas with Cumin and Ginger

Makes 4 to 6 servings

If you'd asked me five years ago how I'd like a nice plate of rice and beans for dinner, I'd have been politely non-committal. Now I get hungry just thinking about these chickpeas and the meal they'll be part of: basmati rice, mango chutney, lime pickle, raita (see adjacent recipe) and a stir-fried green vegetable on the side. The recipe, simplified and adapted, comes from Madhur Jaffrey's Spice Kitchen, *the latest in a string of brilliant and reliable books by the New Delhi-born, New York-based writer.*

3	tablespoons (45 mL) vegetable oil
1	teaspoon (5 mL) cumin seeds
3	medium onions, chopped
3	garlic cloves, chopped fine
⅓	cup (75 mL) canned crushed tomatoes
2	teaspoons (10 mL) finely grated fresh ginger
2	(540-mL) cans chickpeas, drained and rinsed
1¼	cups (300 mL) water
2	jalapeno peppers, seeded and chopped fine
1	teaspoon (5 mL) salt
2	teaspoons (10 mL) roasted cumin seeds, ground (see note)
1	teaspoon (5 mL) garam masala
¼	cup (50 mL) coarsely chopped fresh cilantro
1	tablespoon (15 mL) lemon juice

In large heavy frypan, heat oil over medium-high heat. Add 1 teaspoon (5 mL) cumin seeds and cook for 15 seconds. Add onions; saute for 5 minutes or until onions turn brown at the edges. Add garlic; saute for 1 minute or until golden. Add tomatoes; cook for 1 minute, stirring constantly. Add ginger; cook for 1 minute, stirring constantly.

Add chickpeas, water, jalapeno peppers, salt, ground cumin seeds, garam masala, cilantro and lemon juice; bring to a boil. Reduce heat to low and simmer, uncovered, for 8 minutes, stirring occasionally. Taste and adjust seasoning.

Note: In heavy frypan, roast cumin seeds over medium-high heat for 1 to 2 minutes or until fragrant, shaking pan frequently. Grind in mortar with pestle. ⟳

CUCUMBER RAITA

1	cup (250 mL) plain low-fat yogurt
¾	cup (175 mL) grated peeled cucumber
2	tablespoons (30 mL) chopped cilantro
½	teaspoon (2 mL) salt
½	teaspoon (2 mL) ground roasted cumin
	Pepper to taste

In small bowl, combine all ingredients. Cover and refrigerate until serving time. If desired, garnish with additional chopped cilantro and ground cumin.

Couscous with Chickpeas and Basil Yogurt Sauce

Makes 4 servings

Couscous and chickpeas belong together, and you can check any steaming pot of couscous in Morocco if you don't believe me. Add currants, mushrooms, thin slices of golden squash and strips of red pepper and the result is an entirely satisfying dinner, even before you spoon on the lime, basil and yogurt sauce. Barbary bread (see adjacent) would be a culturally appropriate addition, but any good loaf of bread will do.

1	cup (250 mL) plain low-fat yogurt
3	tablespoons (45 mL) lime juice, divided
4	tablespoons (60 mL) chopped fresh basil, divided
	Salt and pepper
1½	cups (375 mL) plus 2 tablespoons (30 mL) vegetable stock
⅓	cup (75 mL) currants
1½	cups (375 mL) couscous
2	tablespoons (30 mL) olive oil
1	medium onion, chopped
1	jalapeno pepper, seeded and chopped fine
1	garlic clove, chopped fine
¼	pound (125 g) piece butternut squash, peeled and cut into ¼-inch (5 mm) dice
1	medium red bell pepper, cut into thin strips about 3 inches (7 cm) long
1	cup (250 mL) sliced mushrooms
1	cup (250 mL) canned chickpeas, drained and rinsed

In small bowl, combine yogurt, 2 tablespoons (30 mL) lime juice and 2 tablespoons (30 mL) basil. Add salt to taste; set aside.

Put stock in large saucepan; cover and bring to a boil. Stir in currants, remaining 2 tablespoons (30 mL) basil and 1 tablespoon (15 mL) lime juice. Stir in couscous; cover and remove from heat. Let stand for 5 minutes.

Meanwhile, heat oil in large heavy frypan over medium heat. Add onion, jalapeno pepper, garlic and squash; saute for 3 minutes. Add red pepper and mushrooms; saute for 3 minutes or until vegetables are tender-crisp. Stir in chickpeas and heat through.

Add vegetable mixture to couscous; stir to mix. Add salt and pepper to taste. Serve with yogurt mixture. ☾

WHAT IS BARBARY BREAD?

Many Greek and Middle Eastern delis sell a long flat bread topped with sesame seeds that is made by local Iranian bakeries. Barbary bread is made with a minimal amount of fresh yeast. Small balls of dough are allowed to rise twice, then stretched by hand into 500-gram and 300-gram loaves.

Barbary bread should be eaten fresh. If you can't eat it within two days, freeze the bread, then bake it, without thawing, in a 350 F (180 C) oven for no more than five minutes — any longer and it may harden.

Tofu Stir-Fry with Watercress and Cherry Tomatoes

Makes 4 servings

Trevor Hooper, chef-owner of Vancouver's Raku Kushiaki restaurant, brought this brilliantly colored stir-fry into the test kitchen for a story on tofu. Here tofu meets watercress, cherry tomatoes, garlic, ginger, black beans and soy sauce. Serve with steamed rice. To help round out the meal, add grilled or broiled sweet potato: peel and cut the potatoes into inch-thick rounds, rub with olive oil, microwave on high for five minutes and finish on the grill or under the broiler until tender.

2	large bunches watercress
1	tablespoon (15 mL) plus 2 teaspoons (10 mL) vegetable oil, divided
1	teaspoon (5 mL) sesame oil
1	(454-g) block medium tofu, cut into ¾-inch (2 cm) cubes
2	garlic cloves, chopped fine
4	green onions, chopped fine
1	teaspoon (5 mL) finely chopped fresh ginger
2	tablespoons (30 mL) chopped, salted Chinese black beans
1	cup (250 mL) halved cherry tomatoes
1	tablespoon (15 mL) soy sauce
½	teaspoon (2 mL) pepper

Trim and discard about 2 inches (5 cm) of the watercress stems. (You should have about 8 cups or 2 L packed watercress.)

Heat wok over high heat. Add 1 tablespoon (15 mL) vegetable oil and sesame oil; heat until just starting to smoke. Add tofu; fry for 2 minutes, turning once and shaking wok occasionally. Remove and set aside.

Wipe out wok with paper towel. Reheat wok and add 2 teaspoons (10 mL) vegetable oil. Add garlic, green onions, ginger and black beans; stir-fry for 30 seconds. Add watercress and tomatoes; stir-fry for about 1 minute or until watercress is wilted.

Drain accumulated juices from tofu. Gently stir tofu into watercress mixture. Remove wok from heat; gently stir in soy sauce and pepper. ☾

TOFU TYPES

The difference between soft, medium and firm tofu is largely a matter of water. The softer the tofu, the more water it contains. For that reason, soft tofu is also lower in fat, protein and calories.

If you detect a slightly sweeter taste in soft tofu, it's because tofu makers use nigari, *a traditional sea salt, to coagulate it. In medium and firm tofu, the coagulants are calcium sulphate and magnesium chloride.*

Pick soft tofu for soups, sauces, cold dishes and tofu dengaku (see next page), where its custardy texture is important and preparation doesn't involve much handling.

Use medium tofu in stir-fries; mix gently to keep it from breaking.

Choose firm tofu when you want to marinate and grill the tofu.

For a contrast in texture, use diced deep-fried tofu in stir-fries. Sunrise Markets Inc., the biggest tofu maker on the West Coast, fries its medium tofu, cut in chunks, in canola oil to make deep-fried tofu.

Tofu Dengaku with Spinach Salad

Makes 4 servings

What makes this recipe so good that even people who don't like tofu will ask for seconds? Part of the answer is the egg-enriched miso topping over the custard-like texture of grilled soft tofu. But trace tofu dengaku back to its home in Japan and you'll find that it's a traditional street food, a snack to eat while you're sightseeing or visiting a temple. Perhaps it's the matchbox shape or maybe the sprinkling of sesame seeds on top: here or there, this is fun food. Make a meal of it with a cold cooked-spinach salad, steamed rice and thin slices of pickled ginger (buy it by the jar at Asian grocers). Although making this meal becomes quicker with practice, it will still take you a little longer than most recipes in this book: allow about 45 minutes.

Tofu dengaku

2　(300-g) packages soft tofu
　　(4½x3-inch or 11x7-cm block)
3　tablespoons (45 mL) red miso (aka miso)
1　tablespoon (15 mL) sake
1　tablespoon (15 mL) mirin (Japanese rice wine)
1　tablespoon (15 mL) sugar
1　egg yolk
1　tablespoon (15 mL) vegetable stock
2　tablespoons (30 mL) roasted sesame seeds

Spinach salad

1　(300-g) package frozen chopped spinach
¼　cup (50 mL) sesame seeds
2　tablespoons (30 mL) sake
5　teaspoons (25 mL) soy sauce
1　tablespoon (15 mL) sugar
1　tablespoon (15 mL) roasted sesame seeds

Tofu dengaku: Cut each block of tofu in half crosswise, then cut each half block crosswise into 1-inch (2.5 cm) thick slices (12 slices total). Place tofu between clean tea towels to drain.

Combine miso, sake, mirin, sugar and egg yolk in heatproof bowl; set over simmering water in saucepan for 5 to 7 minutes or until mixture thickens, stirring constantly. Add stock and stir to blend. Remove from heat.

WHAT IS MISO?

Miso, a salty, aromatic paste made from fermented soybeans, is one of the most important ingredients in Japanese cooking.

If you're trying miso for the first time, a good rule of thumb is: the lighter the color, the milder the taste.

There are three basic types of miso. Strong-flavored hatcho miso is dark, salty and pungent, made entirely from soybeans. Aka, or barley miso, usually golden red in color and mild, is made from soybeans fermented with barley. And shiro or rice miso is a pale tan color and the mildest of all.

Store miso tightly covered in the refrigerator. It will keep several months. Freezing destroys the aroma and the texture. You'll find miso in health food stores, Asian markets and many supermarkets.

Preheat broiler. Place tofu slices on greased baking sheet; broil for 8 minutes or until dry in appearance and lightly golden, turning once.

Spread tops of tofu slices with miso mixture and broil for an additional 1 minute or until miso starts to bubble. Sprinkle tofu with sesame seeds. Serve with spinach salad.

Spinach salad: Place spinach in bowl. Microwave at high for 2 to 3 minutes or until thawed, but not heated through. Drain spinach and squeeze out excess moisture; set aside.

Put ¼ cup (50 mL) sesame seeds in blender; grind finely.

In large bowl, combine ground sesame seeds, sake, soy sauce and sugar. Add spinach and toss. Transfer to serving bowl and sprinkle with roasted sesame seeds. ⊘

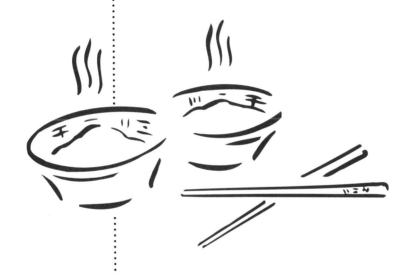

Szechuan Eggplant with Tofu
Makes 4 servings

If you want to stay in the realm of classic Chinese cooking, you don't add tofu to Szechuan-style eggplant. Pork, yes. Tofu, no. But if you want a satisfying vegetarian meal that needs only rice and a stir-fried green vegetable to make it complete, the temptation to sin against the canon is overwhelming. So I offer this recipe with deep apologies to The Cooking of Chinese Delicious Food and Refreshment, *a book I bought 20 years ago in Taiwan and have used ever since. The flavorings, with slight adjustments, are from the book. The tofu is all mine. Use deep-fried tofu, which you can buy packaged; it's already quite dry and will soak up flavor without diluting the sauce.*

¾	**pound (350 g) Japanese eggplants**
6	**tablespoons (90 mL) vegetable oil**
1	**tablespoon (15 mL) chopped garlic**
1	**tablespoon (15 mL) chopped fresh ginger**
4	**teaspoons (20 mL) hot bean sauce**
½	**cup (125 mL) vegetable stock**
5	**teaspoons (25 mL) mushroom soy sauce**
1	**teaspoon (5 mL) sugar**
6	**ounces (170 g) packaged fried tofu, diced**
1½	**teaspoons (7 mL) sesame oil**
1½	**teaspoons (7 mL) Chinese brown vinegar**
3	**tablespoons (45 mL) chopped green onion, divided**

Trim eggplants and cut into 2x½-inch (5x1 cm) pieces.

In large heavy frypan, heat vegetable oil over high heat. Add eggplant; reduce heat to medium-low and stir-fry for 6 minutes or until soft and golden. Remove and set aside.

Add garlic, ginger and bean sauce to frypan; stir-fry for 10 seconds. Add stock, soy sauce and sugar; bring to a boil over medium-high heat. Add tofu; cook for 1 minute.

Return eggplant to frypan and cook for 2 minutes or until sauce has evaporated. Add sesame oil, vinegar and 2 tablespoons (30 mL) green onion; stir until heated through. Sprinkle with remaining 1 tablespoon (15 mL) green onion. ☼

WHAT IS HOT BEAN SAUCE?

You'll find this dark, thick paste under several names, including hot bean sauce and chili bean sauce. It's a potent mix of soy beans, rice, salt, sugar, chilies and soy oil that adds not only heat but depth to Szechuan cooking.

When you're shopping, try to find a Chinese-made hot bean sauce. Southeast Asian versions are usually much hotter. I use Kimlan brand, which is made in Taiwan.

Be careful not to confuse hot bean sauce with chili sauce, a hotter, thinner, bright red condiment that's used as a dipping sauce.

WHAT IS MUSHROOM SOY SAUCE?

There are two main kinds of Chinese soy sauce, light and dark. Light soy sauce is far more salty and more subtly flavored. Dark soy sauce is mixed with molasses and aged longer, which gives it a deeper, richer flavor.

Mushroom soy is made by infusing dark soy sauce with straw mushrooms, which gives the sauce a more complex flavor. The difference in taste is subtle: you can use mushroom soy sauce whenever dark soy sauce is called for, and vice versa.

Spaghetti Squash with Spinach, Feta and Herbed White Beans

Makes 4 servings

WHAT IS SPAGHETTI SQUASH?

Native to South America, but developed as a commercial crop by Japanese plant breeders in this century, spaghetti squash separates into pasta-like strands when you cook it.

Somewhat resembling a golden watermelon, it usually weighs from three to eight pounds, and can reliably be found in company with other winter squashes. Pick one that's an even yellow color; a green tinge means it's not ripe.

Like most winter squashes, spaghetti squash keeps. Store it, uncut, at room temperature for up to three weeks.

Microwaving spaghetti squash is quick: 5 to 6 minutes a pound. Baking it takes longer: at 375 F it will take from an hour to 90 minutes to cook a medium squash.

Anyone who ever questioned the role of divine providence in the invention of pasta need only eat a spaghetti squash to feel a rush of faith. Clearly we were meant to eat food in long thin strands. Because spinach comes with the main course, all you need to add is a loaf of bread.

1	**(398-mL) can navy beans, drained and rinsed**
1	**tablespoon (15 mL) chopped fresh basil**
½	**teaspoon (2 mL) dried oregano**
2	**tablespoons (30 mL) olive oil, divided**
1	**tablespoon (15 mL) white wine vinegar**
1	**(3-pound or 1.5-kg) spaghetti squash**
1	**bunch spinach**
1	**tablespoon (15 mL) butter**
½	**cup (125 mL) chopped onion**
2	**garlic cloves, chopped fine**
½	**cup (125 mL) crumbled feta cheese**
	Salt and pepper
	Grated parmesan cheese

In small bowl, combine beans, basil, oregano, 1 tablespoon (15 mL) oil and vinegar; set aside.

Wash and pierce squash deeply with knife in several places. Place in glass pie plate. Microwave at high for about 15 minutes or until squash yields to pressure, turning squash over after 7 minutes. Let stand for 5 minutes. Cut in half and scrape out seeds and fibres. Pull out long strands of flesh by twisting with a fork; place in large bowl.

Meanwhile, wash and trim stems from spinach. Stack leaves and cut crosswise into ¼-inch (5 mm) wide strips; set aside.

In large frypan, heat butter and remaining 1 tablespoon (15 mL) oil over medium heat. Add onion and garlic; saute for 1 minute. Add spinach and saute for 2 to 3 minutes or until spinach is just wilted. Add feta cheese and bean mixture; heat through. Add salt and pepper to taste.

Add spinach mixture to squash and toss. Transfer to serving platter and sprinkle with parmesan cheese. ⏀

Curried Red Lentils and Cauliflower

Makes 4 servings

Yes, it takes longer to measure the seven spices in this recipe than to spoon out a pre-mixed curry powder. And it will cost you another minute or two if you keep your coriander, cumin and cardamom whole and grind them as you need them. But the payoff in flavor is worth every minute. Take the high road, and the lentils, cauliflower and onions will transform themselves into a main course with a rich and subtle play of tastes. Steamed rice and a raita (see adjacent recipe) or just plain yogurt, make this a satisfying meal. A green salad with oranges and red onions, a selection of chutneys and some store-bought chapatis (whole-wheat Indian flatbread) take it past satisfaction into splendor.

1¼	cups (300 mL) red lentils, rinsed
1½	cups (375 mL) chopped onions
1	teaspoon (5 mL) crushed garlic
2	tablespoons (30 mL) olive oil
1	teaspoon (5 mL) ground coriander
1	teaspoon (5 mL) ground cumin
1	teaspoon (5 mL) turmeric
½	teaspoon (2 mL) chili powder
¼	teaspoon (1 mL) ground cardamom
¼	teaspoon (1 mL) ground cinnamon
	Pinch ground cloves
1	cup (250 mL) vegetable stock
⅓	cup (75 mL) tomato paste
4	cups (1 L) cauliflowerets
	Salt
½	cup (125 mL) unsalted roasted cashews
2	tablespoons (30 mL) chopped fresh cilantro
½	cup (125 mL) plain low-fat yogurt

In covered pot, bring lentils to a boil in generous amount of water; cook for about 5 minutes or until tender. Drain and save cooking liquid.

In large frypan, saute onions and garlic in hot oil until tender. Reduce heat and add coriander, cumin, turmeric, chili powder, cardamom, cinnamon and cloves; stir well. Blend in stock and

ITALO-INDIAN TOMATO RAITA

1	cup (250 mL) plain low-fat yogurt
1	medium tomato, chopped
1	tablespoon (15 mL) finely chopped fresh basil
1	tablespoon (15 mL) finely chopped, drained sun-dried tomatoes (packed in oil)
1	teaspoon (5 mL) finely chopped jalapeno pepper
	Salt and pepper to taste

In small bowl, combine all ingredients. Makes about 2 cups (500 mL).

tomato paste. Add cauliflowerets and mix well. Cover and cook for 8 to 10 minutes or until cauliflower is tender.

Stir lentils into curried mixture in frypan. If necessary, thin sauce with some of the reserved liquid. Add salt to taste. Stir in cashews. Transfer to serving platter and sprinkle with cilantro. Serve with yogurt. ⏁

Great Canadian Beans

Makes 4 servings

What's so Canadian about baked beans? When Nicole Adams of Nanaimo makes them, she uses maple syrup sent by her mother back home in Ontario and tomatoes that she and her fiancé dry at his parents' Okanagan farm. Even if you can't achieve as thoroughly patriotic a spin on this recipe, go ahead and make it anyway: its rich, baked-bean taste came within a few points of winning the vegetarian category of our Six O'Clock Solutions recipe contest.

All you need to add for dinner is a loaf of rustic bread and a green salad. If you'd like more, set out a bowl of radishes before dinner, along with a bit of salt to dip them into. You'll have plenty of time for washing and tearing salad greens while the beans simmer.

1	tablespoon (15 mL) vegetable oil
1	small onion, chopped fine
1	(796-mL) can plum tomatoes (undrained), chopped
	Pinch dried crushed hot red pepper or dash of Tabasco sauce
2	tablespoons (30 mL) maple syrup
1	tablespoon (15 mL) Worcestershire sauce
1	tablespoon (15 mL) Dijon mustard
6	sun-dried tomatoes (not packed in oil), chopped
2	(398-mL) cans navy beans, drained and rinsed
	Salt and pepper

In heavy saucepan, heat oil over medium heat. Add onion and saute for 5 minutes or until tender. Add canned tomatoes, dried red pepper, maple syrup, Worcestershire sauce, mustard, sun-dried tomatoes and beans; simmer for 15 minutes. Add salt and pepper to taste. ⏁

SLICK WORK

If a recipe calls for both oil and honey or molasses, measure the oil first, then use the same measuring implement for the sweetener. It should slide out easily.

If there's no oil in the recipe, you can get close to the same effect by warming the measuring cup or spoons with hot water before you measure the sweetener.

Mustardy Mushroom Stew

Makes 4 servings

Laurel Hickey's prize-winning mushroom stew is a recipe that won't sit still. It started out in life as Mushrooms Berkeley from Anna Thomas's 1970s classic, The Vegetarian Epicure. *By the time it won the vegetarian category of our Six O'Clock Solutions contest, it had become a handsome, highly flavored dish that uses tomatoes spiked with balsamic vinegar in place of the red wine that Thomas suggested. And its assertive flavors include licorice-tasting fennel seeds along with mustard and Worcestershire sauce. When Hickey makes it, the full meal includes potatoes and a spinach salad sprinkled with toasted almonds.*

2	tablespoons (30 mL) olive oil
2	medium onions, cut into rings
3	garlic cloves, chopped fine
1½	pounds (750 g) medium button mushrooms, trimmed and brushed (see note)
1	(398-mL) can tomatoes (undrained), chopped
½	cup (125 mL) dry red wine, optional
⅓	cup (75 mL) brown sugar
2	tablespoons (30 mL) red wine vinegar or balsamic vinegar
2	tablespoons (30 mL) Worcestershire sauce
2	tablespoons (30 mL) Dijon mustard
2	teaspoons (10 mL) fennel seeds
1	tablespoon (15 mL) dried basil
¼	teaspoon (1 mL) pepper or to taste
	Salt
	Chopped fresh parsley

In large heavy frypan, heat oil over medium heat. Add onions and garlic; saute for about 10 minutes or until onions are lightly browned. Add mushrooms and cover; cook for about 5 minutes or until liquid is released, stirring occasionally.

Uncover and increase heat to medium-high. Add tomatoes, wine, sugar, vinegar, Worcestershire sauce, mustard, fennel seeds, basil and pepper; cook for about 8 minutes or until stew is thick. Test for seasonings; add salt to taste. Spoon into serving dish and garnish with parsley.

Note: If mushrooms are large, cut in half. ⟳

WORCEST FEARS

Worcestershire sauce contains tamarind, garlic, soy sauce, onions, molasses, lime juice, vinegar and seasonings. The best known brands also contain anchovies.

Sharwood's, better known for Major Grey mango chutney, does make a vegetarian Worcestershire sauce. It's not easy to find: if you're interested, ask your grocer to stock it.

Or try a vegetarian substitute that's available at some specialty stores: Pickapeppa Sauce, made by the Jamaican Pickapeppa Co. Ltd.

Quick Pizza Dough
Makes 2 pizza crusts

BREAD SHELLS

If you don't have it in you to make even this quick pizza dough, an Italian bread shell will help you bring pizza to the table in record time. Keep a stock of them in the freezer and you're never more than a few minutes away from a complete meal.

Baking instructions on different brands of shells vary. If you're following one of our pizza recipes, use the time and temperature suggested in the recipe. We've tested them and know the toppings will cook in the recommended time.

If you're baking the shell without toppings — for the Fresh Vegetable Pizza or for the Smoked Salmon Pizza — follow the directions on the bag.

All by itself, this recipe justifies having a food processor in the kitchen. Not only will you rapidly recoup the price of the machine by no longer ordering out for pizza, you'll begin to live with the confidence of someone who is never more than half an hour away from a satisfying meal. As long as the pantry is even modestly stocked with pizza makings, you need never go ill-fed.

Most often, I make this bread as a quick pizza meal with whatever toppings I have on hand. But when there's time for a bit of fussing with a soup or salad dinner, I like to bake it as focaccia, topped with caramelized onions or a scattering of roasted red peppers and black olives. There isn't much that conveys contentment and well-being more clearly than hot-from-the-oven bread.

4	cups (1 L) all-purpose flour
2	(8-g) packages instant yeast
2	teaspoons (10 mL) salt
1	teaspoon (5 mL) sugar
	Water
2	teaspoons (10 mL) olive oil

In large-capacity food processor fitted with a steel blade, combine flour, yeast, salt and sugar. Heat 1½ cups (375 mL) water and the oil until hot to the touch, 125 to 130 F (50 to 55 C). With the motor running, gradually pour the hot water mixture through the feed tube. Process, adding up to 2 tablespoons (30 mL) cold water until the dough forms a ball, then process for 1 minute to knead.

Turn dough out on to lightly floured surface, cover with plastic wrap and let rest for 10 minutes.

Divide dough in half. Roll out each piece on lightly floured surface to form a 12-inch (30 cm) circle. Place each in 12-inch (30 cm) pizza pan. ⏱

Fresh Vegetable Pizza

Makes 4 to 6 servings

You might view this pizza as a cunning plan to induce children to eat more raw vegetables, and if that's what you're looking for, fine, it should work. But children weren't part of the equation when we tested this recipe: what we wanted was a pretty, fresh, effortless, good-tasting pizza that would be welcome on any warm day. This is it. All you need to round out the meal is a green salad; spinach-and-mushroom would do nicely.

2	(12-inch or 30-cm) unbaked pizza crusts (Quick Pizza Dough recipe, page 169) or Italian-style bread shells
½	pound (250 g) Danish herb and spice cream cheese
½	cup (125 mL) light mayonnaise
1	small red bell pepper, chopped fine
1	small yellow bell pepper, chopped fine
1	cup (250 mL) finely chopped cauliflower
4	green onions, chopped
4	plum tomatoes, chopped
	Pepper

Using a fork, prick unbaked pizza crusts all over. Bake at 500 F (260 C) for 8 minutes, then slide pizzas from pans directly on to oven rack; bake an additional 1 to 2 minutes or until bottom of crusts are crisp and golden. (Bake bread shells according to package directions.) Let cool for 10 to 15 minutes.

In bowl, beat together cream cheese and mayonnaise.

For each pizza, spread half the cream cheese mixture evenly over baked crust or bread shell; top with half the red and yellow peppers, cauliflower, green onions and tomatoes. Sprinkle lightly with pepper. Cut into 8 wedges. ○

PEPPER POTENTIAL

When a grower lets a green bell pepper ripen into glorious red or yellow it isn't just the taste that improves.

Three ounces of green bell pepper contains a respectable amount of vitamin C — about 80 milligrams, which is more than your entire daily requirement.

Give the pepper a week or two more on the vine and the vitamin C content doubles. Three ounces of red pepper offers about 160 milligrams of vitamin C; and yellow peppers will give you slightly more.

As they turn red and yellow, peppers also gain beta carotene, an antioxidant that appears to have protective powers against disease. Red peppers have nine times more beta carotene than green ones.

Artichoke, Spinach and Goat Cheese Pizza

Makes 4 to 6 servings

Basil Tip

In September, when basil is plentiful and inexpensive, buy several bunches.

Wash and dry them, strip the leaves from the stalks, and put the leaves in a food processor. With the processor running, add enough olive oil to make a smooth paste.

Freeze the basil paste in ice cube trays. When frozen, transfer to a freezer container.

All winter long, you have a close-to-instant source of chopped basil for pesto, pasta sauces and steamed vegetables.

Artichokes and goat cheese occupy an odd territory: unfamiliar enough to seem just slightly exotic, they are also available in long-lasting packages. (Look for vacuum packed goat cheese on the cooler shelves near the camembert and brie.) Keep them on hand, and a quick trip to the market for spinach, fresh basil and a red onion supplies all you need to make a chic little pizza. If you're inclined toward salad, one of belgian endive, orange, fennel and olives (page 72) will do the trick without seeming like a repetition of the spinach on the pizza.

2	**(12-inch or 30-cm) unbaked pizza crusts (Quick Pizza Dough recipe, page 169) or Italian-style bread shells**
4	**tablespoons (60 mL) olive oil, divided**
4	**cups (1 L) shredded spinach**
½	**cup (125 mL) chopped fresh basil**
½	**cup (125 mL) slivered, drained sun-dried tomatoes (packed in oil)**
2	**(170-mL) jars marinated artichoke hearts, drained**
10	**ounces (284 g) soft goat cheese, cut into bite-size pieces**
1	**small red onion, sliced thin**
	Pepper

For each pizza, brush unbaked crust or bread shell evenly with 1 tablespoon (15 mL) oil. Sprinkle half the spinach and basil evenly over crust. Arrange half the sun-dried tomatoes, artichoke hearts, goat cheese and onion on top. Drizzle with 1 tablespoon (15 mL) olive oil. Sprinkle lightly with pepper.

If using home-made dough, bake at 500 F (260 C) for 8 minutes, then slide pizzas from pan directly on to oven rack; bake an additional 1 to 2 minutes or until bottoms of crusts are crisp and golden. (On bread shells, bake at 450 F or 230 C for 10 minutes.) ⟳

Secret-Ingredient Pizza with Porcini Mushrooms and Provolone

Makes 4 to 6 servings

Dried mushrooms intensify in taste. Mixed with a combination of fresh oyster, shiitake, chanterelle or button mushrooms, they add a round and deeply satisfying flavor to this pizza. The secret ingredient? It's the soaking liquid from the dried porcini mushrooms, mixed with sherry, reduced to a quarter cup of thick, dark sauce, and poured over the baked pizzas — like gravy for vegetarians. We found the idea in Deborah Madison and Edward Espe Brown's The Greens Cookbook. *Add a salad of mixed greens, and, if you're making this pizza in the summer, a first course of corn on the cob.*

¾ cup (175 mL) **boiling water**
2 **(10-g) packages dried porcini mushrooms**
3 **tablespoons (45 mL) butter, divided**
4 **medium leeks (white part only), quartered lengthwise and sliced thin**
½ cup (125 mL) **water**
  Salt and pepper
1 **tablespoon (15 mL) olive oil**
6 **cups (1.5 L) thinly sliced mushrooms (oyster, shiitake, chanterelles, button or any combination)**
½ **teaspoon (2 mL) salt**
4 **garlic cloves, chopped fine**
2 **tablespoons (30 mL) chopped fresh thyme, divided**
2 **tablespoons (30 mL) chopped fresh flat-leaf parsley, divided**
¼ cup (50 mL) **dry sherry**
2 **(12-inch or 30-cm) unbaked pizza crusts (Quick Pizza Dough recipe, page 169) or Italian-style bread shells**
  Olive oil
3½ **cups (875 mL) grated provolone cheese**

In large bowl, pour boiling water over dried porcini mushrooms; soak for 15 minutes. Pour mushrooms and liquid into paper coffee filter set in cone over glass measure. Reserve strained liquid (½ cup or 125 mL). Coarsely chop mushrooms; set aside.

WHAT ARE PORCINI MUSHROOMS?

The Italians call them porcini, the French call them cepes. Almost never available fresh in North America, they're most frequently encountered dried, packaged in small, but none the less expensive, amounts.

Use porcini for their rich, earthy flavor. They're not as expensive as they look: an ounce is enough to flavor a soup for four. Choose the bag with the largest, palest mushrooms for best flavor. Soak them in hot water for 15 minutes to soften them before cooking.

In large heavy frypan, heat 2 tablespoons (30 mL) butter over medium-high heat. Add leeks; saute 1 minute. Add ½ cup (125 mL) water and reduce heat to medium-low; cook 8 minutes or until leeks are tender and liquid has evaporated, stirring occasionally. Add salt and pepper to taste; set aside.

In another large frypan, heat 1 tablespoon (15 mL) oil and remaining 1 tablespoon (15 mL) butter over medium-high heat. Add porcini mushrooms; saute for 1 minute. Add fresh mushrooms and ½ teaspoon (2 mL) salt; saute for 2 minutes. Add garlic; saute for 2 minutes or until mushrooms are tender. Add pepper to taste and half the thyme and parsley.

Remove mushroom mixture from frypan and set aside. Increase heat to high; add sherry and reserved mushroom liquid. Bring to boil; cook for about 3 minutes or until juices are reduced to ¼ cup (50 mL). Set mushroom juices aside.

For each pizza, brush unbaked crust or bread shell lightly with oil. Spread with half the leek mixture. Sprinkle with ¾ cup (175 mL) cheese. Top with half the mushroom mixture and sprinkle with 1 cup (250 mL) cheese.

If using home-made dough, bake at 500 F (260 C) for 8 minutes, then slide pizzas from pans directly on to oven rack; bake an additional 1 to 2 minutes or until bottoms of crusts are crisp and golden. (On bread shells, bake at 450 F or 230 C for 10 minutes.)

Remove pizzas from oven; pour half the reserved mushroom juices over top of each pizza. Garnish with remaining thyme and parsley. ⟳

WHAT IS FLAT-LEAF PARSLEY?

In Roman times, common parsley had flat leaves. Parsley-loving gardeners used it to breed a more decorative curly parsley. We still have these forms of parsley today, but in North America at least, flat-leaf parsley (also called Italian parsley) is far from common.

That's a shame, because flat-leaf parsley not only has a stronger and more interesting taste, it's also hardier, more vigorous and more easily grown than curly parsley.

So why do those who seek flat-leaf parsley have to try their luck in specialty markets while curly parsley is available everywhere?

Call it a retail habit. Until the '80s, when home cooks discovered other herbs, curly parsley served as the universal garnish, sprigs of it tucked on to a plate of just about anything, then pushed away uneaten at the end of the meal.

Unless you're interested in purely decorative effects, it's worth seeking out, or better yet, growing, the flat-leaf variety.

Black Bean Pizza with Tomatoes, Pepper and Olives

Makes 4 to 6 servings

Black bean flakes are an add-boiling-water-and-stir miracle that waits on your pantry shelf until you need a smooth paste to make into a dip, tuck into a tortilla, or in this case, spread over a pizza crust. (You could get much the same effect from any cooked black beans, but not without a food processor.)

Cumin, lime and jalapeno-spiked monterey jack cheese take this pizza in a decidedly Tex-Mex direction. You might like to set out corn chips and salsa before dinner. Add a green salad with chopped avocado to eat with the pizza, and dinner's complete.

1½	cups (375 mL) dried black bean flakes
1	cup (250 mL) boiling water
2	tablespoons (30 mL) lime juice
½	teaspoon (2 mL) ground cumin
2	cups (500 mL) grated part-skim mozzarella cheese
1	cup (250 mL) grated jalapeno monterey jack cheese
2	(12-inch or 30-cm) unbaked pizza crusts (Quick Pizza Dough recipe, page 169) or Italian-style bread shells
1	small onion, chopped fine
3	to 4 medium plum tomatoes, sliced
1	medium green bell pepper, cut into thin strips about 1½ inches (4 cm) long
⅔	cup (150 mL) sliced green olives
	Coarsely chopped fresh cilantro

Put bean flakes in bowl and add the boiling water; stir and let stand for 5 minutes. Stir in lime juice and cumin; set aside.

Combine mozzarella and monterey jack cheese; set aside.

For each pizza, spread half the bean mixture evenly over unbaked crust or bread shell. Top with a quarter of the cheese mixture and half the onion, tomatoes, bell pepper and olives. Sprinkle with a quarter of the cheese mixture.

If using home-made dough, bake at 500 F (260 C) for 8 minutes, then slide pizzas from pans directly on to oven rack; bake an additional 1 to 2 minutes or until bottoms of crusts are crisp and golden. (On bread shells, bake at 450 F or 230 C for 10 minutes.) Sprinkle half the cilantro over each pizza. ○

WHAT ARE BLACK BEAN FLAKES?

Sometimes sold as black bean soup mix, these mildly seasoned flakes are the ultimate in bean convenience. Already cooked, all they need is five minutes' soaking in boiling water to be ready to spread on a pizza, wrap in a tortilla or use as the foundation of a bean dip.

For a thick but spreadable paste, use ¾ of a cup of water to one cup of bean flakes.

Many supermarkets stock black bean flakes in what looks like a purple milk carton. You can also buy bulk flakes in natural and bulk-food stores.

Pesto Pizza with Japanese Eggplant

Makes 4 to 6 servings

If you're looking for a quick pizza with the satisfying texture of grilled eggplant, leave the plump, European eggplants alone. They're bitter and need half an hour to mellow out under a sprinkling of salt. Instead, choose long, thin Japanese eggplants that can go straight from the cleaver to the grill. Then pile on the toppings: yellow bell pepper, fresh basil, green olives, sun-dried tomatoes and mozzarella, all resting on a layer of pesto.

There are enough vegetables in the pizza to make salad seem redundant. Instead, add a bowl of hummus with some pita and grilled red peppers to eat while the pizza cooks.

¾	**pound (350 g) Japanese eggplants, cut into ¼-inch (5 mm) thick slices**
1	**tablespoon (15 mL) olive oil**
⅔	**cup (150 mL) fresh pesto**
2	**(12-inch or 30-cm) unbaked pizza crusts (Quick Pizza Dough recipe, page 169) or Italian-style bread shells**
3	**cups (700 mL) grated part-skim mozzarella cheese**
½	**cup (125 mL) drained sun-dried tomatoes (packed in oil), sliced**
1	**medium yellow bell pepper, sliced thin**
½	**cup (125 mL) chopped fresh basil**
⅔	**cup (150 mL) sliced green olives**
	Pepper

Place eggplant slices on greased broiler pan and brush with oil. Broil for 8 minutes or until golden, turning once.

For each pizza, spread half the pesto over unbaked crust or bread shell, leaving ½-inch (1 cm) border all around. Sprinkle with ¾ cup (175 mL) of the cheese. Top with half the sun-dried tomatoes, eggplant, yellow pepper, basil and olives. Sprinkle with ¾ cup (175 mL) of the cheese. Sprinkle lightly with pepper.

If using home-made dough, bake at 500 F (260 C) for 8 minutes, then slide pizzas from pans directly on to oven rack; bake an additional 1 to 2 minutes or until bottoms of crusts are crisp and golden. (On bread shells, bake at 450 F or 230 C for 10 minutes.) ⏲

GUIDE TO
RECIPES BY CATEGORY

Meat

Recipe	Low Fat	Extra Fast	Entertaining	Kids' Faves
Speedy Chili with Sun-Dried Tomatoes (*page 15*)				○
Flank Steak with Chipotle Marinade (*page 16*)		○		
Cheeky Stroganoff with Ground Beef (*page 17*)		○		○
Far-East Burgers (*page 18*)		○		○
Beef Stir-Fry with Chinese Broccoli (*page 20*)	○			
Beef, Bell Pepper and Snow Pea Stir-Fry (*page 21*)		○		
Barbecued Orange Beef (*page 22*)	○		○	
Lone Star Tamale Pie (*page 23*)				○
Almost Beef Picadillo Enchiladas (*page 24*)				○
Beef Fajitas (*page 25*)		○		○
Pork Stir-Fry with Broccoli and Lemon (*page 26*)		○		
Pork Chops with Maple Syrup and Balsamic Vinegar (*page 28*)	○	○		
Pork Chops with Sweet-and-Sour Cabbage (*page 29*)	○	○		
Flash-in-the-Pan Pork Schnitzel (*page 30*)	○	○		
Pork Chops with Papaya Salsa (*page 31*)	○		○	
Barbecued Tenderloin with Plum Sauce and Rosemary (*page 32*)	○		○	
Barbecued Pork Tenderloin with Ginger and Soy Sauce (*page 33*)	○		○	
Pork Tenderloin with Dried Cranberries and Blueberries (*page 34*)	○	○	○	
Lamb Burgers (*page 35*)			○	
Lamb and Eggplant Meal-in-a-Pocket (*page 36*)			○	
Lamb Kebabs with Raspberry Sauce (*page 38*)			○	
Lamb Chops with Honey Rosemary Glaze (*page 39*)	○	○	○	
Lamb Chops with Fresh Mint and Jalapeno Pepper (*page 40*)	○	○	○	
Spaghetti with Beef and Mushrooms (*page 41*)				○

Low-Fat If your eating is based on a good variety of fresh, non-processed foods — emphasizing whole grains, fruit and vegetables — you probably won't have to count your fat or your calories. You have a healthy diet already.

If you have reason to be concerned about your fat intake, however, we've marked the recipes in this book that are particularly low in fat.

Current nutritional recommendations suggest that adults get no more than 30 per cent of their calories from fat. Remember: this refers to a daily allowance, not just a particular food or meal. For the average adult woman (who consumes about 1,900 calories daily) this means 65 grams of fat, or less, per day. For the average adult man (who consumes about 2,700 calories daily) this means 90 grams of fat, or less.

To qualify for our low-fat rating, the recipes marked above had to contain no more than 15 grams of fat per serving.

(Whenever a recipe gives a range of servings — four to six, for example — we calculated the fat content on the smaller number of servings. When a recipe calls for milk or yogurt,

we used 1 per cent. Soups marked low fat, above, are main course meals and not just starters.)

Extra Fast All the recipes in this book are fast — most can be made in 30 minutes or less. The recipes marked Extra Fast can be made in about 20 minutes.

Remember: the first time you make a recipe, allow yourself a few extra minutes; as you gain practice, you'll get faster. Simple steps — like putting pasta water on to heat the moment you enter the kitchen — will also help you get dinner to the table in record time.

Great for Entertaining What you're happy to serve to guests depends on your own taste and style. We've singled out recipes — from fancy to casual — we think have enough pizzazz to please company. But these are just suggestions. Let your judgment prevail; you know your audience better than we do.

Kids' Faves What distinguishes a Kids' Fave? Anything that has to be eaten with fingers. Recipes with lots of cheese. No "weird" ingredients. Simple tastes. We can't guarantee your kids will like these recipes, but we think they're good bets.

	Low Fat	Extra Fast	Entertaining	Kids' Faves
Red, White and Green Rotini with Bacon (page 43)	✓	✓		
Spaghettini with Pork, Shiitake Mushrooms and Sage (page 44)	✓		✓	
Spaghetti with Mushrooms, Pancetta and Sage (page 45)		✓		
Fettuccine with Mushrooms, Prosciutto and Basil (page 46)		✓	✓	
Barbecued Pizza with Pesto, Pepper and Prosciutto (page 47)			✓	
Upside-Down Pizza (page 48)				✓
Pepperoni Pizza with Light Cheese (page 49)				✓

Chicken, Turkey, Duck

	Low Fat	Extra Fast	Entertaining	Kids' Faves
Chicken Noodle Soup with Snow Peas and Fresh Herbs (page 52)	✓			✓
Grilled Chicken and Red Onion Salad with Feta Cheese (page 53)			✓	
Chicken with Balsamic Vinegar and Fresh Basil (page 54)	✓			
Chicken Breasts with Orange Glaze (page 55)	✓		✓	
Chicken with Creamy Lemon Sauce (page 56)	✓		✓	
Glazed Apricot-Walnut Chicken (page 57)	✓	✓		
Cinnamon Chicken with Orange Juice, Raisins and Capers (page 58)	✓			
Raspberry-Vinegar Chicken (page 59)	✓	✓		
Chicken with Ginger, Mint and Yogurt (page 60)	✓			
Chicken with Mushrooms, Lemon and Fresh Rosemary (page 61)	✓			
Chicken Breasts with Mushrooms and Creamy Mustard Sauce (page 62)	✓			
Peanutty Chicken (page 63)				✓
Chicken Strips (page 64)	✓			✓
Chicken Focaccia Burgers (page 65)	✓			✓
Chicken Tortilla Pizzas (page 66)				✓
Spicy Chicken and Bell Pepper Stir-Fry (page 67)	✓		✓	

	Low Fat	Extra Fast	Entertaining	Kids' Faves
Major Grey's Chicken Stir-Fry (page 69)	✓			✓
Thai Stir-Fry with Chicken, Cilantro and Coconut Milk (page 70)			✓	
Pan-Seared Chicken Pasta with Wilted Spinach (page 72)			✓	
Speedy Spirals with Chicken, Tomatoes and Black Olives (page 73)		✓		
Chicken Spaghettini with Broccoli, Pine Nuts and Sun-Dried Tomatoes (page 74)		✓	✓	
Radiatore Pasta with Chicken, Asparagus and Snow Peas (page 75)		✓	✓	
Virtuous Turkey Soup with Tomatoes and Fresh Basil (page 76)				✓
Texan Outrage Turkey Chili (page 77)	✓	✓		✓
Tex-Mex Turkey Lasagne (page 79)				✓
Turkey Fajitas (page 80)				✓
Revisionist Turkey Stroganoff (page 81)		✓		
Fat Fightin' Turkey Burgers (page 82)	✓	✓		✓
Turkey Burgers with Sun-Dried Tomatoes and Fresh Herbs (page 83)	✓	✓		
Turkey with Sage Cranberry Sauce (page 84)	✓	✓	✓	
Turkey with Papaya Ginger Sauce (page 85)	✓	✓	✓	
Turkey with Fruit Chutney (page 86)	✓	✓		
Lemon Sage Turkey (page 87)	✓			
Turkey Sausages with Red Lentils (page 88)	✓			
Pizza with Turkey Sausage and Yellow Bell Pepper (page 89)	✓			✓
Hot Duck Salad with Soy Sesame Vinaigrette (page 90)			✓	
Barbecued Duck Pizza (page 91)			✓	

Seafood

	Low Fat	Extra Fast	Entertaining	Kids' Faves
Chop-Chop Cioppino (page 94)	✓		✓	
Creamy Cod Soup with Leeks and Green Onions (page 95)	✓			

	Low Fat	Extra Fast	Entertaining	Kids' Faves
Seafood Chowder with Pasta Shells *(page 96)*	✓			
Clam and Cauliflower Chowder *(page 97)*	✓	✓		
Dolly Watts' Salmon Soup or Haw'gwil Jem *(page 98)*	✓			
Grilled Salmon and Pecan Salad *(page 98)*		✓	✓	
Salmon Fillets with Mango *(page 100)*	✓	✓	✓	
Salmon Fillets with Lime and Fresh Herbs *(page 101)*	✓		✓	
Broiled Salmon Steaks with Blueberries *(page 103)*			✓	
Barbecued Salmon Steaks with Peach and Berry Salsa *(page 104)*	✓	✓	✓	
Broiled Salmon Steaks with Herbed Almond Butter *(page 105)*		✓	✓	
Maple Roast Sesame Salmon Steaks *(page 106)*		✓	✓	
Jalapeno Salmon Cakes *(page 107)*	✓			✓
Summer Sole with Fresh Tomatoes *(page 108)*	✓	✓		
Cod with Fresh Salsa and Lime Sauce *(page 109)*		✓		
Cod with Wine and Sun-Dried Tomatoes *(page 110)*	✓			
Cod with Capers *(page 111)*	✓	✓		
Spicy Broiled Cod *(page 113)*	✓	✓		
Fast Mexican Snapper *(page 114)*	✓			
Steamed Sea Bass with Black Bean Sauce *(page 115)*	✓	✓	✓	
Halibut with Fresh Rosemary and Pine Nuts *(page 116)*		✓	✓	
Halibut on Fettuccine with Chili-Sesame Sauce *(page 117)*			✓	
Halibut with Strawberry, Lime and Mint Salsa *(page 118)*	✓	✓	✓	
Trout with Herb Butter *(page 119)*		✓	✓	
Seafood with Green Curry and Lemon Grass *(page 120)*	✓		✓	
Scallops in Strawberry, Balsamic Vinegar and Pepper Sauce *(page 121)*	✓	✓	✓	
Sizzling Prawns with Ginger *(page 122)*	✓		✓	

	Low Fat	Extra Fast	Entertaining	Kids' Faves
Clams Provençal *(page 123)*	✓		✓	
Linguine with Clam and Black Olive Sauce *(page 124)*	✓			
Seashell Pasta with Prawns, Feta and Red Peppers *(page 125)*	✓			
In-Your-Face Mussels with Parsley Pesto and Fettuccine *(page 126)*			✓	
Down-Home Spaghetti with Tuna-Tomato Sauce *(page 127)*	✓	✓		✓
Penne with Tuna, Lemon, Capers and Olives *(page 128)*		✓		
Kitchen-Sink Rotini with Tuna and Pine Nuts *(page 129)*		✓		
Fettuccine with Lox, Horseradish and Chutzpah *(page 130)*		✓	✓	
Smoked Salmon Pizza *(page 132)*	✓		✓	
Shrimp Pizza with Mustard, Goat Cheese, Dill and Caramelized Onions *(page 133)*			✓	

Vegetarian

	Low Fat	Extra Fast	Entertaining	Kids' Faves
Orzo and White Bean Soup with Double Tomatoes *(page 136)*	✓			
Bean Soup with Kale and Multi-Colored Pasta *(page 137)*	✓			
Holy Moley Chili *(page 138)*	✓		✓	✓
Penne with Tomatoes, Basil and Goat Cheese *(page 141)*			✓	
Summer's End Pasta *(page 142)*	✓		✓	
Bow-Tie Pasta with Broccoli, Cauliflower and Double-Tomato Sauce *(page 143)*	✓			
Garden Patch Pasta with Curls *(page 146)*				✓
Penne with Broccoli, Mushrooms and Wilted Spinach *(page 147)*	✓		✓	
Penne with White Beans and Tomatoes *(page 148)*	✓			
Spaghetti with Warm Tomato-Avocado Sauce *(page 149)*			✓	
Broccoli Mustard Fettuccine with Lemon *(page 150)*			✓	
Spaghetti Frittata with Broccoli, Goat Cheese and Sun-Dried Tomatoes *(page 151)*				✓
Southwestern Corn Cakes *(page 152)*	✓			✓

	Low Fat	Extra Fast	Entertaining	Kids' Faves
Speedy Cheese Enchiladas (*page 153*)				⏱
Spinach and Broccoli Enchiladas (*page 154*)				⏱
Just in Quesadillas (*page 155*)				⏱
Black Bean Burritos (*page 156*)		⏱		
Polenta with Black Bean Salsa (*page 157*)		⏱	⏱	
Jamaican Black Beans with Pineapple-Pear Salsa (*page 158*)	⏱			
Chickpeas with Cumin and Ginger (*page 159*)			⏱	
Couscous with Chickpeas and Basil Yogurt Sauce (*page 160*)			⏱	

	Low Fat	Extra Fast	Entertaining	Kids' Faves
Tofu Dengaku with Spinach Salad (*page 162*)	⏱		⏱	
Great Canadian Beans (*page 167*)	⏱			
Mustardy Mushroom Stew (*page 168*)	⏱			
Fresh Vegetable Pizza (*page 170*)				⏱
Artichoke, Spinach and Goat Cheese Pizza (*page 171*)			⏱	
Secret-Ingredient Pizza with Porcini Mushrooms and Provolone (*page 172*)			⏱	
Pesto Pizza with Japanese Eggplant (*page 175*)			⏱	

COOKING BEANS

In this cookbook we call for canned beans, one of the most worth while of all convenience foods.

But you can economize by cooking dried beans from scratch. Keep a stock of them in the freezer, and you'll find using them is every bit as convenient as opening a can.

Here's a rough guide to make the translation from drained canned beans to home-cooked beans.

- To replace a 398-mL can of beans, you need about 1½ cups (375 mL) of cooked beans.
- To replace a 540-mL can of beans, you need about 2 cups (500 mL) of cooked beans.
- To replace a 796-mL can of beans, you need about 3 cups (750 mL) of cooked beans.

To cook beans:

1) Clean and wash the beans, picking out any twigs or stones.

2) Cover beans with cold water and either
   - Soak 8 to 12 hours (place in refrigerator in warm weather), OR,
   - Place on stove and boil hard for 2 minutes, then leave to stand in the water for an hour.

3) Drain soaking water and rinse beans again.

4) Cover the rinsed, soaked beans with fresh cold water. Be sure to use a pot large enough to allow for foaming. Bring to boil; boil 5 minutes. Then, skim off any scum or, if you wish, drain and rinse beans once again.

5) Return beans to stove, bring to a boil, then reduce heat, cover pot loosely and let beans simmer until tender. (Do not cover tightly or pot will boil over. A little oil will also help prevent this.)

Cooking times will vary depending on type and age of bean. Some beans will cook in as little as 45 minutes, others will require 90 minutes or more.

About 1 cup (250 mL) of dried beans will yield 2 to 2½ cups (500 to 625 mL) cooked beans.

Measuring pasta

As a general rule, we call for 3 ounces (85 g) of dried pasta per person, or three-quarters of a pound (350 g) of pasta to serve four.

Here's a quick way to measure spaghetti, or any other long skinny dry pasta: grasp a handful of pasta tightly at one end, then measure the diameter. If it's about 1½ inches (4 cm) across, you have three-quarters of a pound (350 g).

If you want to substitute fresh pasta for dried, use about 1½ times the amount called for in the recipe. For four people, buy about 1¼ pounds (625 g). Remember that fresh pasta cooks in a fraction of the time, so don't put it in the pot until your sauce is almost ready.

Cooking dry pasta

- Cook pasta in a big pot in lots of boiling water. Use at least 5 quarts (5 L) of water for a pound (500 g) of pasta.
- Add the salt when you add the pasta. Use 1 or 2 teaspoons (5 or 10 mL) for ¾ of a pound (350 g) of pasta.
- Drain pasta as soon as it's cooked. Don't worry about removing every drop of water; some water should cling to the pasta to help distribute the sauce. Do not rinse.
- Here's a rough guide to cooking times for dry pasta; the brand you use will determine the exact cooking time:

  Broad noodles: 5 to 8 minutes
  Spaghettini: 8 to 10 minutes
  Linguine: 9 to 11 minutes
  Bow-tie pasta: 10 to 12 minutes
  Rotini: 10 to 12 minutes
  Penne: 10 to 14 minutes
  Spaghetti: 10 to 14 minutes
  Orzo: 10 to 16 minutes

Small pasta shells: 12 to 14 minutes
Fettuccine: 12 to 15 minutes
Fusilli: 12 to 15 minutes

Substituting dried herbs

Many of the recipes in this book call for fresh herbs. If you need to substitute the dried variety, be sure to use less: drying usually concentrates flavor.

Start with one part dried to replace three parts fresh, then adjust to suit your taste.

Mail order sources

South China Seas Trading Co. specializes in spices, sauces, condiments and other ingredients used in Asian, Indian, African and Caribbean cooking. No catalogue; accepts Visa only for mail orders.

South China Seas Trading Co.
Granville Island Public Market
125-1689 Johnston Street
Vancouver, B.C.
V6H 3R9
Telephone: (604) 681-5402

Great Culinary Adventures Inc. offers more than 200 specialty food items, including sun-dried tomatoes, dried blueberries and cranberries, olive oils and balsamic vinegars, as well as French copper cookware and Portuguese knives. Free catalogue; write or call to order a copy.

Great Culinary Adventures Inc.
1856 Pandora Street
Vancouver, B.C.
V5L 1M5
Telephone: (604) 255-5119
Fax: (604) 253-1331

INDEX

(Boldface type denotes recipe by its full name)

A

Almost Beef Picadillo Enchiladas, 24
**Almost Instant Broiled
    Salmon Steaks**, 102
Anchovy paste, about, 73
Anglo-Indian Curried Lamb, 37
Appetizers
    bruschetta with oyster mushrooms
      and rosemary, 147
    bruschetta with tomatoes and
      bocconcini, 123
    chutney dip for raw vegetables, 82
    creamy herb dip, 79
    guacamole, 25
    honeydew melon, hot and cold, 21
    hummus, 36
    pappadams, 118
    parmesan poppy seed bread, 141
Apples, baked, 97
Apricots, dried, chocolate-dipped, 121
**Artichoke, Spinach and Goat Cheese
    Pizza**, 171
Artichokes
    braised, 87
    on pizza with spinach and goat
      cheese, 171
Arugula
    about, 140
    in salad, with pears and
      Brie cheese, 75
Asian-influenced dishes
    beef stir-fry, bell pepper and snow
      peas, 21
    beef stir-fry with Chinese
      broccoli, 20-21
    chicken, with peanut sauce, 63
    chicken stir-fry, Major Grey's, 69
    chicken stir-fry, Thai, 70
    chicken stir-fry, with bell pepper, 67
    chicken stir-fry, with broccoli, 68-69
    curried red lentils and
      cauliflower, 166-67
    Far East burgers, 18
    lamb curry, 37
    pappadams, 118
    pork tenderloin, barbecued, 32, 33
    prawns with ginger, 122

    satay beef and bok choy stir-
      fry, 18-19
    sea bass, with black bean sauce, 115
    seafood with green curry and lemon
      grass, 120
    tofu, and Szechuan eggplant, 164
    tofu, with watercress and cherry
      tomatoes, 161
    tofu dengaku, with spinach
      salad, 162-63
Asparagus
    about, 43
    with radiatore pasta and chicken, 75
    with rotini and bacon, 43
Avocado
    about, 149
    guacamole, 25
    and tomato spaghetti sauce, 149

B

Bacon
    pancetta, about, 45
    pancetta, on spaghetti with
      mushrooms and sage, 45
    prosciutto, on barbecued pizza, 47
    prosciutto, on fettuccine, with
      mushrooms and basil, 46
    with red, white and green rotini, 43
Baked Apples, 97
Baked Pears, 96
Balsamic vinegar, about, 54
Balsamic Vinegar with Strawberries, 39
Banana-Mint Raita, 37
Barbary bread, about, 160
Barbecue
    chicken, grilled, with red onion
      salad, 53
    duck, barbecued, on pizza, 91
    lamb kebabs, with raspberry
      sauce, 38
    orange beef, 22
    pizza, with pesto, pepper and
      prosciutto, 47
    pork tenderloin, with ginger and soy
      sauce, 33
    pork tenderloin, with plum sauce
      and rosemary, 32

    salmon, grilled, with pecan
      salad, 98-99
    salmon steaks, with peach and
      berry salsa, 104-5
Barbecued Duck Pizza, 91
Barbecued Orange Beef, 22-23
**Barbecued Pizza with Pesto, Pepper
    and Prosciutto**, 47
**Barbecued Pork Tenderloin with
    Ginger and Soy Sauce**, 33
**Barbecued Pork Tenderloin with
    Plum Sauce and Rosemary**, 32
**Barbecued Salmon Steaks with
    Peach and Berry Salsa**, 104-5
Basil, about, 171
Basmati rice, about, 155
Bean flakes, about, 174
Bean sauce, hot, 164
**Bean Soup with Kale and Multi-Colored
    Pasta**, 137
Beans. *see also* Chili
    black bean burritos, 156
    black bean pizza, 174
    Canadian, 167
    cooking, 179-80
    curried lentils and
      cauliflower, 166-67
    de-gassing, 148
    flakes, 174
    hot bean sauce, 164
    Jamaican black, with pineapple-pear
      salsa, 158
    kidney, white, 15
    soup, with kale and pasta, 137
    soup, with orzo, 136
    and tomatoes, with penne, 148
    turkey sausages with red lentils, 88
    vegetarian chili, 138
    white, and avocado salad, 140
Beef. *see also* Ground beef
    barbecued orange beef, 22
    chili, with sun-dried tomatoes, 15
    enchiladas, 24
    fajitas, 25
    Far East burgers, 18
    flank steak with chipotle
      marinade, 16
    satay beef and bok choy stir-fry,
      18-19
    spaghetti with beef and
      mushrooms, 41

stir-fry, with bell pepper and
snow peas, 21
stir-fry, with Chinese broccoli, 20-21
stroganoff, 17
tamale pie, 23
upside-down pizza, 48
**Beef, Bell Pepper and Snow Pea
Stir-Fry**, 21
Beef Fajitas, 25
Beef Stir-Fry with Chinese Broccoli,
20-21
Bell peppers, about, 170
Berries
blueberry sauce, and broiled
salmon steaks, 103
fruit vinegars, 59
and peach salsa, 104
pork tenderloin, with dried
cranberries and blueberries, 34
raspberry sauce, 38
turkey and sage cranberry sauce, 84
Best Brussels Sprouts, 84
Black Bean Burritos, 156
**Black Bean Pizza with Tomatoes,
Pepper and Olives**, 174
**Black Bean Soup with Hot Italiam
Sausage and Spinach**, 14
Blueberries
dried, with pork tenderloin, 34
sauce, and broiled salmon steaks, 103
Bocconcini cheese
about, 99
bruschetta with tomatoes and, 123
Bok choy
about, 19
stir-fry, with satay beef, 18-19
**Bow-Tie Pasta with Broccoli,
Cauliflower and Double-
Tomato Sauce**, 143
Braised Baby Artichokes, 87
Bread
barbary, 160
bruschetta, with oyster mushrooms
and rosemary, 147
bruschetta, with tomatoes and
bocconcini, 123
focaccia, 65
pappadams, 118
parmesan poppy seed, 141
pizza dough, 169
seasoned crumbs, 55
shells, for pizza, 169
Broccoli
about, 145
and cauliflower, with pasta and
tomato sauce, 143
with chicken and spaghettini, 74
Chinese, about, 20
Chinese, stir-fry with beef, 20-21

mustard fettuccine, with lemon, 150
with penne, mushrooms and wilted
spinach, 147
and spaghetti, with pepper and
tomato, 145
and spaghetti frittata, 151
and spinach enchiladas, 154-55
stir-fry, with pork and lemon, 26
**Broccoli Mustard Fettuccine
with Lemon**, 150
**Broiled Salmon Steaks with
Blueberries**, 103
**Broiled Salmon Steaks with Herbed
Almond Butte**r, 105
Broiling, about, 102
Bruschetta
with oyster mushrooms and
rosemary, 147
with poppy seeds and grated
parmesan cheese, 141
with tomatoes and bocconcini
cheese, 123
**Bruschetta with Tomatoes and
Bocconcini**, 123
Brussels sprouts, cooking, 84
Bulgur, about, 138
Burgers
chicken focaccia, 65
cooking, 18
Far East, 18
hamburger disease, 18
lamb, 35
no-stick, 83
turkey, 82, 83
using pita bread for buns, 64
Burritos
about, 24
black bean, 156
Butter, herbed almond, 105
**Buttermilk Vinaigrette with Garlic
and Dill**, 89

C

**Cabbage Salad, with Apple and
Onion**, 77
Capers, about, 111
Cardamom-Yogurt Fruit Sauce, 88
Cauliflower
about, 144
and broccoli, with pasta and
tomato sauce, 143
and clam chowder, 97
and curried red lentils, 166-67
and linguine, 144
Cheeky Stroganoff with Ground Beef, 17

Cheese
bocconcini, 99
feta, 133
goat, 133
jalapeno, 156
low-fat, 49
parmesan, 78, 129
ricotta, 154
Chicken
with apricot-walnut glaze, 57
with balsamic vinegar and
fresh basil, 54
breasts, boneless, 53
breasts, with mushrooms and creamy
mustard sauce, 62
breasts, with orange glaze, 55
cinnamon, with orange juice, raisins
and capers, 58
with creamy lemon sauce, 56
focaccia burgers, 65
with ginger, mint and yogurt, 60
with mushrooms, lemon and
fresh rosemary, 61
noodle soup with snow peas and
fresh herbs, 52
pan-seared, with pasta and wilted
spinach, 72-73
and peanut sauce, 63
pounding, 61
and radiatore pasta, asparagus and
snow peas, 75
raspberry-vinegar, 59
and rotini, with tomatoes and
black olives, 73
and rotini with dill and
pecan pesto, 71
salad, with red onion and
feta cheese, 53
and spaghettini with broccoli, 74
stir-fry, Major Grey's, 69
stir-fry, Thai, 70
stir-fry, with bell pepper, 67
stir-fry, with broccoli, 68-69
strips, 64
tortilla pizzas, 66
**Chicken and Rotini with Dill and
Pecan Pesto**, 71
**Chicken Breasts with Mushrooms and
Creamy Mustard Sauce**, 62
Chicken Breasts with Orange Glaze, 55
Chicken Focaccia Burgers, 65
**Chicken Noodle Soup with Snow Peas
and Fresh Herbs**, 52
**Chicken Spaghettini with Broccoli,
Pine Nuts and Sun-Dried
Tomatoes**, 74
Chicken Strips, 64
Chicken Tortilla Pizzas, 66

Chicken with Balsamic Vinegar and Fresh Basil, 54
Chicken with Creamy Lemon Sauce, 56
Chicken with Ginger, Mint and Yogurt, 60
Chicken with Mushrooms, Lemon and Fresh Rosemary, 61
Chickpeas
    with couscous and basil yogurt sauce, 160
    with cumin and ginger, 159
Chickpeas with Cumin and Ginger, 159
Children
    guide to recipes for (Kids' faves), 176-79
    picky eaters, 48
Chili
    with sun-dried tomatoes, 15
    turkey, 77
    vegetarian, 138
Chinese broccoli
    about, 20
    and beef stir-fry, 20-21
Chipotle peppers, 16
Chives, freezing, 119
Chocolate-Dipped Dried Apricots, 121
Chop-Chop Cioppino, 94
Chutney, about, 86
Chutney Dip for Raw Vegetables, 82
Cilantro, about, 153
Cinnamon Chicken with Orange Juice, Raisins and Capers, 58
Clam and Cauliflower Chowder, 97
Clams
    and cauliflower chowder, 97
    cioppino soup, 94
    and olive sauce, on linguine, 124
    provençal, 123
Clams Provençal, 123
Cod
    with capers, 111
    creamy soup, with leeks and green onion, 95
    with fresh salsa and lime sauce, 109
    with fresh tomato and tomatillo sauce, 112
    spicy broiled, 113
    with wine and sun-dried tomatoes, 110
Cod with Capers, 111
Cod with Fresh Salsa and Lime Sauce, 109
Cod with Fresh Tomato and Tomatillo Sauce, 112
Cod with Wine and Sun-Dried Tomatoes, 110
Cold Cucumber Salad, 70
Condiments. *see* Herbs, spices and condiments

Cooking and food preparation
    beans, cooking, 179-80
    beans, de-gassing, 148
    broiling, 102
    burgers, no-stick, 83
    chili peppers, handling, 61
    cumin, dry roasting, 113
    dicing, 66
    dry pasta, measuring and cooking, 180
    E. coli bacteria, in ground beef, 18
    fruit, baking, 96, 97
    fruit, grilling, 146
    frypans, non-stick, 152
    grilling, 104, 131, 146
    iron, combining food for absorption of, 158
    leeks, cleaning, 52
    lemon or lime zest, 101, 128
    lemons or limes, juicing, 157
    marinating, high-speed, 33
    measuring liquids, 167
    measuring spoons, 58
    onions, slicing, 23
    orange peel, drying, 22
    pounding poultry, 61
    steamer, improvising, 115
    stir-fry, cutting meat for, 26
    stir-frying vegetables, 63
    storing in ice-cube trays, 150, 157
    turkey, ground, 81
Coriander, about, 153
Corn
    cakes, 152
    polenta, with black bean sauce, 157
    in quinoa salad, with cucumber and lime, 139
    removing from cob, 142
Couscous
    about, 69
    with chickpeas and basil yogurt sauce, 160
Couscous with Chickpeas and Basil Yogurt Sauce, 160
Crackers
    papadams, 118
    shrimp, 122
Cranberries
    dried, 34
    pork tenderloin, with dried cranberries and blueberries, 34
    and sage sauce, 84
Creamy Cod Soup with Leeks and Green Onions, 95
Creamy Herb Dip, 79
Cucumber Raita, 159
Cucumber salad, 70
Cumin, roasting, 113

Curried Red Lentils and Cauliflower, 166-67
Curry
    lamb, 37
    red lentils and cauliflower, 166-67
    seafood with green curry and lemon grass, 120

D

The Dance of Life: The Other Dimension of Time, 6
Dates, with cream cheese, 125
Dengaku tofu, with spinach salad, 162-63
Desserts
    apples, baked, 97
    cardamom-yogurt fruit sauce, 88
    chocolate-dipped dried apricots, 121
    dates, with cream cheese, 125
    grilled fruit, 146
    orange slices, with liqueur, 105
    pears, baked, 96
    strawberries with balsamic vinegar, 37
Dicing, about, 66
Dijon mustard, about, 62
Dips
    chutney, 82
    creamy herb, 79
    guacamole, 25
    hummus, 36
Dobson, Austin, 11
Dogfish, about, 109
Dolly Watts' Salmon Soup or Haw'gwil Jem, 98
Double Oranges, 105
Down-Home Spaghetti with Tuna-Tomato Sauce, 127
Duck
    barbecued, on pizza, 91
    breasts, buying, 90
    hot salad with soy semsame vinaigrette, 90-91

E

E. coli bacteria, in ground beef, 18
Eggplant
    and lamb meal-in-a-pocket, 36
    on pesto pizza, 175
    and tofu, 164

Enchiladas
  about, 24
  beef, 24
  cheese, 153
  spinach and broccoli, 154-55
Endive salad, 72
Entertaining, guide to recipes for, 176-79
Extra-Fast, guide to recipes, 176-79

F

Fajitas
  beef, 25
  turkey, 80
Far East Burgers, 18
Fast Mexican Snapper, 114
Fast recipes, guide to, 176-79
Fat-Fightin' Turkey Burgers, 82
Fennel, about, 94
Feta cheese, about, 133
**Fettuccine with Lox, Horseradish and
  Chutzpah**, 130
**Fettuccine with Mushrooms,
  Prosciutto and Basil**, 46
Fish
  anchovy paste, 73
  cod, spicy broiled, 113
  cod, with capers, 111
  cod, with fresh salsa and
    lime sauce, 109
  cod, with fresh tomato and
    tomatillo sauce, 112
  cod, with wine and sun-dried
    tomatoes, 110
  dogfish, about, 109
  halibut, on fettuccine with chili-
    sesame sauce, 117
  halibut, with fresh rosemary and
    pine nuts, 116
  halibut, with strawberry, lime and
    mint salsa, 118
  Mexican snapper, 114
  salmon, smoked, on pizza, 132
  salmon, smoked, with frittata, 131
  salmon and pecan salad, 98-99
  salmon cakes, jalapeno, 107
  salmon fillets with lime and
    fresh herbs, 101
  salmon fillets with mango, 100
  salmon steaks, barbecued, 104-5
  salmon steaks, broiled, 102, 103, 105
  salmon steaks, maple roast
    sesame, 106
  sea bass, with black bean sauce, 115
  seafood with green curry and
    lemon grass, 120

  sole, with fresh tomatoes, 108
  trout, with herb butter, 119
  tuna, with penne, 128
  tuna, with rotini, 129
  tuna-tomato sauce, on spaghetti, 127
Fish sauce, about, 68
Fish soups
  cioppino, 94
  creamy cod, 95
  salmon, 98
Flank Steak with Chipotle Marinade, 16
Flash-in-the-Pan Pork Schnitzel, 30
Flounder, about, 116
Focaccia bread
  about, 65
  with chicken burgers, 65
Franklin, Benjamin, 5-6, 7
Fresh Vegetable Pizza, 170
Frittata
  and smoked salmon, 131
  spaghetti, with broccoli, 151
Fruit. *see also* names of specific fruit;
    Desserts; Sauces
  baked, 96, 97
  grilled, 146
Frypans, non-stick, 152

G

Gai lan (Chinese broccoli)
  about, 20
  and beef stir-fry, 20-21
Garden Patch Pasta with Curls, 146
Garlic powder, about, 30
Ginger, storing, 67
Glazed Apricot-Walnut Chicken, 57
Goat cheese, about, 133
Great Canadian Beans, 167
**Grilled Chicken and Red Onion Salad
  with Feta Cheese**, 53
Grilled Salmon and Pecan Salad, 98-99
Grilling, about, 104, 131, 146
Ground beef. *see also* Beef
  chili, with sun-dried tomatoes, 15
  enchiladas, 24
  Far East burgers, 18
  and mushroom sauce, on
    spaghetti, 41
  stroganoff, 17
  tamale pie, 23
  upside-down pizza, 48
Guacamole, 25

H

Halibut
  cioppino soup, 94
  on fettuccine with chili-sesame
    sauce, 117
  with fresh rosemary and
    pine nuts, 116
  with strawberry, lime and
    mint salsa, 118
**Halibut on Fettuccine with Chile-Sesame
  Sauce**, 117
**Halibut with Fresh Rosemary and
  Pine Nuts**, 116
**Halibut with Strawberry, Lime and
  Mint Salsa**, 118
Hall, Edward, 6
Hamburgers. *see* Burgers
Haw'gwil Jem (salmon and potato soup),
  98
Herbs, spices and condiments.
    see also Sauces
  anchovy paste, 73
  balsamic vinegar, 54
  basil, 171
  capers, 111
  chives, freezing, 119
  chutney, 86
  cilantro, 153
  coriander, 153
  cumin, roasting, 113
  Dijon mustard, 62
  dry, as substitution for fresh, 180
  fresh herbs, 10-11
  fruit vinegars, 59
  garlic powder, 30
  ginger, storing, 67
  horseradish, 130
  oregano, 95
  parsley, flat-leaf, 173
  pepper, 106, 151
Hoisin sauce, 91
Holy Moley Chili, 138
Honeydew melon, hot and cold, 21
Hors d'oeuvres. *see* Appetizers
Horseradish, about, 130
Hot and Cold Honeydew Melon, 21
**Hot Duck Salad with Soy Sesame
  Vinaigrette**, 90-91
Hummus, 36

I

In-Your-Face Mussels with Parsley Pesto and Fettuccine, 126
Iron, in food, 158
Italian-influenced dishes.
  see also Pasta; Pizza
  black bean soup with hot sausage and spinach, 14
  chicken, and radiatore pasta, 75
  chicken, and rotini, 71
  chicken, with balsamic vinegar and fresh basil, 54
  chicken, with pasta and wilted spinach, 72-73
  chicken, with spaghettini and broccoli, 74
  cod, with wine and sun-dried tomatoes, 110
  halibut, with fresh rosemary and pine nuts, 116
  polenta, with black bean sauce, 157
  pork chops, Sicilian style, 27
  pork stir-fry, with broccoli and lemon, 26
  seafood cioppino soup, 94
  turkey soup, with tomatoes and basil, 76
Italo-Indian Tomato Raita, 166

J

Jalapeno cheese, about, 156
Jalapeno peppers, about, 16, 40
Jalapeno Salmon Cakes, 107
Jamaican Black Beans with Pineapple-Pear Salsa, 158
The Joy of Cooking, 8
Just in Quesadillas, 155

K

Kale, about, 137
Ketjap manis (Indonesian soy sauce), about, 38
Kids, guide to recipes for, 176-179
Kitchen Sink Rotini with Tuna and Pine Nuts, 129

L

Lamb
  burgers, 35
  chops, with fresh mint and jalapeno pepper, 40
  chops, with honey rosemary glaze, 39
  curried, 37
  kebabs, with raspberry sauce, 38
  meal-in-a-pocket, with eggplant, 36
Lamb and Eggplant Meal-in-a-Pocket, 36
Lamb Burgers, 35
Lamb Chops with Fresh Mint and Jalapeno Pepper, 40
Lamb Chops with Honey Rosemary Glaze, 39
Lamb Kebabs with Raspberry Sauce, 38
Leeks
  cleaning, 52
  in creamy cod soup, 95
Lemon and Basil Vinaigrette, 42
Lemon grass, about, 120
Lemon Sage Turkey, 87
Lemons
  juice, 150, 157
  zest, 128
Lentils
  curried, and cauliflower, 166-67
  red, with turkey sausages, 88
Limes
  juice, 157
  zest, 101
Linguine with Clam and Black Olive Sauce, 124
Lone Star Tamale Pie, 23
Low-fat
  cheese, 49
  guide to recipes, 176-79
Lox, about, 132

M

Mail order sources, 180
Major Grey's Chicken Stir-Fry, 69
Mangoes
  buying, 100
  and salmon fillets, 100
Maple Roast Sesame Salmon Steaks, 106
Maple syrup
  about, 28
  in Canadian beans, 167
  pork chops, with balsamic vinegar, 28

  on salmon steaks, with sesame seeds, 106
Marinades
  beef satay stir-fry, 19
  grilled salmon, 99
  lamb kebabs, 38
  maple syrup sesame, for salmon, 106
Marinating, high-speed, 33
Measuring
  liquids, 167
  spoons, 58
Meat
  guide to recipes by category, 176-77
  Almost Beef Picadillo Enchiladas, 24
  Anglo-Indian Curried Lamb, 37
  Barbecued Orange Beef, 22-23
  Barbecued Pizza with Pesto, Pepper and Prosciutto, 47
  Barbecued Pork Tenderloin with Ginger and Soy Sauce, 33
  Barbecued Pork Tenderloin with Plum Sauce and Rosemary, 32
  Beef, Bell Pepper and Snow Pea Stir-Fry, 21
  Beef Fajitas, 25
  Beef Stir-Fry with Chinese Broccoli, 20-21
  Black Bean Soup with Hot Italiam Sausage and Spinach, 14
  Cheeky Stroganoff with Ground Beef, 17
  Far East Burgers, 18
  Fettuccine with Mushrooms, Prosciutto and Basil, 46
  Flank Steak with Chipotle Marinade, 16
  Flash-in-the-Pan Pork Schnitzel, 30
  Lamb and Eggplant Meal-in-a-Pocket, 36
  Lamb Burgers, 35
  Lamb Chops with Fresh Mint and Jalapeno Pepper, 40
  Lamb Chops with Honey Rosemary Glaze, 39
  Lamb Kebabs with Raspberry Sauce, 38
  Lone Star Tamale Pie, 23
  Penne with Hot Sausage, Red Pepper and Broccoli, 42-43
  Pepperoni Pizza with Light Cheese, 49
  Pork Chops Sicilian Style, 27
  Pork Chops with Maple Syrup and Balsamic Vinegar, 28
  Pork Chops with Papaya Salsa, 31
  Pork Chops with Sweet-and-Sour Cabbage, 29
  Pork Stir-Fry with Broccoli and Lemon, 26

Pork Tenderloin with Dried
   Cranberries and Blueberries, 34
Red, White and Green Rotini
   with Bacon, 43
Satay Beef and Bok Choy Stir-Fry,
   18-19
Spaghetti with Beef and
   Mushrooms, 41
Spaghetti with Mushrooms,
   Pancetta and Sage, 45
Spaghettini with Pork, Shiitake
   Mushrooms and Sage, 44-45
Speedy Chili with Sun-Dried
   Tomatoes, 15
Upside-Down Pizza, 48
Medjool Dates with Cream Cheese, 125
Mexican-influenced dishes
   burritos, black bean, 156
   chicken, cinnamon, 58
   chicken tortilla pizzas, 66
   chili, vegetarian, 138
   cod, with fresh salsa and
      lime sauce, 109
   cod, with fresh tomato and
      tomatillo sauce, 112
   enchiladas, beef, 24
   enchiladas, cheese, 153
   enchiladas, spinach and broccoli,
      154-55
   fajitas, beef, 25
   fajitas, turkey, 80
   flank steak with chipotle
      marinade, 16
   guacamole, 25
   quesadillas, 155
   snapper, 114
   tamale pie, 23
   turkey lasagne, 79
Middle Eastern-influenced dishes
   hummus, 36
   lamb meal-in-a-pocket, 36
   couscous with chickpeas, 160
Miso, about, 162
Mozzarella cheese, about, 99
Mushroom soy sauce, about, 164
Mushrooms
   with chicken, lemon and fresh
      rosemary, 61
   with chicken breasts, and creamy
      mustard sauce, 62
   and chicken pasta with wilted
      spinach, 72-73
   and fettuccine, prosciutto and
      basil, 46
   oyster, and rosemary bruschetta, 147
   with penne, broccoli and wilted
      spinach, 147
   porcini, about, 172-73
   porcini, on pizza, 172-73

shiitake, about, 44
shiitake, and spaghettini,
   with pork and sage, 44
stew, 168
Mussels
   about, 126
   with pasta, and parsley pesto, 126
Mustard, Dijon, about, 62
Mustardy Mushroom Stew, 168

N

No-Oil Yogurt Salad Dressing, 56

O

Oil, vegetable, about, 80
Olives, about, 124
Omelets
   smoked salmon, and red pepper
      frittata, 131
   spaghetti frittata, with broccoli, 151
Onions, slicing, 23
Orange and Belgian Endive Salad, 72
Orange peel, drying, 22
Oranges, sliced, with liqueur, 105
Oregano, about, 95
Orzo, about, 76
**Orzo and White Bean Soup with
   Double Tomatoes**, 136
**Oyster Mushroom and Rosemary
   Bruschetta**, 147

P

**Pan-Seared Chicken Pasta with
   Wilted Spinach**, 72-73
Pancakes, corn, 152
Pancetta
   about, 45
   and spaghetti with mushrooms
      and sage, 45
Papayas
   about, 31
   and ginger sauce, 85
   salsa, 31
   types, 85
Pappadams, about, 118
Parmesan cheese, about, 78, 129
Parmesan Poppy Seed Bread, 141

Parsley, flat-leaf, about, 173
Pasta. *see also* Italian dishes
   about, 127
   in bean soup with kale, 137
   in beef stroganoff, 17
   bow-tie, with broccoli, cauliflower
      and tomato sauce, 143
   with cauliflower and hot pepper, 144
   and chicken, with asparagus and
      snow peas, 75
   and chicken, with dill and
      pecan pesto, 71
   and chicken, with wilted spinach,
      72-73
   cooking, 180
   fettuccine, broccoli mustard, 150
   fettuccine, with lox and
      horseradish, 130
   fettuccine, with mushrooms,
      prosciutto and basil, 46
   garden patch, 146
   and halibut, with chili-sesame
      sauce, 117
   lasagne, turkey, 79
   linguine, with clam and black olive
      sauce, 124
   matching with sauce, 71
   measuring, 180
   with mussels and parsley pesto, 126
   orzo, about, 76
   orzo, with white bean soup, 136
   penne, with broccoli, mushrooms
      and wilted spinach, 147
   penne, with hot sausage, red pepper
      and broccoli, 42-43
   penne, with tomatoes, basil and goat
      cheese, 141
   penne, with tuna, lemon, capers and
      olives, 128
   penne, with turkey sausage, 78
   penne, with white beans and
      tomatoes, 148
   with prawns, feta and
      red peppers, 125
   rotini, with bacon, 43
   rotini, with chicken, 73
   rotini, with tuna and pine nuts, 129
   in seafood chowder, 96
   spaghetti, with beef and
      mushrooms, 41
   spaghetti, with broccoli, pepper and
      tomato, 145
   spaghetti, with mushrooms, pancetta
      and sage, 45
   spaghetti, with tuna-tomato
      sauce, 127
   spaghetti, with warm tomato-
      avocado sauce, 149
   spaghetti frittata, with broccoli, 151

spaghettini, and chicken, with broccoli, 74
spaghettini, with pork, shiitake mushrooms and sage, 44
summer's end, 142
Peaches, and berry salsa, 104
Peanut sauce, 63
Peanutty Chicken, 63
Pear, Arugula and Brie Salad, 75
Pears, baked, 96
Pemmican, about, 34
Penne with Broccoli, Mushrooms and Wilted Spinach, 147
Penne with Hot Sausage, Red Pepper and Broccoli, 42-43
Penne with Tomatoes, Basil and Goat Cheese, 141
Penne with Tuna, Lemon, Capers and Olives, 128
Penne with White Beans and Tomatoes, 148
Pepper
    grinding, 151
    Szechuan peppercorns, 106
Pepperoni Pizza with Light Cheese, 49
Peppers
    bell, 170
    chili, handling, 114
    chipotle, 16
    jalapeno, 16, 40
Pesto
    dill and pecan, 71
    parsley, 126
    using fresh, about, 175
Pesto Pizza with Japanese Eggplant, 175
Pine nuts, about, 74
Pineapple-pear salsa, 158
Pita bread
    as hamburger buns, 64
    lamb meal-in-a-pocket, with eggplant, 36
Pizza. *see also* Italian-influenced dishes
    artichoke, spinach and goat cheese, 171
    barbecued, with pesto, pepper and prosciutto, 47
    barbecued duck, 91
    black bean, 174
    chicken tortilla, 66
    dough, 169
    fresh vegetable, 170
    pepperoni, with light cheese, 49
    pesto, with eggplant, 175
    with porcini mushrooms and provolone, 172-73
    smoked salmon, 132
    toppings, 47
    turkey sausage, with yellow bell pepper, 89

upside-down, 48
using bread shells, 169
Pizza with Turkey Sausage and Yellow Bell Pepper, 89
Plum sauce, about, 32
Polenta with Black Bean Salsa, 157
Poor Richard's Almanacks, 5-6
Porcini mushrooms, about, 172
Pork
    barbecued pizza, with pesto, pepper and prosciutto, 47
    chops, Sicilian style, 27
    chops, with maple syrup and balsamic vinegar, 28
    chops, with papaya salsa, 31
    chops, with sweet-and-sour cabbage, 29
    fettuccine with mushrooms, prosciutto and basil, 46
    pancetta, about, 45
    rotini with bacon, 43
    schnitzel, 30
    spaghetti with mushrooms, pancetta and sage, 45
    and spaghettini, shiitake mushrooms and sage, 44
    stir-fry, with broccoli and lemon, 26
    tenderloin, barbecued with ginger and soy sauce, 33
    tenderloin, with dried cranberries and blueberries, 34
    tenderloin, with plum sauce and rosemary, 32
Pork Chops Sicilian Style, 27
Pork Chops with Maple Syrup and Balsamic Vinegar, 28
Pork Chops with Papaya Salsa, 31
Pork Chops with Sweet-and-Sour Cabbage, 29
Pork Stir-Fry with Broccoli and Lemon, 26
Pork Tenderloin with Dried Cranberries and Blueberries, 34
Poultry. *see also* Chicken; Duck; Turkey
    guide to recipes by category, 177
    Barbecued Duck Pizza, 91
    Chicken and Rotini with Dill and Pecan Pesto, 71
    Chicken Breasts with Mushrooms and Creamy Mustard Sauce, 62
    Chicken Breasts with Orange Glaze, 55
    Chicken Focaccia Burgers, 65
    Chicken Noodle Soup with Snow Peas and Fresh Herbs, 52
    Chicken Spaghettini with Broccoli, Pine Nuts and Sun-Dried Tomatoes, 74
    Chicken Strips, 64

Chicken Tortilla Pizzas, 66
Chicken with Balsamic Vinegar and Fresh Basil, 54
Chicken with Creamy Lemon Sauce, 56
Chicken with Ginger, Mint and Yogurt, 60
Chicken with Mushrooms, Lemon and Fresh Rosemary, 61
Cinnamon Chicken with Orange Juice, Raisins and Capers, 58
Fat-Fightin' Turkey Burgers, 82
Grilled Chicken and Red Onion Salad with Feta Cheese, 53
Hot Duck Salad with Soy Sesame Vinaigrette, 90-91
Lemon Sage Turkey, 87
Major Grey's Chicken Stir-Fry, 69
Pan-Seared Chicken Pasta with Wilted Spinach, 72-73
Peanutty Chicken, 63
Pizza with Turkey Sausage and Yellow Bell Pepper, 89
pounding, 61
Pronto Penne with Turkey Sausage, 78
Radiatore Pasta with Chicken, Asparagus and Snow Peas, 75
Raspberry-Vinegar Chicken, 59
Revisionist Turkey Stroganoff, 81
Speedy Spirals with Chicken, Tomatoes and Black Olives, 73
Spicy Chicken and Bell Pepper Stir-Fry, 67
Stir-fried Chicken with Broccoli, 68-69
Tex-Mex Turkey Lasagne, 79
Texan Outrage Turkey Chili, 77
Thai Stir-Fry with Chicken, Cilantro and Coconut Milk, 70
Turkey Burgers with Sun-Dried Tomatoes and Fresh Herbs, 83
Turkey Fajitas, 80
Turkey Sausages with Red Lentils, 88
Turkey with Fruit Chutney, 86
Turkey with Papaya Ginger Sauce, 85
Turkey with Sage Cranberry Sauce, 84
Virtuous Turkey Soup with Tomatoes and Fresh Basil, 76
Prawns
    cioppino soup, 94
    with ginger, 122
    with seashell pasta, feta and red peppers, 125
Pronto Penne with Turkey Sausage, 78
Prosciutto
    about, 46

on barbecued pizza with pesto and
  pepper, 47
and fettuccine, mushrooms
  and basil, 46

Q

Quesadillas, 155
Quick Pizza Dough, 169
Quinoa, about, 139
**Quinoa Salad with Corn, Cucumber
  and Lime**, 139

R

**Radiatore Pasta with Chicken,
  Asparagus and Snow Peas**, 75
Raita. *see also* Yogurt
  about, 107
  banana-mint, 37
  cucumber, 107, 159
  tomato, 166
Raspberries
  raspberry-vinegar chicken, 59
  sauce for lamb, 38
Raspberry-Vinegar Chicken, 59
**Red, White and Green Rotini
  with Bacon**, 43
Revisionist Turkey Stroganoff, 81
Rice
  basmati, 155
  cooking, 60
Ricotta cheese, about, 154
Rombauer, Irma and Marion, 8

S

Salad dressings
  buttermilk vinaigrette with garlic
    and dill, 89
  chutney dip for raw vegetables, 82
  creamy herb dip, 79
  lemon and basil vinaigrette, 42
  no-oil yogurt, 56
  orange vinaigrette, 35
  soy sesame vinaigrette, 90-91
  yogurt, 77
Salads, main
  chicken, with red onion and
    feta cheese, 53

grilled salmon and pecan, 98-99
hot duck, with soy sesame
  vinaigrette, 90-91
quinoa, with corn, cucumber
  and lime, 139
white bean and avocado, 140
Salads, side
  cabbage, with apple and onion, 77
  cucumber, 70
  orange and Belgian endive, 72
  pear, arugula and Brie cheese, 75
  spinach, 27, 162-63
Salmon
  availability, 103
  barbecued steaks, with peach and
    berry salsa, 104-5
  broiled steaks, with herbed almond
    butter, 105
  broiled steaks with blueberries, 103
  cakes, jalapeno, 107
  cold-smoked, 132
  fettuccine, with lox and
    horseradish, 130
  fillets, with mango, 100
  fillets with lime and fresh herbs, 101
  lox, about, 132
  and pecan salad, 98-99
  and potato soup (Haw'gwil Jem), 98
  smoked, with red pepper frittata, 131
  smoked salmon pizza, 132
  steaks, broiled, 102
  steaks, maple roast sesame, 106
  in West Coast native legends, 98
**Salmon Fillets with Lime and
  Fresh Herbs**, 101
Salmon Fillets with Mango, 100
Salsa. *see also* Sauces
  papaya, 31
  peach and berry, 104
  pineapple-pear, 158
  strawberry, lime and mint, 118
Satay Beef and Bok Choy Stir-Fry, 18-19
Sauces. *see also* Pesto; Salsa
  apricot-walnut glaze, 57
  banana-mint raita, 37
  basil-yogurt, 160
  blueberry, for salmon steaks, 103
  cardamom-yogurt fruit, 88
  chili-sesame, 117
  chipotle marinade, 16
  clam and black olive, 124
  creamy lemon, 56
  creamy mustard, 62
  cucumber raita, 107, 159
  fish sauce, about, 68
  herb butter, 105, 119
  hoisin, about, 91
  matching with pasta, 71
  mushroom soy, 164

orange glaze, 55
papaya ginger, 85
plum, about, 32
raspberry, for lamb, 38
satay, 18, 19
tomato raita, 166
tuna-tomato, 127
worcestershire, about, 168
Sausages
  hot, with penne, 42-43
  Italian, in black bean soup, 14
  pepperoni pizza, with
    light cheese, 49
  turkey, in chili, 77
  turkey, on pizza, 89
  turkey, with penne, 78
  turkey, with red lentils, 88
**Scallops in Strawberry, Balsamic Vinegar
  and Pepper Sauce**, 121
Sea bass, with black bean sauce, 115
Seafood
  guide to recipes by category, 177-78
  Almost Instant Broiled Salmon
    Steaks, 102
  Barbecued Salmon Steaks with Peach
    and Berry Salsa, 104-5
  Broiled Salmon Steaks with
    Blueberries, 103
  Broiled Salmon Steaks with Herbed
    Almond Butter, 105
  Chop-Chop Cioppino, 94
  Clam and Cauliflower Chowder, 97
  Clams Provençal, 123
  Cod with Capers, 111
  Cod with Fresh Salsa and
    Lime Sauce, 109
  Cod with Fresh Tomato and
    Tomatillo Sauce, 112
  Cod with Wine and Sun-Dried
    Tomatoes, 110
  Creamy Cod Soup with Leeks and
    Green Onions, 95
  Dolly Watts' Salmon Soup or
    Haw'gwil Jem, 98
  Down-Home Spaghetti with
    Tuna-Tomato Sauce, 127
  Fast Mexican Snapper, 114
  Fettuccine with Lox, Horseradish
    and Chutzpah, 130
  Grilled Salmon and Pecan Salad,
    98-99
  Halibut on Fettuccine with
    Chile-Sesame Sauce, 117
  Halibut with Fresh Rosemary and
    Pine Nuts, 116
  Halibut with Strawberry, Lime and
    Mint Salsa, 118
  In-Your-Face Mussels with Parsley
    Pesto and Fettuccine, 126

Jalapeno Salmon Cakes, 107
Kitchen Sink Rotini with Tuna and
    Pine Nuts, 129
Linguine with Clam and Black
    Olive Sauce, 124
Maple Roast Sesame Salmon
    Steaks, 106
Penne with Tuna, Lemon, Capers
    and Olives, 128
Salmon Fillets with Lime and
    Fresh Herbs, 101
Salmon Fillets with Mango, 100
Scallops in Strawberry, Balsamic
    Vinegar and Pepper Sauce, 121
Seafood Chowder with
    Pasta Shells, 96
Seafood with Green Curry and
    Lemon Grass, 120
Seashell Pasta with Prowns, Feta and
    Red Peppers, 125
Shrimp Pizza with Mustard,
    Goat Cheese, Dill and
    Caramelized Onions, 133
Sizzling Prawns with Ginger, 122
Smoked Salmon and Red Pepper
    Frittata, 131
Smoken-Salmon Pizza, 132
Spicy Broiled Cod, 113
Steamed Sea Bass with
    Black Bean Sauce, 115
Summer Sole with Fresh
    Tomatoes, 108
Trout with Herb Butter, 119
Seafood Chowder with Pasta Shells, 96
**Seafood with Green Curry and
    Lemon Grass**, 120
**Seashell Pasta with Prowns, Feta and
    Red Peppers**, 125
Seasoned Bread Crumbs, 55
**Secret-Ingredient Pizza with
    Porcini Mushrooms and
    Provolone**, 172-73
Sesame seeds, about, 117
Shallots, about, 108
Shrimp
    crackers, 122
    pizza, 133
**Shrimp Pizza with Mustard,
    Goat Cheese, Dill and
    Caramelized Onions**, 133
Sizzling Prawns with Ginger, 122
Skinny Orange Vinaigrette, 35
**Smoked Salmon and Red Pepper
    Frittata**, 131
Smoked-Salmon Pizza, 132
Snapper, Mexican, 114
Sole, with fresh tomatoes, 108

Soups
    bean, with hot Italian sausage
        and spinach, 14
    bean, with kale and pasta, 137
    bean, with orzo, 136
    chicken noodle, with snow peas and
        fresh herbs, 52
    clam and cauliflower chowder, 97
    cod, with leeks and green onions, 95
    mushroom stew, 168
    salmon and potato
        (Haw'gwil Jem), 98
    seafood chowder with
        pasta shells, 96
    seafood cioppino, 94
    turkey, with tomatoes and basil, 76
Sour cream, yogurt as substitute for, 17
Southwestern Corn Cakes, 152
Soy sauce, Indonesia (Ketjap manis), 38
Soybean products
    miso, 162
    tofu, 161
**Spaghetti Frittata with Broccoli,
    Goat Cheese and Sun-Dried
    Tomatoes**, 151
Spaghetti spoons, about, 41
Spaghetti squash, about, 165
**Spaghetti Squash with Spinach, Feta and
    Herbed White Beans**, 165
Spaghetti with Beef and Mushrooms, 41
**Spaghetti with Broccoli, Pepper
    and Tomato**, 145
**Spaghetti with Mushrooms, Pancetta
    and Sage**, 45
**Spaghetti with Warm Tomato-Avocado
    Sauce**, 149
**Spaghettini with Pork, Shiitake
    Mushrooms and Sage**, 44-45
Speedy Cheese Enchiladas, 153
**Speedy Chili with Sun-Dried
    Tomatoes**, 15
**Speedy Spirals with Chicken, Tomatoes
    and Black Olives**, 73
Spices. *see* Herbs, spices and condiments
Spicy Broiled Cod, 113
**Spicy Chicken and Bell Pepper
    Stir-Fry**, 67
Spinach
    in black bean soup with
        Italian sausage, 14
    and broccoli enchiladas, 154-55
    with chicken pasta, 72
    with penne, broccoli and
        mushrooms, 147
    on pizza with artichokes and
        goat cheese, 171
    salad, Japanese, 162-63
    salad, suggestions for, 27

with spaghetti squash, feta and
    herbed white beans, 165
Spinach and Broccoli Enchiladas, 154-55
Squash, spaghetti, with spinach, 165
**Steamed Sea Bass with Black
    Bean Sauce**, 115
Steamer, improvising, 115
Stir-fried Chicken with Broccoli, 68-69
Stir-fry
    beef, bell pepper and snow peas, 21
    beef, with Chinese broccoli, 20-21
    chicken, Major Grey's, 69
    chicken, Thai, 70
    chicken, with bell pepper, 67
    chicken, with broccoli, 68-69
    cutting meat for, 26
    green vegetables, 63
    pork, with broccoli and lemon, 26
    satay beef and bok choy, 18-19
    tofu, with watercress and cherry
        tomatoes, 161
Stock
    about, 29
    vegetable, about, 136
Strawberries, in balsamic vinegar
    as dessert, 39
    with scallops, 121
Stroganoff
    beef, 17
    turkey, 81
**Summer Salad with White Beans
    and Avocado**, 140
Summer Sole with Fresh Tomatoes, 108
Summer's End Pasta, 142
Szechuan Eggplant with Tofu, 164
Szechuan peppercorns, about, 106

T

Tacos, about, 24
Tahini
    about, 117
    hummus, 36
Tamale pie, 23
Tex-Mex Turkey Lasagne, 79
Texan Outrage Turkey Chili, 77
**Thai Stir-Fry with Chicken, Cilantro
    and Coconut Milk**, 70
Tofu
    about, 161
    dengaku with spinach salad, 162-63
    and Szechuan eggplant, 164
    with watercress and cherry
        tomatoes, 161
Tofu Dengaku with Spinach Salad,
    162-63

Tofu Stir-Fry with Watercress and
Cherry Tomatoes, 161
Tomatillos, about, 112
Tomatoes
chopping, 14
storing, 143
sun-dried, 110
Tortillas
about, 24
Tex-Mex turkey lasagne, 79
Tostadas, about, 24
Trout with Herb Butter, 119
Tuna
with penne, lemon, capers
and olives, 128
with rotini and pine nuts, 129
and tomato sauce,
with spaghetti, 127
Turkey
burgers, 82, 83
chili, 77
fajitas, 80
with fruit chutney, 86
lasagne, 79
lemon sage, 87
with papaya ginger sauce, 85
pounding, 61
with sage cranberry sauce, 84
sausage, with penne, 78
sausage pizza, with yellow
bell pepper, 89
sausages, with red lentils, 88
soup, with tomatoes and basil, 76
storage of ground, 81
stroganoff, 81
Turkey Burgers with Sun-Dried
Tomatoes and Fresh Herbs, 83
Turkey Fajitas, 80
Turkey Sausages with Red Lentils, 88
Turkey with Fruit Chutney, 86
Turkey with Papaya Ginger Sauce, 85
Turkey with Sage Cranberry Sauce, 84

U

Upside-Down Pizza, 48

V

Vegetable oil, about, 80
Vegetables. see also names of
specific vegetables
grilling, 131

stir-frying, 63
stock, 136
Vegetarian
guide to recipes by category, 178-79
Artichoke, Spinach and Goat Cheese
Pizza, 171
Bean Soup with Kale and Multi-
Colored Pasta, 137
Black Bean Burritos, 156
Black Bean Pizza with Tomatoes,
Pepper and Olives, 174
Bow-Tie Pasta with Broccoli,
Cauliflower and Double-Tomato
Sauce, 143
Broccoli Mustard Fettuccine
with Lemon, 150
Chickpeas with Cumin
and Ginger, 159
Couscous with Chickpeas and Basil
Yogurt Sauce, 160
Curried Red Lentils and Cauliflower,
166-67
Fresh Vegetable Pizza, 170
Garden Patch Pasta with Curls, 146
Great Canadian Beans, 167
Holy Moley Chili, 138
Italo-Indian Tomato Raita, 166
Jamaican Black Beans with
Pineapple-Pear Salsa, 158
Just in Quesadillas, 155
Mustardy Mushroom Stew, 168
Orzo and White Bean Soup with
Double Tomatoes, 136
Penne with Broccoli, Mushrooms
and Wilted Spinach, 147
Penne with Tomatoes, Basil and
Goat Cheese, 141
Penne with White Beans and
Tomatoes, 148
Pesto Pizza with Japanese
Eggplant, 175
Polenta with Black Bean Salsa, 157
Quick Pizza Dough, 169
Quinoa Salad with Corn, Cucumber
and Lime, 139
Secret-Ingredient Pizza with
Procini Mushrooms and
Provolone, 172-73
Southwestern Corn Cakes, 152
Spaghetti Frittata with Broccoli,
Goat Cheese and Sun-Dried
Tomatoes, 151
Spaghetti Squash with Spinach, Feta
and Herbed White Beans, 165
Spaghetti with Broccoli, Pepper
and Tomato, 145
Spaghetti with Warm Tomato-
Avocado Sauce, 149
Speedy Cheese Enchiladas, 153

Spinach and Broccoli Enchiladas,
154-55
Summer Salad with White Beans
and Avocado, 140
Summer's End Pasta, 142
Szechuan Eggplant with Tofu, 164
Tofu Dengaku with Spinach Salad,
162-63
Tofu Stir-Fry with Watercress and
Cherry Tomatoes, 161
Winter Linguine with Cauliflower
and Hot Pepper, 144
Vinaigrette. see Salad dressings
Vinegar
balsamic, 54
fruit, 59
Virtuous Turkey Soup with Tomatoes
and Fresh Basil, 76

W

Walnuts, about, 57
Williams, William Carlos, 9
Winter Linguine with Cauliflower and
Hot Pepper, 144
Worcestershire sauce, about, 168

Y

Yogurt. see also Raita
cardamom-yogurt fruit sauce, 88
chicken with ginger, mint and
yogurt, 60
creamy herb dip, 79
extra thick, 17
no-oil salad dressing, 56
salad dressing, 77

Z

Zest
lemon, 128
lime, 101